Action Research: a Methodology for Change and Development

Bridget Somekh

Open University Press

Open University Press
McGraw-Hill Education
McGraw-Hill House
Shoppenhangers Road
Maidenhead, Berkshire
England SL6 2QL

email: enquiries@openup.co.uk
world wide web: www.openup.co.uk

and Two Penn Plaza, New York, NY 1012–2289 USA

First published 2006

A catalogue record of this book is available from the British Library

ISBN 10: 0 335 21658 7 (pb)   0 335 21659 5 (hb)
ISBN 13: 978 0335 216581 (pb)   978 0335 21659 8 (hb)

Library of Congress Cataloging-in-Publication Data
CIP data has been applied for

Typeset by BookEns Ltd, Royston, Herts.
Printed and bound by Bell & Bain Ltd, Glasgow

For Robert

Contents

Acknowledgements

I would like to thank all those from schools, universities and public and private companies who have worked with me on action research projects over the years. This is your work as well as mine and working with you has been a powerful learning experience for me.

I would also like to thank those who read draft chapters and responded with comments, particularly Terry Carson, Andy Convery, Dave Ebbutt, Gabriel Goldstein, Margaret Ledwith, Cathy Lewin, Di Matthews-Levine, Diane Mavers, Julienne Meyer, Bob Munro, Angel Perez, Peter Posch, Tim Rudd, Peter Seaborne and Barbara Zamorski.

Finally, I would like to thank John Elliott whose name appears in many chapters of this book as my inspirational teacher and colleague.

Introduction

This book is about the many ways in which social science researchers can use action research methodology to overcome the limitations of traditional methodologies when researching changing situations. Action research combines research into substantive issues, such as how to improve the quality of children's learning in a state-maintained education system or how to give good access to health care to all members of a community, with research into the process of development in order to deepen understanding of the enablers of, and barriers to, change. It is a means whereby research can become a systematic intervention, going beyond describing, analysing and theorizing social practices to working in partnership with participants to reconstruct and transform those practices. It promotes equality between researchers from outside the site of practice and practitioner–researchers from inside, working together with the aspiration to carry out research as professionals, with skilful and reflexive methods and ethical sensitivity.

Change is an inevitable and continuous process in social situations, locally, nationally, globally … the problem is to understand the extent to which we can have any control over its nature (what kinds of things the change involves) and its direction (where it is taking us). This is particularly important when there is a deliberate attempt to introduce something new in order to bring about improvement. Because of the complexity of human experience and social relationships and institutions, it will probably always be impossible to plan changes and implement them exactly as intended, but action research provides a means of generating knowledge about the implementation of the initiative and using this to keep it on track as far as possible. It is a methodology integrating social science inquiry with participants' practical action so that all concerned have a sense of agency rather than constructing themselves as powerless.

In this book I am presuming that readers will already be familiar with much of the existing literature on action research. My aim is to build on the considerable body of knowledge about, and experience of conducting, action research developed in many fields of the social sciences in the second half of the twentieth century. Since different groups have developed different approaches to action research, sometimes with very little aware-ness of others, I have been able to draw on divergent rather than conver-gent ideas, and will inevitably challenge the assumptions of some groups. The book is grounded in my own experience of working on action research projects for 25 years, always working flexibly and exploring new possibili-ties for project design rather than developing and refining any orthodoxy. As an editor, since 1992, of the international journal, *Educational Action Research* (EAR), and involved for many years in co-ordinating the Collaborative Action Research Network (CARN), I have needed to maintain a broad, inclusive definition of action research and this has linked well with my personal aspiration to follow Francis Bacon's vision of how to be a life-long ('late') learner in his essay 'On Custome and Education' (1625):

> For it is true, that late Learners, cannot so well take the Plie: Except it be in some Mindes, that have not suffered themselves to fixe, but have kept themselves open and prepared, to receive continuall Amendment, which is exceeding Rare.
>
> (Bacon 1625)

Much of my research has been focused on change in relation to the introduction of information and communication technologies into educa-tional settings. This interest goes back to the early 1980s when, as a teacher of English, I carried out action research into children's use of word process-ing for story writing. Computers in classrooms are interestingly disruptive of traditional practices, but schools as institutions are robust in resisting fundamental structural change. This inherent conflict between forces for change and processes of institutional–cultural reproduction has proved a fascinating focus for my research over the years. Although not all my ICT-related projects have adopted an action research methodology, they have all drawn upon insights from action research, and in both my early and my most recent work I have adopted an explicitly action research approach, because it has provided a credible and methodologically coherent solution to working between the visions of policy makers and the potential disap-pointments of the implementation of those visions in the education system.

An important consideration in claiming, as I do in this book, that action research should be the methodology of choice for social science researchers focusing on innovation, is the quality and reliability of the knowledge it generates. I am interested in knowledge that has the capacity to transform social practices and in the ways in which action research can gain access to the intimate and passionate purposes of individuals whose lives and work construct those practices. And I am interested, too, in the ways that participant–researchers can generate and communicate knowledge to those who seek it out of need. Early in my research career I learnt something important about the generalizability of knowledge generated from research. Here is the story:

During 1985–6 I was working at the Cambridge Institute of Education on the 'Support for Innovation Project',[1] which involved supporting senior management teams and their staff in 12 high schools in the professional development of teachers engaged in implementing a large number of innovatory programmes simultaneously. I had been working on the project for about six months when I received a phone call from the Deputy Head of another high school in a neighbouring county who said he had heard about our project and would like me to visit the school and talk to the senior management team about possible strategies for undertaking similar work of their own. It was perhaps my first consultancy, at any rate I was very nervous when I set out to drive to the school. The meeting took place in the Head's office and involved a discussion between myself and four or five senior managers (I think, from memory, all men). As soon as they began talking about the issues that confronted them, I found the need to question them to find out more. Were teachers likely to say … ? Did the pupils tend to respond by … ? Did they find that heads of department felt that … ? Was one of the problems for the senior management team that … ? They responded very openly and I easily recognized the underlying significance of points they were making and empathized with their assumptions and constraints. I was able to offer advice based on my knowledge of what other schools were doing in similar circumstances. Central issues included: communication (who had access to what information and how could they broaden access); territoriality (who 'owned' which rooms and could these boundaries be made more flexible); and informal power networks (who influenced who, and how could the creative energy of individuals be harnessed). At the end of the meeting the Head said to me something along the lines of, 'It's amazing, I can't believe you have never been to our school before, you seem to know so much about the way our school works.' I remember walking to my car feeling so tense after one and a half hours of total concentration and fright-induced adrenalin in my bloodstream that I was literally sick on the way home. But I had learnt that the knowledge acquired from qualitative research is generalizable to similar settings (this school was similar in size to the project schools and governed by the same regulatory and political context) and that knowledge acquired from

---

[1] SIP was funded by Norfolk and Suffolk County Council Local Education Authorities from the government's TRIST grant for in-service training of teachers.

research involving close partnership with participants is quickly validated and appropriated by those in similar settings who recognize its immediate usefulness.

Living through the looking glass and looking back on Wonderland

In Lewis Carroll's *Alice in Wonderland*, when Alice went down the rabbit hole she emerged into a world where reality was transformed. Her perceptions of her experience were radically shifted by wild changes in her relative size and dramatic shifts in power and control away from herself as a privileged child to those she had assumed were powerless like rabbits and the kings and queens in a pack of playing cards. My introduction to action research as a teacher in 1978 was in lots of ways my own experience of entering Wonderland. Many of my assumed realities shifted, particularly my understandings of my role as a teacher engaged in working interactively with young people. Much of this centred upon issues of power and control as I came to realize that learning is closely related to a sense of personal efficacy and that children needed to be freed of my authority and given autonomy and encouraged to take responsibility for their own learning. But in Carroll's later book, *Through the Looking Glass*, when Alice passed through the mirror she was radically re-challenged, finding herself this time in a world where reality had seriously shifted once again. As a mathematician, Carroll enjoyed the game of applying mathematical logic to social settings and inventing new realities that challenged the assumptions of his Victorian adult readers. Alice was removed from the playful world of Wonderland to the more serious looking-glass world of social commentary and political satire; and in a similar way, new understandings of philosophical issues such as the nature of reality, truth and being have radically shifted my thinking and made it impossible for me to inhabit the same world as I did when I first became an action researcher. What was it like for Alice looking back on Wonderland from this new reality? Lewis Carroll doesn't tell us, leaving instead untidy links between Alice's two worlds so that characters from one appear unexpectedly in the other. For me, writing this book is a personal journey of revisiting Wonderland from the perspective of a looking-glass world. My current understandings of action research, embedded in recent and current projects, are very different from my understandings 15 years ago. I need to reflect on these changes and make personal meanings from the contradictions and inconsistencies embedded in the shifts. The effect is daunting and exciting, a revisiting of the past in the light of new understandings of the present. And, as for Alice, my two worlds are not unconnected.

Meanwhile, the political ideology of the world in which I am working as a researcher has also changed over that time. Theories that drive contemporary social science research are very radical by comparison with those that seemed radical 15 years ago. Yet the policy context has moved in the other direction, ideologically framed now in more totalitarian assumptions of traditional research practices than was the case in the 1970s and 1980s. Across the English-speaking world, in Britain, North America and Australia, the expectations of educational policy makers are locked in unrealistic assumptions of the application of natural science research methods to social situations; there is a belief in a process of incremental knowledge building to construct a technology of definite educational solutions for generalized application across contexts, through processes such as EPPI[2] reviews. This extends to policy-makers' vision of teachers engaging in 'evidence-based practice' either by applying the outcomes of traditional research to their classrooms or carrying out their own research to develop and implement solutions to practical problems. The latter is similar in many ways to my own early action research while still a teacher, but whereas in the 1980s action research flourished in England through links with departments of education in universities and colleges and was confined to a small number of regions, in the late 1990s and first years of this century the British government has funded teacher research through initiatives such as Best Practice Research Scholarships and built up a support infrastructure through bodies such as the Teachers' Research Panel and events such as the teacher research conference sponsored by the Teacher Training Agency in spring 2004. The result has been the growth of a culture of research in the teaching profession across the whole country.

The current British policy context and government initiatives are inspired by a vision of equality of educational opportunities for all children and a vision of greater social justice. The means of achieving these aims often appear to social science researchers like myself to be over-simplistic and mechanistic, but the basic vision is similar to my own. There are spaces created by these policies for evidence-based practice and school improvement in which transformative action research has a chance to grow. My aim is to work with – and within – policy initiatives rather than mounting disapproving critiques from the sidelines. My approach is to work within the system and aim to educate policy makers by engaging them in research in some form, even if it is no more than as members of project steering

---

[2]   The Evidence for Policy and Practice Information (EPP) reviews adopt a systematic approach to the organization and review of evidence-based work on social interventions. For a critique of this approach, see Maclure, M. (2005) 'Clarity bordering on stupidity': where's the quality in systematic review? *Journal of Education Policy* (in press).

groups. An important part of my current work involves evaluating innova-tive initiatives for ICT in education sponsored by the Department for Education and Skills of the British government; and in one case this includes integrating action research carried out by teachers in the design of a large-scale evaluation study (see Chapter 8). In this way I am able to find spaces to engage creatively with policy makers, support the implementa-tion of policies in ways that are consistent with their underpinning values of social justice and work even in small ways towards transformation in the education system.

Methodological principles for action research

This shift in my vision and understanding over a period of 20 years, together with the radical changes over the same period in social policy and the politics of sponsored research, forced me to fundamentally rethink what I wanted to say about action research before starting to write this book. To do this I have engaged in reading and reflection, the latter focused mainly on reading writings I published while still a teacher and the raw data from six research projects in which I have explicitly adopted an action research methodology. My other experience as an evaluator of major gov-ernment initiatives has necessarily been influential in my thinking.

The eight methodological principles presented here are the outcome of that process. For clarity and simplicity they are stated briefly and they are definitive for me, personally, at the time of writing this book. However, they are underpinned by ideas that are the subject of continuing debate among action researchers, many of whom will wish to take issue with either the principles themselves or their wording. Chapter 1 deals with some of this complexity and, ideally, the principles should be read in con-junction with Chapter 1.

The broad, inclusive definition of action research adopted in this book rests on eight methodological principles

Action research integrates research and action in a series of flexible cycles involving, holistically rather than as separate steps: the collection of data about the topic of investigation; analysis and interpretation of those data; the planning and introduction of action strategies to bring about positive changes; and evaluation of those changes through further data collection, analysis and interpretation ... and so forth to other flexible cycles until a decision is taken to intervene in this process in order to publish its out-comes to date. Because action research is an integral part of the ongoing activities of the social group whose work is under study, the cyclical process is unlikely to stop when the research is 'written up,' although the extent of data collection and intensity of the inquiry is likely to reduce.

Action research is conducted by a collaborative partnership of participants and researchers, whose roles and relationships are sufficiently fluid to maximize mutual support and sufficiently differentiated to allow individuals to make appropriate contributions given existing constraints. These partnerships can be of many kinds. They may be between a practitioner–researcher and students/clients and colleagues in that researcher's field of professional practice. Or they may be made up of different combinations of 'insiders' and 'outsiders', establishing their own working relationships. However, there always needs to be a recognition of how power is constituted and accessed within the partnership and an aspiration to establish equality of esteem. Ethical practices are of paramount importance, given the blurring of insider and outsider roles and the unusually open access this gives the researchers to personal and micro-political data.

Action research involves the development of knowledge and understanding of a unique kind. The focus on change and development in a natural (as opposed to contrived) social situation, such as a workplace, and the involvement of participant–researchers who are 'insiders' to that situation gives access to kinds of knowledge and understanding that are not accessible to traditional researchers coming from outside. The publication of this knowledge makes it available for others to use, particularly when the details of the original context are fully described so that judgements can be made about its potential usefulness in other settings.

Action research starts from a vision of social transformation and aspirations for greater social justice for all. Action research is not value neutral; action researchers aim to act morally and promote social justice through research that is politically informed and personally engaged. They construct themselves as agents able to access the mechanisms of power in a social group or institution and influence the nature and direction of change. This does not mean that they believe naïvely that they can easily implement a set of actions that will solve all problems, but it orients them to move the change process forward as positively as possible while increasing understanding of whatever limitations may arise.

Action research involves a high level of reflexivity and sensitivity to the role of the self in mediating the whole research process. The self of the researcher can best be understood as intermeshed with others through webs of interpersonal and professional relationships that co-construct the researcher's identity. This distributed definition of self recognizes that individuals can position themselves politically and strategically within a social situation and construct themselves as relatively more, rather than less, powerful. Through action research individuals work with colleagues to change aspects of their day-to-day activities (their practices) with the aspiration to improve working processes, relationships and outcomes.

Action research involves exploratory engagement with a wide range of existing knowledge drawn from psychology, philosophy, sociology and other fields of social science, in order to test its explanatory power and practical usefulness. This approach to existing knowledge is important: it is not accepted without question, assumed to be useful and applied to the situation under study; rather, it is explored and tested in relation to the data being collected from the situation under study and becomes an integral part of analysis and interpretation in the action research. In this way, the accumulated knowledge and wisdom of others, from past and present generations, is built upon and refined and used to shed light on the situated data from a specific field of study.

Action research engenders powerful learning for participants through combining research with reflection on practice. The development of self-understanding is important in action research, as it is in other forms of qualitative research, because of the extent to which the analysis of data and the interpretive process of developing meanings involves the self as a research instrument. Primarily, this is a matter of ensuring the quality of research through understanding how personal values and assumptions shape research findings. However, because of the focus on their practice, action research also necessarily involves powerful personal–professional learning for the participant–researchers about the impact of their own assumptions and practices on work outcomes and relationships with colleagues. For 'outsiders' this form of learning may be less intense than for 'insiders', but the new relationships and practices involved in carrying out the action research will lead to reflection on their research role and activities and hence to personal–professional learning.

Action research locates the inquiry in an understanding of broader historical, political and ideological contexts that shape and constrain human activity at even the local level, including economic factors and international forces such as the structuring power of globalization. The advantage of working in teams with insider–participants and outsiders collaborating together is that it is easier to adopt this broader perspective, not necessarily because outsiders bring specialist knowledge but because insiders are necessarily constrained in their analysis of the larger framework in which the site of study is located by being enmeshed in its institutional culture and assumptions.

Overview of the book

The book is divided into this introduction and nine chapters.

Chapter 1 discusses some methodological issues relating to agency, change and the generation of actionable knowledge that are important in designing and implementing action research projects. It draws on a wide range of literature but is also grounded in my own work. The eight methodological principles contained in this Introduction should be read in conjunction with Chapter 1.

Chapter 2 extends this analysis by reviewing the range of different approaches to action research that have developed since the early work of the 1940s. It argues that action research is necessarily different in different contexts and illustrates this by drawing on work from 'southern' countries and other social science disciplines such as health, management and social work.

Chapters 3 presents extracts from two action research studies I carried out as a teacher 20 years ago, the first into teaching and learning in my own classroom and the second, with the support and involvement of colleagues, into the processes of power and decision making in the school as a whole. The chapter is written in two voices: that of my former school teacher self and my present-day university researcher and teacher self.

Chapters 4–8 each focus on the work of a particular project, carried out between 1988 and 2005, in which I adopted action research methodology and customized it to different specific purposes and contexts. Each incorporates discussion of the theories and methods that shaped the work of the research team and/or emerged from the project's research.

Chapter 9 reflects back on the process of writing the book, looking particularly at the nature and role of personal narrative and the integration of discussions of theory with the praxis of action and reflection. It ends by inviting readers to engage critically with these accounts of action research projects and to use to them to design new work that will surpass my own for creativity, reflexive sensitivity and transformative impact.

1 Agency, Change and the Generation of Actionable Knowledge

In this chapter, I want to discuss some methodological issues that are problematic for action researchers. As much as anything, this is in order to destabilize the certainties that may have been suggested by the eight principles of action research presented in the Introduction, so that in wishing to achieve clarity I do not lose sight of complexity. Incompatible, maybe, but both clarity and complexity are key aims of this book.

The nature of action

A difficulty for action research is that the early theoretical work assumed an unproblematic link between cause and effect in social situations. In Lewin's (1946) original cyclical model action research began with a process of reconnaissance to identify key features that shaped the activities of the social group under study. The data collected at this stage were used to identify problems and hypothesize solutions based on theoretical insights that could be tested by planning and implementing action strategies. The validity of the hypotheses could then be established by evaluating the impact of the action strategy, on the assumption that failure to achieve the intended impact would demonstrate that the theoretical insight on which it was based was invalid (Altrichter *et al.* 1993: 77). This was never suggested to be a simple process, but one that would involve successive actions in a cycle of testing and improvement. However, in recent years the belief in the competence of human beings to plan and implement change through a rational process of planning and action has been fundamentally challenged by a wide range of contemporary theorists. For example, many no longer believe there is any such thing as 'truth' or 'reality' existing 'out there' that can be identified and measured independently of the human minds that construct them as the product of experience. Smith summarizes the problem in terms of the loss of any clear basis for the justification of moral action:

> There is no possibility of theory-free observation and theory-free knowledge, (...) the duality of subject and object is untenable, and

> (...) there can be no external, extra-linguistic referent to which we can turn to adjudicate knowledge claims. In the end (...) we can never know, or most certainly never know if we know, reality as it actually is. And (...) there is no possibility of an appeal to an independently existing reality to resolve our differences.
>
> (Smith 2004: 47)

Hence, the human instinct to make meaning from complexity, reduce uncertainty and construct cause-and-effect explanations is seen as no more than that — a manifestation of a basic instinct that deludes us into the construction of naïve over-simplifications. It follows that these cannot be the basis for effective action.

In a curious way, however, the arguments that are used to undermine the concept of a separate, identifiable reality, which can be researched to provide explanations for human behaviour and serve as the basis for planned actions, are themselves dependent upon a rational – and therefore equally flawed – line of argument. The disproval of truth and reality proves as problematic as their establishment. Moreover, the critique of the modernist origins of action research is over-simplistic. The tradition of action research is rooted both in Lewin's social psychology, which conceived of action as emerging from a process of group exploration of social interactions rather than solely from rational deduction, and in John Dewey's theory of 'learning by doing' (Dewey 1973). Berge and Ve (2000) in assessing the importance of both Dewey and George Herbert Mead in the history of action research, emphasize the priority they gave to children learning through experimentation and play and more generally to the social nature of action:

> Another crucial part of their theory of action is that they leave behind the idea of a society made up of isolated individuals (...). The pragmatists' main point is collective creativity.
>
> (Berge and Ve 2000: 25)

Theories of action in action research also draw heavily on the European philosophers, Habermas, Gadamer and Arendt. For Habermas, communicative action was the goal and moral purpose of human endeavour, at its best based upon a process of individuals reaching understanding of each other's 'lifeworlds', derived from their different 'culturally ingrained preunderstandings' (Habermas 1984: 99–101). The problem lay in the constraints for free, equal discourse created by 'relations of force' and 'intrapsychic as well as interpersonal communicative barriers.' (Habermas 1979: 119–20). Hence, he developed the concept of the 'ideal speech situation' in which the conditions for this kind of discourse could be created – by giving all participants equal rights to speak, excluding no views, allowing for the expression of feelings and wishes, and ensuring that all can hold each other account-able for their views (1970). His ideas formed the basis for the critical theory that Carr and Kemmis (1983) used to develop their ideal of emancipatory action research. This reconstructs professional practice as an endeavour 'based on theoretical knowledge and research', undertaken by those who have 'an overriding commitment to the well-being of their clients', and in the control of the professionals themselves who 'reserve the right to make autonomous and independent judgements, free from external non-professional controls and constraints ...' (Carr and Kemmis 1983: 220–1). Gadamer's philosophy drew on the tradition of textual hermeneutics and saw action as emerging from a continuous process of critical reflection, so that experience itself became 'scepticism in action' (Gadamer 1975: 317). This became the basis for Elliott's conceptualization of professional practice as 'a practical science' in which professionals are able to cope with uncer-tainty and change, take decisions in situations that are unpredictable, exer-cise 'practical wisdom' to decide on the most appropriate course of action and exercise 'situational understandings' to decide on which actions will be consistent with 'realizing professional values in a situation' (Elliott 1993: 66–7). For Elliott, action research is a process whereby, through the collec-tion and interpretation of data, in the light of personal reflection and self-evaluation, individuals can establish 'situational understanding,' as the basis for action which integrates practical aims with moral understanding. Coulter (2002) points to the importance for action research of a third philosopher, Hannah Arendt, who carried out her early work in Frankfurt with Habermas and Gadamer but then emigrated to the United States as a refugee from Hitler's Nazis. Arendt's most important contribution for action research theory lies in her insistence that the highest form of human action is located in practice rather than in the sphere of ideas. Coulter uses her the-ories to make a useful distinction between *labour*, *work* and *action*, seeing the first as oriented towards 'survival', the second towards 'creation of some object' and only the third, *action*, as 'exercising human freedom' within conditions of 'plurality', that is, in Arendt's terms, in and with others (Coulter 2002: 199). It is the third of these that Coulter identifies as 'edu-cational action research'.

So, far from drawing on naïve realism, for example to define action as the introduction of treatments to overcome problems defined in simple terms of cause and effect, action research is underpinned by a substantial body of literature that has built up complex theories of action as the prac-tical instantiation of moral ideals and human aspirations. A core concept is the integration of intellectual and theoretical engagement in *praxis*, which Noffke (1995: 1) defines as 'the practical implications of critical thought, the continuous interplay between doing something and revising our thought about what ought to be done'. Such action is seen very often as an explicitly collaborative endeavour. This literature continues to grow as writers seek resolutions to the challenges posed by postmodernist approaches. A particularly interesting contribution comes from Schostak (1999: 401), whose typology of kinds of action is based on the assumption that 'competent action is simply not possible for anyone' and that 'because one cannot foresee all events, action cannot be the product of a total rationality, a complete grasp of a given situation, or state of affairs'. Schostak cites Tragesser's (1977) concept of 'prehension', which covers 'those situations where the grasp of something is incomplete, but not arbitrary and can provide a basis for action.' In practice, this is always the position for action researchers: the collection and analysis of data provide a much better basis for taking action than is ever normally available, but action researchers are always in the position of taking decisions on the basis of prehension rather than full apprehension of the situation.

The nature of the self

The quality of action research depends upon the reflexive sensitivity of the researchers, whose data collection, analysis and interpretations will all be mediated by their sense of self and identity. Although some, such as Whitehead (1989), see an exploration of the self and improvement of one's own practice as the central purpose of carrying out action research, in my view this tips the balance too much towards professional development rather than research. For me, the importance of self-enquiry in action research is a matter of research quality. The self can be said to be a 'research instrument' and action researchers need to be able to take into account their own subjectivity as an important component of meaning making. There is a considerable body of literature on the nature of the self and methods for developing self-knowledge. Of particular interest to me is Feldman's appropriation of existentialism to re-orient teacher education through a process of self-study as 'a moral and political activity' towards 'changing who we are as teachers' (Feldman 2003: 27–8). Many writers place emphasis on writing as a self-revelatory and creative process and the research diary or journal as an essential companion to the process of carrying out action research (O'Hanlon 1997; Altrichter and Holly 2005).

But what exactly is the nature of self and identity? When I first became an action researcher, while still a teacher, I assumed that my 'self' was a unique core identity, akin in many ways to the idea of a 'soul' which had been a major part of my upbringing as a Christian. This self embodied values and beliefs, it was responsible for its actions (here the Christian concept of sin fitted well) and had a 'voice' that could be heard – or not – depending on whether I was accorded respect and rights by participating in a democratic community. In my early work, I presumed this definition of the self more or less unproblematically, believing that action research could empower the individual self and entitling the teachers' publications in the Pupil Autonomy in Learning with Microcomputers (PALM) project, (1988–90) the *Teachers' Voices* series (see Chapter 3). The theories of action embedded in both the emancipatory action research of Carr and Kemmis (1983) and the practical science of Elliott (1993) were also primarily based on an assumption of a unitary self, although both theories stressed the importance of individual selves working in groups and engaging in what Habermas calls 'communicative action'.

In more recent years I have come to see that conceptualizing the self as socially constructed and multiple rather than unitary provides many useful insights into the nature of action in action research. It enables new ways of understanding agency, which I am defining here as the capability of a self to take actions that will have an impact on a social situation. Moving to this new conceptualization of the self was a revelatory process in my learning. I had early on been alerted to the patterned nature of human behaviour through a simple method of interpreting data transcripts called 'pattern analysis' (Ireland and Russell 1978). These patterns are very easily observable in any social situation involving human interaction (Garfinkel 1984). It quickly became clear to me that much human behaviour is strongly routinized and that this has the enormous advantage that we can function effectively in situations that make multiple demands on us (for example, as a manager or a teacher) by off-loading a large proportion of our behaviour to automatic actions and utterances. It also has disadvantages. At a trivial level, for example, we may find ourselves driving somewhere we go everyday when we actually intended to go somewhere quite different. At a more fundamental level the routines established in professional practice – what we say, how we stand, our attitudes to children, to their parents, to colleagues and how we speak to them – are likely to be largely unconscious and may actually be counter-productive to our espoused intentions (Argyris and Schon 1974). Freud's tripartite model of the self is useful in exploring how these routine behaviours are established: the 'ego' or conscious self co-exists with the 'super-ego', which constantly invokes the voice of authority to regulate and control the 'ego', and the 'id' or sub-conscious, which incorporates the basic drives of survival towards food, sex and self-protection and, oblivious to the super-ego, constitutes an uncontrollable force that constantly subverts the intentions of the ego (Freud 1986). Using this model of the self, some of our routine behaviours can be seen as originating in the 'unconscious' and therefore signifying the duality of our purposes in a kind of continual struggle between the civilized and subconscious, uncontrollable elements of our self, mutually constrained by the intrusive and controlling authority of the super-ego. In Freudian analysis, action is always motivated by the self, but the motivation may originate in the id and be largely hidden from, and unacknowledged by, the ego.

The starting point for my re-conceptualization of the self was my reading of the work of George Herbert Mead. His alternative tripartite model of the self provides a different set of insights from those deriving from Freud and allows a different kind of analysis of routinized behaviour. For Mead (1934) the self can be conceptualized as comprising the 'I', which is active, the 'me', which is reflective and the 'generalized other', which constitutes the responses of those with whom the 'I' interacts. Mead's theory of 'symbolic interactionism' explains human action in terms of interactions with others, in which behaviours symbolize intentions and stimulate responses. Using these theories, it becomes clear that routinized behaviours are not specific to individuals but are generated interactively between the self and others. In stimulating our responses and becoming an integral part of our behavioural routines, 'others' become in a very real sense a part of the self. Moreover, the self is not unitary but multiple, since the generalized other is not constant but constantly changing. Here was the explanation for an uncomfortable experience I had had as a child when I invited two friends who did not know each other to play at my house on the same day. I was caught in an unexpected dilemma because I was in the routine of behaving in quite different ways with each of my friends. I couldn't be the expected 'I' to both, because I was in fact different 'I's for each of them. Reading Mead years later was a revelation in relation to this one memory and also gave me new tools for analysing research data from human interactions.

Mead's concept of the self is useful in understanding why change is so often resisted. A good example comes from my early work focused on the introduction of computers into schools and society more generally. It was clear that they aroused a great deal of strong emotions and many people were resistant to using them. The most obvious early use was as a word processor and it might have been expected that those whose work involved writing would be eager to use this facility. There was, of course, the problem of keyboarding, but it seemed that this was only a small part of the reasons for resistance. More fundamental was the disruption to daily routines that would follow from using a computer. Personal space would need to be rearranged, one's favourite pen would no longer be the mediating tool for writing, the socio-cultural ambiance of one's desk with its symbolic items such as a loved-one's photograph, an ornamental paper-weight and a souvenir coffee-cup mat would be invaded by intrusive new presences – a computer and printer – that would need to be centrally positioned to be of use. Work routines would also completely change and new skills need to be learnt and become part of routine behaviour before the computer could be integrated into work as a mediating tool (Wertsch 1998). It was clear to me that these objects and their associated routines had a kind of ritual status and were constitutive of the self's identity (Somekh 1989). Only those who were highly motivated to use computers, often because of their affordances in terms of status or career opportunity, adopted them enthusiastically; for most others, adopting a computer disrupted the routines of behaviour and their ritualistic power in constructing and reconstructing self-identity.

The concept of multiple selves, derived from the work of Mead, is also helpful in understanding the complexities of professional action, for example of teachers, nurses and managers. Moving between many different groups during the course of a working day, managers need to construct themselves in a variety of ways to interact effectively with each group. The power relations will be differently constituted; discourses will need to shift to accommodate more or less formal relationships; different conventions of clothing (jacket on or off), seating (behind the desk or in the easy chair) and hospitality (who makes the coffee) will be appropriate in each case. It became clear that management – and indeed all professional work – involves a process of frequently positioning and repositioning the self to be as effective as possible in a range of working tasks and relationships. This can be seen as a component element of Elliott's (1993) 'situational under-standing' (see Chapter 6 of this book). Moreover, professionals who engage in action research can learn to be more effective in this process of self-posi-tioning as well as other elements of situational understanding. The danger is that this ability to change the nature of the relationship with others through strategic positioning of the self will be exercised manipulatively. As in the exercise of other management strategies, there is a moral imperative to act in the best interests of clients (e.g. children, patients) and colleagues, which becomes increasingly important with increasing levels of skill.

The nature of power

An important issue for action research is the way that power is conceptual-ized, since power is an integral part of the interactions in any group or organization and an active constituent of any process of change. My own early understanding of power followed the work of Lukes (1974) and par-ticularly his 'three-dimensional view', which takes account of a whole host of subtle ways in which power is exercised consciously or unconsciously by individuals within organizations. These include the exercise of power over another 'by influencing, shaping or determining his very wants' (Lukes 1974: 23), and the recognition that 'an apparent case of consensus [may not be] genuine but imposed' (Lukes 1974: 47). This enabled me to reach a deeper understanding of the operation of power between the PALM project team and participating teacher researchers (Somekh 1994) (see Chapter 4). The simple idea that power resided with the members of the external team based in the university, and that participating teachers were necessarily powerless by comparison, was an important part of the initial project design, based on Elliott's combined model of first-order and second-order action research (Elliott 1988), which safeguards teachers' autonomy by formalizing the division of labour. This separation of roles proved to be untenable in the PALM project because the operation of power between members of the team (some of whom were teachers seconded for the life of the project to work at the university) and participating teacher–researchers, and the power relations between the latter and their colleagues in school, created a much more complex terrain. This is not to suggest that power was ever seen by action research theorists as simple. For example, Habermas' critical theory has been very influential in the development of action research methodology (1973; 1974), and considerations of power lie at the heart of Habermas' theory of communicative action (1984) in which power is seen as a contaminating and largely insoluble problem that prevents the establishment of an ideal speech situation. Increasingly, those engaging in action research in whole organizations, as opposed to small focused sites such as hospital wards and classrooms, include an analysis of the operation of micro-politics as a significant factor in the operation of power. The study of 'micropolitics' concerns 'the overt and covert processes through which individuals and groups in an organization's immediate environment acquire and exercise power to promote and protect their own interests' (Malen 1994: 147). By its very nature micro-political power consists in a complex and poorly defined set of relationships and actions that can best be explained by means of observation and interviewing data rather than being formally stated in documents. However, micro-political theories still assume that power is a one-way, and largely negative, force in which the powerful impose on the powerless (Somekh *et al.* 1997) (see Chapter 5).

A more complex and much more subtle way of conceptualizing power is presented by Foucault. Difficult to categorize since his work spans philosophy, sociology and political analysis, Foucault's ideas have been revolutionary in social science research through his influence on postmodernist and deconstructive theories of social formation. His work has become increasingly important in my understanding of action research, particularly in relation to his theory of discourse and its implications for knowledge and power and how this affects the process of social change. His starting point is how power is constructed by the process of categorization and ordering within human cultures (Foucault 1970: xv–xx). To name something, such as mental illness, is the first step in creating a technology of control which becomes a means of exercising power over the mentally ill. Groups are constituted by the technologies and discourses that they construct and sustain. A discourse incorporates words and concepts that instantiate the values and assumptions of the group so that words take on a symbolic value as indicators of adherence to a 'regime of truth' (Foucault 1972: 131), which the group uses to define its purposes and meaning. Hence when the British government redefined teacher education as teacher training it was taking an intentionally meaningful action that had hostile implications for those who categorized themselves as teacher educators. Over time, with some success, it also re-branded teaching in the public mind as a technical rather than a professional activity (training having strong cultural associations with the teaching of low-level skills) and by further development of this discourse (through persistent use in public documents and policy statements of terms such as 'delivery' of the curriculum, 'attainment targets,' 'key skills,' 'key stages,' 'national tests') the culture of training as a technical activity was produced and marketed and the professional autonomy of teachers was reduced and their power eroded.

Interestingly, Foucault does not conceptualize power as negative. Rather, he sees it as a productive social construction that is inherent to human interaction (Foucault 1977: 194). It may be either negative or positive in its impact. It is also not something that is done by one person to another; oppression is a function of the group as much as any one individual and self-categorization is always a factor, individuals are therefore complicit in the exercise of power as it affects them negatively as well as positively. These ideas provide an important set of tools for the analysis of change, often in ways that are counter to the assumptions of participants in organizations.

Action research for agency in organizational change

The origins of action research in Lewin's work with communities and its long tradition in the field of management as a means of bringing about organizational change have established its importance as a methodology that supports systemic change rather than necessarily focusing on tightly bounded, local sites of study such as classrooms. By 'systemic change' I mean simply that individuals and groups always work within socio-cultural, political and economic structures that themselves are regulated by organizational, regional, national and international frameworks, so change initiatives have to be undertaken across all these levels or at least consciously take them into account. Elliott's early work showed that teachers could not change their practice in classrooms without the support of senior managers in their school and that groups of teachers could work most effectively by involving parents, governors and pupils in action research (Ebbutt and Elliott 1985). In developing their concept of emancipatory action research, Carr and Kemmis advocated that teachers should engage with the broader ideological and political structures in which their schools and classroom practice are embedded, with the aim of establishing a more just and democratic society of the kind envisaged by Habermas' concept of communicative action. Elliott was consciously accessing these broader levers of power when he established in 1978 the Classroom (now Collaborative) Action Research Network (CARN). More recently, Posch has analysed the impact of changes in society on schools and carried out action research to develop 'dynamic networking' as a means of producing local knowledge that takes account of the larger system and impacts directly on practice (Posch 2000). In a powerful critique of simplistic assumptions, commonly held by politicians across the world, that the economic success of nations depends on improving educational standards in terms of test scores, Elliott (2000: 184) points to the work of Posch and his colleagues as an alternative approach to change that is 'grounded in a comprehensive analysis of social and economic change in advanced industrial societies'.

A major issue for social scientists is the extent to which change can be brought about by the agency of individuals and the extent to which individual action is determined by the institutional structures within which they live and work. From a Marxist point of view (Marx 1977: 249–51) the power of capital enforces the oppression of workers through the mechanism of the labour market. Individual workers are unable to exercise agency. Indeed, through the power of institutions such as the state and organized religion they become willing participants in their own subservience. Part of the process by which this is achieved is by 'false consciousness' whereby those who are oppressed are unable to perceive the object of their oppression. A sense of agency is therefore illusory. For Marx, the only way to make workers free was through revolutionary change to replace the oppressive powers of capitalism with a system of common ownership in which all are equal.

A Foucauldian analysis of power suggests that agency should as a first step involve deconstructing the discourses and regimes of truth that construct social action and his concept of power as an energy emerging from social interaction perhaps opens up possibilities for action research to move from deconstruction to action. Giddens' structuration theory directly confronts the structure–agency debate by suggesting that these two forces, previously seen as separate, are actually inter-related:

> According to the notion of the duality of structure, the structural properties of social systems are both medium and outcome of the practices they recursively organize.
>
> (Giddens 1984: 25)

The institutional structures, whether of school, education system, state or multi-national company are not monolithic and rigid, but fluid and incrementally changing. As Altrichter and Salzeber (2000: 108) put it: 'Organizations, in our understanding, are webs woven from concrete interactions of (self-) interested actors.' They are formed in fact by the practices of the people who work within them, which continuously construct and reconstruct them, since they are constituted by people as much as by regulations, held together as Foucault suggests by the complicity of those who work within them. Thus in organizations where resistance to change is deep rooted (as in the case of the institutional resistance of education systems to fundamental changes in working practices using computer technologies), it originates in, and is sustained by, processes of cultural reproduction in which neither the formal structures of the institution nor the informal networks of individuals are capable of circumventing the resistance of the other (Somekh 2004). By the same token, by taking concerted action linked to the development of understanding of their own processes, schools can come to see themselves 'as agents of change, not as objects of change' and take on the role of 'knowledge-building schools' (Groundwater-Smith 2005: 342).

To unlock agency of individuals and groups and promote and sustain change in an organization, action research needs to adopt a systemic approach. The work of Argyris (1993), particularly his theory of 'double-loop learning', suggests that groups should work interactively and reflectively to go beyond their personal learning and aim for a broader impact on improving working methods and practices across their whole workplace. Senge's (1993) theory of the learning organization implies the need for cross-departmental and inter-functional collaboration and development. In some of my own work, I have adopted this approach by developing a systemic approach to action research, involving partnership between action research leaders who between them have access to many of the different levers of power in their organization (see Chapter 5). The important point here is that all the leaders carry out action research in relation to their own roles, to promote change within their own area of influence, rather than those of higher status planning and managing the action research to be carried out by colleagues of lower status. There is the need to be prepared for the potential difficulties of collaboration and ready to negotiate issues openly but with sensitivity, for example such collaborations often involve agreements of confidentiality between team members, including a procedure for individuals to give formal 'clearance' before information and reports that refer to them are made available beyond the group.

Another useful way of understanding the relationship between agency and institutional structures is through socio-cultural theories drawing on the work of Vygotsky, whose starting point is that human action is always mediated by cultural tools (Wertsch 1998: 25–30) (see Chapter 8). Action may be 'internal' or 'external' and does not originate in the human agent alone but is jointly produced in tension between the agent and the cultural tool. To explain this Wertsch gives the example of pole vaulting, in which the athlete can only jump the bar by using the pole, but it is almost impossible to think of any human activity that is not dependent on tools in a similar way. Socio-cultural tools are embedded in historical practices and institutional structures and their affordances either enable or constrain the actions of individuals. Drawing on cultural tools, individual agents are oriented towards achieving objects and capable of action within the constraints of the larger activity system which frames their actions. Engeström has developed a method of Developmental Work Research (DWR) that uses cultural–historical activity theory (CHAT) as the basis for working with those who share in a common area of practice (such as care for children with chronic multiple health needs) to generate knowledge about their work practices, identify points of contradiction in the activity system and use these as the basis for refining and improving it (Engeström 2005). In terms of the theories of action I have been discussing, activity theory is particularly helpful because it gives priority to collaborative decision making on the basis of sharing knowledge about identified 'contradictions'.

A further development of these theories is the concept of 'distributed cognition' (Salomon 1993), which gives emphasis to the generation of knowledge by an activity system as a whole rather than by individuals working within it. In practice, few have gone so far as to reject the significance of individual minds of learners/workers in shaping the activity system, but many see an additional significant role for distributed cognition as groups carry out joint activity, sometimes moving to a point – as in the example of air traffic controllers – where no one individual holds the knowledge and skills to carry out the whole of the activity and it can be said to be jointly carried out by the group as a whole who share responsibility for it between them (Hutchins and Klausen 1996).

Socio-cultural theories, drawing as they do on the inter-related and embedded nature of action and the way in which it is shaped by socio-cultural tools and historically derived practices, make it clear why the simple model of an individual planning and implementing change by undertaking action research in isolation from others is unrealistic. The systemic nature of human activity makes it critically important for action research to be undertaken collaboratively.

Collaboration and emancipation

Another of the key concepts in action research, which has tended to be adopted too simplistically, is collaboration. The importance of social rather than individual action is frequently assumed in the literature (Mead 1934; Dewey 1944; Habermas 1984) and for Carr and Kemmis (1983) collaboration was an essential component of emancipatory action research. When engaging in action research projects it would seem that the starting point is often an assumption that the process of collaboration will be supportive and unproblematic. This was certainly my own position when embarking on the PALM project (see Chapter 4). It was necessary for us to learn about the problematics of collaboration through the conduct of the research. It was not just the operation of power that constrained our working relationships with teachers, but the fundamental differences in how we understood the world. What we came to learn was that our collaboration should not aim to 'empower' the teachers by inducting them into new understandings of our world, but that each side of the partnership should learn to respect the others' values and assumptions in a participatory process that involved moving between and inhabiting each other's worlds. There is after all something inevitably patronizing in the concept of others needing to be emancipated, particularly as the literature always assumes that the university-based partners will be the leaders in emancipating those characterized as 'practitioners.' It is hard to escape the implication in this discourse that practice is of lower status than theory and this is clearly contrary to the espoused values of action researchers.

Sumara and Luce-Kapler (1993) provide a detailed analysis of the process of collaboration in action research, starting with the original meaning of the word, 'co-labouring', and using this to illuminate the discomfort and difficulties of collaboration described by many writers. They see these apparent problems as 'healthy and productive, for it is during moments of disagreement, of negotiation, of *labouring over that which is difficult* that we gain insights into ourselves, each other, and whatever enterprise binds us together. (Sumara and Luce-Kapler 1993: 394). This concurs with my own finding that episodes of substantial friction are frequently the starting point for deeper level collaboration (Somekh 1994: 266–7). They are, of course, an indication of the deep seriousness with which both sides of the partnership view their joint endeavour. The friction is sometimes the result of anxiety that we are being pulled by our partners towards actions that are mistaken, other times it is a consequence of too much holding back and forced politeness so that emotions are suppressed and frustration levels build up. Sumara and Luce-Kapler's metaphor of action research as a 'writerly text' is a good one, for the process of grappling with a difficult reading and being forced to co-construct meanings with the text is similar to 'co-labouring' with partners when we 'encounter many "knots" (Murray 1990, p. 80) of discomfort, difficulty and frustration'. They conclude:

> We believe that this is the fundamental power of action research as a writerly text: it expects research to be like our reading of *The English Patient*:[1] unpredictable, often uncomfortable, challenging, yet always infused with the possibility of what the next page will bring.
>
> (Sumara and Luce-Kapler 1993: 394)

---

[1]   Ondaatje, M. (1997) *The English Patient*. London: Macmillan.

Socio-cultural theories of learning also shed useful light on the process of collaboration in action research. For example, Lave and Wenger's (1991) analysis of communities of practice as sites for 'legitimate peripheral participation' models the process of learning through joint activity alongside expert role models rather than through overt instruction. Although the notion of experts and novices at first appears to imply inequality, the process as described by Lave and Wenger is mutually respectful. In his later book, Wenger (1998) analyses the characteristics of a productive community of practice as involving: a 'joint enterprise', which is negotiated and for which all partners are mutually accountably; 'mutual engagement', which involves diversity between the participants but a commitment to doing things together; and a 'shared repertoire' of stories, artifacts, discourses and concepts, which are built up over time and engender a sense of community – for example through laughing *with* each other over shared memories (Wenger 1998: 72–85). Wenger, too, emphasizes the inevitability and often desirability of disagreements and stresses that sometimes these can be accepted and tolerated rather than being the subject of negotiation, depending, of course, on the seriousness of the disagreement and whether or not it has the potential to undermine the joint enterprise. In analysing the tensions arising from cross-national collaboration and our resulting inter-cultural learning in a European project, Pearson and I used Wenger's model of a community of practice as an analytical framework (Somekh and Pearson 2002).

Social justice and democracy

No research is ever neutral, but action research because it embodies an imperative for change is always explicitly value laden. Noffke (1997) begins her review of action research literature with a quotation from Martin Luther King, deliberately adopting a political stance oriented towards social justice, while acknowledging that, for some action researchers, the main impetus is professional and for others personal. Her three categories are not, of course, mutually exclusive and because all action research is rooted in aspirations for improvement it always has an inescapable moral purpose. What varies greatly is the extent to which action researchers engage explicitly with the larger political structures that play a part in shaping local action. The sites of struggle in contemporary society such as gender and social class, ethnic identity and sexual orientation, are inscribed in larger patterns of the global economy, multi-national enterprises, mass communications media and international agencies. Action research takes place in local contexts, involving individuals and groups working together to improve aspects of practice; but the day-to-day experience of those groups and the action research process itself are always embedded in these larger social structures.

What has changed over time is not the inescapable social justice imperative underpinning action research, whether or not explicitly stated, but the level of awareness of action researchers about the social justice implications of their work and the rejection of over-simplistic notions about equity and emancipation. When I had been working for a year on the PALM project Melanie Walker came to the University of East Anglia from South Africa and joined our project team as an adviser. Having just completed a major study of action research as a means of empowerment for teachers working in the Bantu education system within the South African political structures of apartheid, her primary interest was not in if and how teachers could use computers to help children to become more autonomous learners, but in whether or not our action research was exploring the social and political implications of the policy that had put computers into schools in the first place. Her questions were challenging for me on two levels. First, they raised my awareness of my own possible collusion in oppressive practices were I not to address questions of this kind explicitly; second, they signalled for me the radical differences in our points of view and how these had been constructed by the social and political contexts in which we had both worked, first as teachers and later as leaders of action research projects. Political structures and differences rooted in personal experiences both need to be addressed explicitly in action research. Whose interests will be served by the work? What are the hegemonic structures within which it will be carried out? What are the differences in background and experience of the different partners and their client groups?

Moreover, my new understandings of the formation and operation of power within organizations and groups, stemming from the work of Foucault and Giddens, has increased my understanding of the complexity of social justice issues. It is no longer sufficient to operate with simple concepts such as equity, partnership, empowerment and 'giving voice,' since these are what Stronach and McNamara (2002: 156) call 'political weasel words'. As Walker points out:

> discourses are never closed fields; there are always many ways of seeing and understanding, some of which accord with dominant, hegemonic discourses which then appear 'natural' and appeal to 'common sense'. Other discourses challenge the common-sense view.
>
> (Walker 2001: 12)

So the pursuit of social justice in action research involves keeping open definitions for the organizing concepts and categories we develop, remaining sensitive to the different interpretations that individuals bring to words and actively seeking to identify and respect difference and diversity. It is

Arendt's insight of plurality (Arendt 1978: 187) that provides us with our most reliable organizing principle, as well as her understanding that it is through our actions that we make meanings rather than through words. Fascination with idiosyncrasy, respect for difference, effort to understand the experience of others within their own terms not ours, constant vigilance against falling into complacency and the ability to catch ourselves out in unthinking, routinized power play – these are all qualities that we should strive for if we are serious about social justice. Put more simply it's about taking delight in the diversity of human beings while recognizing our commonality of experience. As Griffiths puts it so eloquently:

> It is difficult to balance the knowledge that we are all the same in being human, with the knowledge that part of being human is, precisely, our unquenchable agency, our lovely creativity, our need and ability to make societies and communities: so that we are all – humanly – different.
>
> (Griffiths 2003: 7)

There is a necessary intellectual toughness, too. As Walker points out (1995: 17) there is the need to use scholarship to challenge any easy acceptance of 'common sense' understandings and to recognize that making meanings on the basis of experience alone is insufficient. She advocates 'passionate scholarship' … to prevent action research from being 'domesticated' and 'congealing into hegemonic orthodoxy'.

The concept of democracy is particularly problematic since its meaning has become blurred by politicians' habitual use of it to claim a moral highground. The unthinking application of the concept of democracy as a solution to the problems of third world countries is an example of what Fals-Borda and Mora-Osejo (2003a) call 'Eurocentrism'. They identify the need to develop regulatory structures and governmental practices that are sensitive to the complexity of developing countries' cultures and practices, and call upon participatory action research as a means of resisting the unthinking operation of hegemonic power by countries such as the USA. Gergen (2003) presents a particularly intriguing and insightful analysis of the concept of democracy in which he starts by defining 'first order democracy' in the context of many participatory action research projects as no more than 'effective coordination,' an essential first step in ensuring the functionality of society, but containing within itself an impetus to exclude and dominate (Gergen 2003: 51). He argues that what is needed is 'second order democracy' in which easy categorization of practices is resisted. His key concept is 'relational responsibility':

> The proposal in this case is that we bracket the tradition of indi-

vidual autonomy, out of which the presumption of individual responsibility, blame, alienation, and guilt arise. Rather, we may justifiably foreground our responsibility to ongoing processes of relating. (...) When we are responsible to the process of relating in which meaning is indeed given birth, we essentially support the possibility of a good life, society or world.

(Gergen 2003: 53)

Knowledge generation in action research

As this chapter draws to a close I want to return to the key issues about the nature of knowledge that have already been touched on in the section on 'the nature of action'. The starting point for this book is that action research provides a means whereby research can become a systematic intervention, going beyond describing, analysing and theorizing social practices to working in partnership with participants to reconstruct and transform those practices. This presupposes that it is possible to generate actionable knowledge which is trustworthy in providing the foundation for improvement. As already discussed earlier in this chapter, this is not an easy position to hold at a time when the nature of knowledge is strongly contested. Yet, rather than seeing action research as unsustainable in the light of these challenges, I see it as benefiting from a much more complex understanding of what counts as actionable knowledge and what may be accepted as a trustworthy foundation for improvement. There is much to be gained by adopting a dual approach: generating contextualized knowledge on the basis of careful, systematic inquiry and evaluating this through action oriented towards improvement; while at the same time maintaining a critical scepticism and openness to different interpretations that iteratively challenge the action research 'findings' in terms of both the appropriateness of the action and any claims to improvement. This is in line with Haraway, who argues that we need

> simultaneously [...] a critical practice for recognizing our own 'semiotic technologies' for making meanings, *and* a no-nonsense commitment to faithful accounts of a 'real' world.
>
> (Haraway 1991: 187)

Far from weakening my argument for the importance of action research as a research methodology for the social sciences, new understandings of the nature of knowledge can be seen to strengthen it. If it is no longer possible to establish truths which are generalisable across contexts, it is no longer a disadvantage to have a methodology which always generates contextualized knowledge. Because of its contextualized nature, knowledge generated from action research is cautious in its claims, sensitive to variations and open to reinterpretation in new contexts. It is, therefore, not only more useful than traditional forms of knowledge as the basis for action but also more open than traditional forms of knowledge to accepting the challenge of its own socially constructed nature and provisionality.

Giddens strengthens this argument further by providing a new theoretical basis for understanding the nature of generalizable knowledge and its relation to action. In the introduction to the book in which he sets out structuration theory to explain the nature and power of human agency, he makes the point that 'the uncovering of generalizations is not the be-all and end-all of social theory' (Giddens 1984: xix). He goes on to argue that there are two 'poles' of generalization 'with a range and variety of possible shadings between them'. His argument is that many generalizations 'hold because actors themselves know them – in some guise – and apply them in the enactment of what they do'. These generalizations don't need to be discovered although 'the social science observer [...] may give a new discursive form to them'. Other generalizations, he continues, 'refer to aspects of circumstances, of which agents are ignorant and which effectively "act" on them, independent of whatever the agents may believe they are up to'. He further argues that generalizations of this second kind 'are mutable in respect to what those agents can learn knowledgeably to "make happen". From this derives the (logically open) transformative impact which the social sciences can have on their "subject matter".' In other words, Giddens opens up the possibility of a kind of social science methodology that transforms the understandings of participants in a social situation and gives them new personal knowledge and insights as the basis for agency to improve social practices. Action research can be seen as a methodology that uniquely enables and facilitates this process of knowledge transformation as the basis for powerful social action. A good example of this is Noffke's account (Noffke and Somekh 2005) of multiple levels of action research involving teachers, parents, students and an administrator in a school, as well as the whole of the local community. The overlapping understandings of the various parties developed from different perspectives: 'Yet in each story, the process of research is cyclical and focused both on producing new knowledge and on creating actions which will affect directly the social situation in which the issue emerges' (Noffke and Somekh 2005: 92).

Elliott's work over nearly 30 years focuses in particular on the nature of practitioner knowledge and gives a firmer basis to understanding this transformative process. He argued first that theorizing was a core activity of teaching (Elliott 1976: 35) and that teachers' theories were of practical value through a process of 'naturalistic generalization' whereby other teachers can 'intuitively' relate the case to their own context (Elliott 1985: 13). As already discussed, in his later work, drawing on Dreyfus, he provided a detailed analysis of educational action research as a method for managers, teachers and other professionals to develop 'situational understanding' (Elliott 1993: 71–83). This can be seen as a kind of knowledge very similar to the deeper level understanding that Giddens suggests should be the aim of social science interventions in practice. More recently Elliott has revisited his definition of actionable knowledge in the light of Arendt's theory of action. He argues: 'my account of action research includes rather than excludes theoretical activity as an aspect of the practical' and he builds on the work of Macmurray to show that through reflection knowledge in action research includes both the 'intellectual mode' and the 'emotional mode' and that 'it is this mode of theoretical reflection which lies at the heart of the action research process' (Elliott 2004: 21–3). This more holistic definition of knowledge, involving emotion, is similar to Winter's definition of 'theory' in action research as 'speculative play with possible general explanations of what we experience and observe' (Winter 2002: 27). Like Elliott, Winter sees involvement in the production of actionable knowledge as crucial to being a citizen in a civil society. He writes:

> This is a form of theory which is integrative, critical and political; it is both personal and collective, a synthesis of values and understandings, and a response to the many methodological dimensions of practical action in complex organizations profoundly influenced by external political forces.
>
> (Winter 2002: 41).

Elliott (1989), in common with other action research theorists, explains the nature of professional action drawing on Aristotle's ways of knowing, in particular drawing a distinction between *techne* (technical knowledge involving building something new) and *phronesis* (knowledge that combines reason and moral understanding as the basis for action). Carr and Kemmis (1983) further explain the distinction for the Greeks between the kind of practical action (*poietike*) that draws on *techne* and the practical, morally informed action (*praxis*) that draws on *phronesis* (Carr and Kemmis 1983: 33–4). In my own work, I have further explored another of Aristotle's five ways of knowing, *nous* (an unreasoned state of intuitive knowledge) to show that it provides the best explanation of Dreyfus' 'situational understanding'. Action research enables the transformation of the unthinking routines of practice, which may have been established at a time when an individual was undertaking something new (for example, practice placements during pre-service teacher education) and not capable of acting with sensitivity and moral judgement, into the finely tuned intuitive actions grounded in depth of understanding (*nous*) that are characteristic of the best professional practice (Somekh and Thaler 1997: 151–2).

In the Introduction to this book I told a story about my own early induction into the power of personal knowledge generated through action research to generalize to another similar context, through a process of inter-personal mediation and negotiation. This is the process of 'communicative validation' described by Altrichter *et al.* (1993) or Elliott's 'naturalistic generalization' referred to earlier. Case studies that focus on the day-to-day experience of individuals in a particular setting, and involve the collection of a wide range of data to allow in-depth analysis, uncover the multifaceted complexity of human behaviour in groups and organizations. If they are used to generate multiple interpretations and these are engaged with and interrogated by the participants in other settings to provide alter-native explanatory theories, this constitutes a process of communicative validation and strengthens their potential for transformative action.

There is, however, a problem in converting this personal, contextual knowledge into knowledge that can be easily made available to a wide audi-ence. The problem lies in a dilemma relating to the nature of case study texts: while it is clear that case study knowledge is capable of being com-pared across cases, and that Stenhouse's (1981) vision of a library of case studies should, as he claimed, make it possible to establish trends across cases and create a multiplier effect in terms of impact, case studies, as texts, are too demanding of the reader to be read in large numbers. The genre of case study demands the reader's full focus of attention and invites a kind of constructive, interactive reading, akin to what Sumara and Luce-Kapler (1993) call 'writerly reading'. Case studies are not often 'writerly texts' in the sense of being complex and difficult, but they require a similar kind of engagement from the reader so that a process of communicative validation can take place leading to naturalistic generalization. Discussing this problem in relation to the nature of knowledge generated by teachers in the PALM project, I have argued the need for a process of 'dialectical interpre-tation' that generates a substantial body of knowledge, communicatively validated and capable of becoming the basis for action (see Chapter 4).

The alternative approach is to draw the case study reports together, engage all participants in carrying out a cross-case analysis and to produce a succinct summary of the knowledge outcomes. All the individual action researchers will, of course, have produced knowledge actionable in their own context, and indeed integral to their leadership of the whole process of action and change, but taking this a step further to publish that knowledge and thereby make it available to a wider audience is crucially important.

2 Doing Action Research Differently

Because action research is a methodology that closely involves participants in a social situation it is necessarily strongly influenced by their values and culture. The history of the group, its traditions, the kinds of tools it uses to mediate its activities, its dominant discourses and regimes of truth, the institutional structures in which it is framed and the political constructions of power and ideology that enable and constrain its activities, all play a part in determining how action research methodology is shaped to the group's purposes and the kinds of knowledge that are generated by action research projects. In Chapter 1 I discussed many of the theoretical concepts that underpin this statement. In this chapter I will explore the implications for action research methodology of this cultural fluidity and responsiveness.

The chapter is divided into three sections, the first on action research in 'southern' or 'developing' countries, the second on action research in health and social care settings, and the third on action research in business settings. All these settings are, of course, educational since education is a life-long process that incorporates the continuous development and learning of adults in their work places and communities. Each section begins with a personal narrative of my experience of action research in this setting and what interests me about it. This is followed by a short sub-section discussing some of the theoretical resources I have found most helpful in understanding it. I am using this term in the Stenhousean sense of 'resources to think about the problems of living rather than objects of mastery' (Elliott 1998: 116). So these short sub-sections enable me to engage in what Elliott (1990: 5) calls 'a dialectical process' of drawing out 'meaning and significance' from knowledge developed by others and 'reconstructing' it in the light of my own 'historically conditioned consciousness'. Each section ends with a commentary on some published reports in order to illustrate action research practices in the particular setting.

It is important to say that these studies of action research in different settings have not been chosen to be representative of work in these fields as a whole and there is no intention to make judgements of the relative value of the different approaches. They have been chosen, rather, because I see them all as being of high quality and particular interest to me personally. The chapter as a whole ends with reflections on what can be learnt from these examples about the culturally responsive nature of action research. Readers from across different professions will, I hope, bring their own examples to their reading of this chapter and further explore this diversity of action research practice.

Action research in 'southern' or 'developing' countries

A personal narrative

I have never spent long in a 'southern' country and I am very aware that I am ill-equipped to relate to the culture and values of being 'southern' or 'developing', and the experience for those who live there of being categorized as such by Eurocentric people such as myself. Since many of my readers will share this 'otherness' I want to sketch how I remember my experience of two visits that I made to Brazil and South Africa, both more than 10 years ago. My intention is to show what I learnt as this influences how I will write this section. My selective memories may also be useful in revealing the assumptions and values that I brought to these experiences.

I first visited a 'southern' county in 1989 when attending a conference in Brazil on the use of computers in education. It was organized jointly by the Federal University of Rio de Janeiro and the Rio branch of the Catholic University, PUCE. I arrived on the evening when the outcomes of the first round of the presidential election had just been announced and the right-wing candidate, Color, and the communist, Lula, had emerged as the two to go forward to the second ballot. During the next week I was hosted alternately by faculty members from the software engineering department of the university and employees of IBM Brazil, which had sponsored my visit. It was an excellent introduction to Brazilian politics. At a time when the inflation rate was so high that taxis had a sliding-scale chart pinned to the interior of the back window to enable you to calculate your fare, and when the fall of the Berlin wall had just radically changed the global power balance, the election issues were sharply drawn: the positive impact of multi-national companies like IBM which created jobs was counter-balanced by their habit of paying taxes overseas rather than in Brazil; the power of the USA was potentially threatening in a post-Soviet world and communists looked to Cuba for leadership; poverty was endemic, with a large proportion of the population living in *favellas* with no proper sanitation scattered among and between the housing areas for the rich and the middle classes; schools were so packed that students only attended for half a day and the 'morning students' and their teachers vacated the building at lunch time to make room for the 'afternoon' cohort – and many children did not attend school at all as was clear from watching the child labourers working on the construction site that adjoined the school where I visited for a day. My own assumptions and values were jolted out of Eurocentric complacency by this visit. My political, ideological and educational assumptions shifted ground. I was intrigued and excited to learn that if Lula won the election he intended to appoint Paulo Freire as Minister of Education. I was surprised and impressed to find that philosophy was a subject on the high school curriculum, something that I had never at that time encountered in Britain and that was certainly not the case in the newly established national curriculum for England and Wales.

In 1993, I visited South Africa immediately following the election of Nelson Mandela as President in the first democratic elections. This time the purpose was to assist in building research capacity among academic staff at the University of the Western Cape where Melanie Walker was at that time head of the Department of Academic Development. UWC had played a leading role in the 'struggle' against apartheid in support of the ANC (African National Congress) and several members of its senior management, including the Rector, had just left to join Mandela's government as senior advisers. I spent the majority of my time working with four female members of academic staff on an evaluation of the Communities Partnership Project (CPP), which was funded by the Kellogg's Foundation to improve the quality of professional education in nursing and occupational therapy. Specifically, CPP was developing community-based professional education for student nurses and occupational therapists (OTs) who as a result were based for a substantial part of their training in a nearby black African township called Mfleni. The day ended early because travel home across the Cape Flats to Melanie's house where I was staying was dangerous after dark. In the evenings I was entertained by my working colleagues who belonged variously to the different previously segregated communities of white, Asian, black and coloured, and were experiencing the shifts in power that were signalled by the recent elections for each of their groups. I was introduced to several people who could tell stories of their time in prison on Robben Island, one of whom on hearing I was half Irish told me how he and fellow prisoners had been inspired by reading the poetry and plays of Yeats, O'Casey and other Irish writers from the time of the 1916 'rising' against the English colonial power.

In Brazil I had only been able to visit schools and talk to teachers from schools and the university, but in South Africa I engaged in an evaluation of CPP over a two-week period in partnership with staff from the faculties of nursing and OT at UWC, with two months further follow-up time to write the report together, using email to keep us linked, after I had returned to England. We used a highly collaborative approach, designing the study together and analysing data in group workshops. Our research team visited

Mfleni to observe the students working in community clinics and children's homes. We collected data by interviewing students, members of university staff and community-based nurses and OTs; two of us worked together in all cases because I needed to be accompanied by a translator; the notes from interviews and observations were written up and jointly analysed and discussed. I was able to see for myself how our data reflected the shifting politics and ideologies of that unique period in South Africa, so that many times I needed the help of colleagues to understand the values and assumptions embedded in discourse and the maelstrom of recent experiences and mixed fear–guilt–exultation–hope that constructed responses to events in the data such as a sudden loud bang outside the health centre in Mfleni. In discussion with the director of CPP and through the process of writing up the research in a public document, I acquired some understanding of the way in which overseas aid constructs the possibilities and boundaries for a development project in a 'southern' country.

Theoretical resources for understanding the experience or action research in 'southern' countries

How to make sense of my experiences in Brazil and South Africa? Perhaps my predominant response was a feeling of inadequacy, a kind of collectively engendered guilt that merely by being white and from a 'northern' developed country I was colluding in the oppression of the poor. In *Pedagogy of the Oppressed* (1972), the Brazilian educational philosopher and activist, Paulo Freire, in many ways confirms me in this role of the oppressor. For Freire, the poor are systematically oppressed by the rich, colluding in their own oppression by desiring the kind of 'banking concept of education' that is delivered by schools. Teachers have 'narration sickness' (Freire 1972: 45) endlessly delivering information to 'fill' the heads of their students, whereas genuine education can only be experienced through 'praxis', that is combined reflection and action through which the consequences of action 'become the object of critical reflection' (Freire 1972: 41). Education needs to be of a different kind to liberate the oppressed, specifically it needs to be 'problem-posing education', which is itself 'the practice of freedom' (Freire 1972: 52–4). At the computers in education conference I attended in Brazil undercurrents of tension had been observable between those who shared Freire's vision of education and those who were impatient to roll out a package of development through equipping schools with computers. Freire conceives of oppression as 'cultural invasion' (Freire 1972: 121), which he sees as a complex process whereby even those whose intention is to liberate will perpetuate oppression unless they engage consciously in praxis, in partnership with the oppressed, rather than as their intended benefactors. This, too, rings true with my perception in Brazil: oppression originated in the political and economic structures of Brazil itself, as well as the political and economic structures imposed on Brazil from overseas; but compared with my experience in the UK, there was a much higher level of consciousness of poverty and crime, and tension between those who constructed this as oppression and those who preferred to lay blame at the door of the oppressed themselves.

Fals-Borda (2001) has been a leader in taking Freire's ideas forward and developing an 'alternative paradigm' of participatory action research (PAR) which is focused on achieving 'transformations' and replaces what he calls the 'fetish-like idea of Science as Truth' with 'our *praxis-inspired commitment*' (Fals-Borda 2001: 28–9). His energy and idealism break out of the measured discourse of academic writing and strongly signal for me a passionate Latin-American intellectualism and activism – very much an embodiment of the praxis that both he and Freire advocate. 'PAR is not only a research methodology but also a philosophy of life' he writes, and a few pages on refers to the PAR researchers as 'the rising universal brotherhood of critical intellectuals – women and men' (Fals-Borda 2001: 34) which will overcome the combined evils of the world. This belief in the power of agency resonates well with the enthusiasm and hope which I found amongst those in South Africa who were reminiscing about their times in the 'struggle' and their hopes for the 'new South Africa', but it is his references to paradigm struggles between praxis-inspired commitment and a more traditional reliance upon science to uncover truth which strike truer to my experience of working on the evaluation of CPP, a project in which participants had to manoeuvre between the values and purposes of an international donor agency, the university's shifting political and academic standing in the emerging state, and the range of conflicting values and aspirations of academic staff in the nursing and OT departments, student nurses and OTs with a mix of white, Asian and coloured heritages, and community-based professionals of African heritage in Mfleni.

When I returned from South Africa I went straight into an interview for an academic post in a well-established British university. 'Culture shock' in the sense of a sudden and complete change in the discourse/values of my 'generalized other' and hence a reorientation of my identity was, I think, a factor in my not getting the job. My experience in South Africa and my work in the CPP evaluation had sensitized me to issues of social justice and raised my political awareness; I may have lost some of my first world academic detachment and lost touch somewhat with the discourse of British university education faculties. Even if it was not a determining factor in my losing the job, I was strongly aware of looking at issues in a different light. Fals-Borda and Mora-Osejo (2003a) provide an interesting analysis of the divergence in academic culture, and in particular in understandings of the nature of knowledge, between their own country of Columbia and Eurocentric countries such as the USA, Britain and Australia. They describe how during the 1950s their knowledge of 'the unique characteristics of the tropical milieu in the Amazonian and Andean regions' was challenged by orthodox scientific knowledge developed in first world countries. Context influences the construction of knowledge not only in the social sciences but in the natural sciences too, they contend. They argue for the importance of recognizing the 'fragility and complexity' of the tropics in regard to climate, soil and ecosystems' which 'in turn conditions human behaviour and enriches cultural patterns' (Fals-Borda and Mora-Osejo 2003a: 34–5). This, they argue, is an important ingredient in 'the Participatory Action Research (PAR) school that we developed in the so-called Third World' (Fals-Borda and Mora-Osejo 2003a: 36).

Examples of action research in 'southern' countries

I have chosen two published accounts of action research in 'southern' countries as the basis for reflecting on the nature of action research in these settings. They are drawn from South Africa and Brazil.

1 Images of Professional Development *by Melanie J Walker, published by the Human Sciences Research Council, Cape Town, South Africa, 1996 (Walker 1996)*

Walker's study engages directly with the question: To what extent is any external intervention intended to improve an oppressive education system inevitably itself oppressive, particularly if the intervention is grounded in knowledge from the developed world and is being applied to a 'southern' or 'third world' country? Walker's book presents a critical reflection on the action research study she carried out with teachers in the Bantu education system that existed in South Africa until the end of apartheid in 1993. The original study was her doctoral thesis; the book contains considerable additional material including reflections on extracts from the thesis. She writes as a white South African whose purpose in carrying out action research with teachers in black African schools was to assist their professional development. She is explicit that the experience of working with them was also powerful in terms of her own professional development.

In her study, Walker draws substantially on knowledge from first world countries, but a significant body of references (43 out of approximately 190) are to authors who have worked and published in South Africa. There are also two references to books by Freire published in London. The orientation of the whole book is towards promoting social justice and struggling to minimize the power differentials that constructed Walker's relationship with the teachers. The action research process she engaged in with the teachers is described in considerable detail, with extended sections consisting of transcripts of discussions and extracts from her field notes. This is a highly reflexive study that makes few claims for its own efficacy in bringing about change. She describes how her work is caught in the tension that is historically embedded in action research between an impetus to empower and an impetus to 'a social engineering element' (Walker 1996: 208). Her aim is to work with teachers on terms of mutual respect and equality, but she illustrates very fully how this aim is unattainable given the oppressive structures of the Bantu education system in which her teacher–partners are encultured. The teachers' attitudes to their work and to her as a 'white woman' are constructed by the power relationships inscribed in the ideology of apartheid. Moreover, Walker suggests, drawing on the work of Ellsworth, that her action research methodology with its aims of empowering teachers and giving them 'voice' is perpetuating the '"the repressive myths" of a critical pedagogy' (Walker 1996: 115). The teachers inevitably accept their own lack of agency and initially prefer to blame the absence of resources in their own school for limitations in their teaching rather than try out the new teaching practices that Walker is suggesting.

Nevertheless, although she believes that the impact of the action research is limited, Walker identifies occasional 'transforming moments' in which individual teachers appear to move towards greater criticality and some sense of their own agency. One of these occurs after she has demonstrated a new pedagogic approach and several teachers have in turn tried it out in their own classrooms. In her commentary on the transcript, Walker says that she is interested in the way one of the teachers 'accounts for her own development' (Walker 1996: 147) rather than the accuracy or distortion of her account of reality. Here Walker's thinking can be compared with Fals-Borda's rejection of traditional ways of validating knowledge in the natural sciences. She also explains that her work took place within a context in which many South Africans would reject an attempt, such as hers, to improve the existing oppressive education system as 'liberal/reformist' and inherently itself oppressive. She was carrying out her work in a divided culture in which many black Africans agreed with Freire that revolutionary change was the only way to overcome oppression, and anything less radical merely reinforced the teachers' own conformity with the existing system and collusion in their own oppression. In struggling to come to terms with this dilemma she reminds us that, despite many differences, people across different cultures have always crossed boundaries and 'overlapped and influenced one another' (Walker 1996: 155). Nevertheless, the issue of racism is painfully inscribed in her identity as a white South African – and, through her access to Eurocentric knowledge, a proxy member of the oppressive 'northern' peoples. The social justice that underpins her action research in this study and in all her work is eloquently summarized when she writes:

> Racism is a set of values steeped in the history of colonialism and slavery which oppress black people in whatever system they

happen to live. What is at stake here is for white democrats to confront, however painfully, that the dreadfully warped nature of apartheid society did not pass us by. We must needs face our own raced identity not merely with a rhetorical move or two, declaring oneself say, on the side of the oppressed, while ignoring the socially constructed basis of such inequalities. What is demanded is to work in practice to establish friendship and respect across differences.

(Walker 1996: 156)

Whereas Fals-Borda makes strong claims for the liberatory power of participatory action research, led by himself and his network of colleagues many of whom come from 'southern' countries, Walker points to the importance for both northern and southern researchers to 'be wary of claiming one right way to do action research, or some essentializing form'. Her ideas are in line with my own belief in the responsiveness and flexibility of action research methodology when she concludes: 'Nonetheless, through comparative local accounts, we can read interpretations of possibilities of a shifting dynamic of action research in different places and times by different people' (Walker 1996: 232).

2 Popular knowledge and academic knowledge in the Brazilian peasants' struggle for land by Gelsa Knijnik, University do Vale do Rio dos Sinos, Brazil, in Educational Action Research (5)3: 501–511 (Knijnik 1997)

Well, my friends, in the research we had done in the townships and favellas … we realized that what our settlement companions really need is mathematics. … They look for mathematics the same way they look for a medicine for a hurt because they know where the hole of the projectile is, by which they are exploited.

(from a speech by an MST monitor)

Knijnik's article examines the theoretical issues underpinning her work as a mathematics educator with the Brazilian Landless People's Movement (MST). The main focus of the article is on the nature of mathematical knowledge, but she emphasizes the practical context by opening with this quotation from 'a monitor (…) a young peasant living in a camp [who had been] surveying rates of illiteracy among his male and female comrades as well as the most pressing educational requirements of the camps and settlements connected to the Movement' (Knijnik 1997: 501). A lengthy footnote gives statistical information on school attendance rates, numbers in the camps and the educational levels of the monitors (elementary school only) and teachers (500 out of 1500 have a teaching certificate and 40 have a university degree). The footnote also contains the MST's original slogan: 'occupying, resisting, producing' and its revized slogan: 'land reform: everyone's struggle'.

The article shows clearly the influence of Paulo Freire's liberatory pedagogy. The emphasis is on praxis, through engaging landless people in critical examination of mathematical knowledge closely related to their practical needs. The knowledge base on which the article draws is largely Latin American, only three of the references being to British or North American publications, two of these to book chapters on ethnomathematics written by Knijnik herself and another Brazilian. There are also a small number of references to Spanish and Portuguese publications. Social justice is the driving motivation behind the article whose discourse is structured around concepts such as 'struggle,' 'subordination,' 'power,' 'legitimacy' and 'culture'. Like Walker, Knijnik's analysis of power and the nature of knowledge is subtle; she avoids dichotomizing issues and uses the tools of contemporary sociology such as the concept of 'social and cultural capital' to analyse the needs of MST in relation to mathematical knowledge (Bourdieu is her one wholly 'first world' reference).

Her starting point is that mathematics is 'a cultural system permeated with power relations' within which academic mathematics is just one form among many deriving from different cultural groups. However, it has legitimacy in the dominant culture that has power to allocate jobs and wealth. She draws on Julia Verela's analysis of the status given by the Jesuits to decontextualized knowledge to illustrate that 'knowledges are legitimately constituted and become dominant knowledges through a social process rather than because they are inherently superior, more refined and "scientific" versions of reality.' To illustrate popular mathematical knowledge in Brazil she gives the example of *Cubação*, a system for estimating the size of a piece of land that produces comparable results to academic mathematics, rounded upwards.

Knijnik gives a clear overview of three approaches to popular knowledge: first the 'ethnocentric' which defines knowledge from the standpoint of the dominant class and defines 'popular mathematics' as 'a deficiency, a backwardness, "non-cultures" – like "non-mathematics"'; second, 'ethnomathematics', which approaches popular mathematics as a coherent cultural system that should be described 'from a point of view which is not external to the context in which they are produced', so that the values, codes which give them meaning and, in turn, give meaning to such mathematics, can be described within their own logic; and third, 'cultural legitimacy', which does not disregard the differential social status that attaches to academic and popular mathematics and suggests 'interpreting popular cultures from the standpoint of their relationship with the legitimate culture'. These three standpoints imply different pedagogical approaches and it is the third that Knijnik describes as characterizing her work with MST.

Knijnik's article demonstrates her meticulous scholarship in the way she constructs her arguments, drawing on both leading Latin-American theorists of pedagogy and ethnomathematics and contemporary 'northern' theories of knowledge. For example, in her conclusion she writes:

> Here is an aspect which I find important to stress: analogously to the non-glorification of popular knowledge, I have been watchful not to glorify academic knowledge as the only meta-narrative which could explain and present solutions – preferably a single one – to all problem-situations of the concrete world.
>
> (Knijnik 1997)

The approach she adopts in her work with MST is to involve her students in investigating the traditions and practices of popular mathematics, for example *Cubação*, alongside teaching them the alternative practices for estimating land using academic mathematics, so that they can work with her 'to analyse the power relations involved in the use of both these kinds of knowledge' (Knijnik 1997). This process has led her and her students to evaluate the strengths and weakness of *Cubação* by comparison with the traditional 'northern' approach to estimating size. It has the disadvantage that it becomes less and less accurate the further the piece of land moves away from being rectangular; its advantage is that it is very quick and efficient to use which outweighs other considerations when the land is of poor quality and its value does not vary greatly with small variations in size. In summarizing the importance and meaning of working in this way for MST members, in particular in terms of establishing mutual respect and relevance to their needs, towards the end of her article Knijnik quotes what one of her students said following a discussion of some teaching support materials she had produced:

> We were talking about the differences of a text you just produced, in this case to help our discussion ... We see part of us in it, but we see in it also a very large contribution from you to the situation we live in, for our practices. So, we feel a mix in that text: there is part of our life, part of your life, of the more elaborate knowledge you already had ... you have already absorbed some things through contact with the people's causes to which you have always paid attention. You left your story to hear our people's stories. And, now, your stories already have a bit of a mix of our stories.
>
> (from the testimony of an MST student)

Action research in health, social care and community settings

A personal narrative

So why have I chosen to look next at health, social care and community settings? I suppose there are two reasons: first, that I became involved in my role as Co-ordinator of the then Classroom Action Research Network in a movement within the UK to increase the involvement of the nursing profession in research and then later as an editor of the journal, *Educational Action Research*, was able to observe the growth in a grass-roots literature of nurse action researchers; second, that this involvement was one of the things that helped me to understand how responsive action research methodology is to culture and context – action research in health care settings was simply different from action research in education. My interest in action research in social care and community settings came later, but again fascinated me because social care, in the UK, is located within cultural and regulatory frameworks that are different again from those of nursing; and community work, in contrast, is more grass-roots based, less well-resourced and more emancipatory.

My involvement in health started with a letter in 1989 from Dr Alison Kitson of the UK's National Institute for Nursing, inviting me to join the Advisory Board for an action research project at the John Radcliffe Hospital in Oxford. The focus of the work was on a fundamental change to nursing practice known as patient-centred nursing, in which as I remember one of the strategies was to be for every patient to have a named 'primary nurse' who would hand over care of the patient to the named 'associate nurse' rather than to the ward sister at the change of shift. This was to ensure that patients had continuity of care and a new kind of relationship with named nurses. The project was led by Alison Binnie, a ward sister at the Radcliffe and Angie Titchen, a former physiotherapist who by that time was a full-time researcher at the Institute of Nursing. This would involve a fundamental shift in nurses' understandings of their work to ensure that there were significant changes to practice rather than merely technical or 'cosmetic' changes. The action research took place primarily in the general medical ward for which Alison had responsibility and involved the participation of all staff. Angie was also registered for a doctor of philosophy degree at the University of Oxford with Donald McIntyre as her research supervisor. The three meetings a year of the Advisory Board took place at the Institute of Nursing and served as my introduction to action research in health and social care settings. These meetings were extremely interesting. Angie and Alison regularly produced discussion papers that dealt sequentially over the two years with the action research design and methodology, methodological issues arising from work in progress and the generation and validation of knowledge. Discussions at the meetings were lively, in part because of Alison and Angie's passionate engagement with the work, and in part as a result of the critical questions that Donald McIntyre raised and pursued relentlessly. Donald had a particular interest in social science research methods but did not count himself as an advocate of action research. Angie was his doctoral student so the Advisory Board meetings inevitably became extensions to his teaching and, as Ron Elder was to say in 2002 when he presented Donald for an honorary degree at the University of Dundee: 'Doing a thesis with Donald is like being dragged through an intellectual hedge longways. You emerge as a different and wiser person.'

I learnt an enormous amount from my very peripheral participation in this action research project. I came to a new understanding of the importance of action research as a methodology for researching the process of change in social practices and the meticulous care needed to ensure that action research went beyond the professional development of the participants and contributed to the generation of knowledge to inform others engaged in the same or similar changes to nursing practice. At the same time, I was introduced vicariously to the pressures under which nurses worked within the British National Health Service (NHS), to their proud tradition of caring for patients and the complex ethical considerations raised by the effort to combine this with efficiency of service provision within limited budgets and resources. Over the two years, meetings often involved Alison and Angie discussing the impact of policy changes emanating from central government, which at the time involved the introduction of new ways of tracking efficiency and cutting down 'waste' by the introduction of an element of competition through setting up 'an internal market' between service providers and 'clients'. The shifts in discourse, underpinning values and regulatory frameworks paralleled similar changes being introduced at the same time into the education service in which I was primarily working. Alison Kitson, who as project director chaired the Advisory Board meetings, had frequent access to policy makers and at the time was developing on behalf of government a new system for auditing nursing practice in the NHS. This public service discourse was in sharp contrast to the discourse of the 'medical model', which instantiated the hegemony of the consultants (the most senior medical practitioners), who were in daily contact with nurses on the ward but in most cases held themselves aloof from the action research being undertaken there. The medical model was based on concepts of illness/disease and treatment and was predicated on realist assumptions about the nature of knowledge; it set methodological norms for research design involving randomized controlled trials to establish statistically the percentage of patients likely to respond positively to a specific treatment. It seems to me that the shadow of the medical model hung over the daily enactment of the action research project, setting an expectation of academic rigour of a kind that Titchen and Binnie both rejected and respected.

Theoretical resources for understanding the experience or action research in health, social care and community settings

Because health and social care are fairly new fields of action research, they have tended to draw on the theoretical writing from education, whereas action research in community settings has drawn on the work of writers such as Horton and Freire (1990). The work of Carr and Kemmis (1983), Kemmis and McTaggart (1988) and Winter (1989) has been particularly important in health. My focus here, however, is on theoretical resources that *raise issues* directly relating to action research in health, social care and community settings. I have chosen three issues: the authorial voice in action research reports; the way that knowledge generation is conceptualized; and the interplay between a social justice imperative and the politicization of work practices. I have chosen one of my texts from the work of Yoland Wadsworth (2001), an Australian whose work involves participatory action research with disadvantaged communities and aboriginal groups. By moving outside health into community development I hope to sharpen the issues and clarify what is characteristic of action research in both of these settings.

The choice of texts to illustrate these issues has necessarily been arbitrary and personal and, lest what I have to say does not do justice to the richness and diversity of the work, I suggest that readers may like to consult two significant reviews of action research in health settings (Waterman *et al.* 2001; Whitelaw *et al.* 2003) and the series of case studies in Winter and Munn-Giddings (2001, Part II: 63–204).

My first focus is on *the authorial voice in reporting action research*. It is normal practice for action research reports to be written in the first person singular, incorporating reflexive passages that account for the 'self' of the author and open up issues regarding the relationship between the various partners in the research and the values that the author or authors and their partners brought to the work. Yet, I am aware that many writers who wish to publish their work in journals in the field of nursing have run into problems because the traditions of the medical model call for depersonalized 'third person' accounts. Chiu (2003: 165–83) provides an interesting example of one such writer who adopts the tricky strategy of adopting an impersonal voice without actually referring to herself as 'the researcher'. In an account of using focus groups in three action research projects to improve the access to breast and cervical screening of women from minority ethnic groups she adopts the passive voice almost throughout, but is unable to sustain it to the end – in the final section she allows the personal voice to emerge when she addresses an aspect of knowledge production that is entirely dependent upon the involvement of selves: 'I have drawn on particular examples from my research projects to illustrate the dialectical process of knowing and doing embedded in PAR ...' The same issue is dealt with very differently in a chapter by Wadsworth (2001: 420–32). Authorial voice is still a problematic issue for her and she refers early in the chapter to her memories of being expected at the start of her career to adopt 'the mantle of the scientific "We"'. She rejects this because it led to what she calls 'the presumptive and ultimately unscientific ventriloquism' of writing about other people's lives and perceptions 'without them being actively present in that process'. However, the point she mainly wants to raise is the inappropriateness of using 'I' when writing about participatory action research projects. She puts forward the view that using 'I' undermines one of the main mechanisms for establishing the validity of knowledge claims, since it is in the 'intersubjective nature of truth-construction' that their 'trustworthiness and "objectivity"' lie. For Wadsworth the key issue has become how to use 'we' as a genuinely participatory 'we' rather than a merely cosmetic 'we'. This has fundamental implications for the whole action research process which must become fully participatory and be collaboratively led.

This has clear links with my second focus on *approaches to knowledge generation*. The difference between Wadsworth's point of view on authorial voice and that of Chiu points to a fundamentally different standpoint on the nature of knowledge. Like Chiu, Wadsworth is seeking to validate knowledge claims but sees this as a process that is dependent upon participation with those who are participants in the field of study. Her location in community-based social care rather than health care studies constructs the issues very differently. For Wadsworth 'the genuine achievement of a sense of "we" or "us" becomes ... an indicator of ... trustworthiness', but this has to include the group selecting its own facilitator and taking the leading role in the conduct of the action research rather than herself as facilitator being predominantly in control. In community work it is possible to make such an approach consonant with the fundamental values and purposes of an action research project, in a way that I have come to understand it certainly cannot be in the pressured context of action research in the British National Health Service. Chiu's approach to the validation of knowledge is both more traditional and more complex. She presents what she calls 'an extended epistemological framework', which she says is necessary because: 'PAR writings appear to be long on ideology but short on methodology.' Her epistemology incorporates an explicit commitment to a clearly defined, realist theory of truth and recognition of the valuable knowledge contributions made by her close medical colleagues researching in a positivist tradition. Yet, her 'extended' epistemology also incorporates the 'knowledge, experience and practice' generated by participants that is the central factor in change processes. As with her choice of authorial voice, she appears to experience tensions in attempting to reconcile action research methodology with the medical model in which she is encultured.

What is interesting is that both Wadsworth and Chiu are concerned with generating knowledge and ensuring its validity. This has implications for my third focus on *the interplay between a social justice imperative and the politicization of work practices* in action research in health and social care settings. Wadsworth places social justice at the centre of her work as a facilitator of action research and, like both Walker and Knijnik sees her facilitation role as that of a co-learner with the participants, rather than someone coming from outside with the aim of empowering them. There are strong overlaps between her community work with impoverished groups and aboriginal people in Australia and the work of those leading PAR in 'southern' countries such as South Africa and Brazil. Action research in the context of the British national health service is necessarily very different. It is responsive to the politicized context of public service provision in a 'northern' country where since around 1980 there has been an ideological imperative to increase 'value for money' and cut costs in order to reduce taxation. Chiu has a social engineering rather than a social justice purpose, in that she conceives of the improved access to services of women from ethnic minority groups as an unquestionable good to be brought about by her work rather than a focus for participatory critical praxis. Other British writers such as Bridges and Meyer (2000) and Kemp (2000) adopt a much more collaborative approach than Chiu, but like her their focus is on bringing about solutions to specific problems arising from negative aspects of policy rather than more holistic development issues. Kemp's study is of the provision of training for unqualified support workers who are employed in community care centres for the long-term mentally ill. The radical change in policy in Britain in the early 1990s, which closed down residential care homes for the mentally ill, produced a crisis situation, but Kemp's work addresses the immediate practical problem rather than the larger policy issues. In a very similar way, Bridges and Meyer's paper focuses on the improvement of care for elderly people in an accident and emergency service department of a large hospital, at a time when hospitals in the United Kingdom were in crisis because of the reduction in resources (beds and nurses) resulting from policy changes that prioritized efficiency and tax cuts. Both are carefully executed studies aimed at improving services but in Freire's terms they are oppressive rather than liberatory because they accept the structured injustices in the system rather than tackling the underlying policy issues. I see this judgement as narrowly conceived and unfair, however. I agree with Walker who, in her action research with teachers in the Bantu education system in a pre-democracy South Africa, saw the possibility of professional learning to improve the working lives of those involved and the educational opportunities of a small number of children, even if there was no opportunity to make radical changes to the system. Moreover, much of the action research in health care settings in Britain is carried out under sponsorship of government or influential charities and the knowledge it generates is fed back into policy development. As the ideological tide begins to turn, as it surely will, this knowledge will support the case of those wishing to develop new policies.

Examples of action research in health and community settings

I have chosen two published accounts of action research in health and community settings. The first presents an action research project in the field of nursing in Britain. The second is a book about a community-led movement that began in 1987 in Ivanhoe, a town in the rural Appalachian area of the USA, and was partly inspired and facilitated by the Highlander Research and Education Centre, founded by Myles Horton, which had played an influential part in supporting the Civil Rights movement in the 1960s.

1 Creating a Learning Culture: a story of change in hospital nursing *by Angie Titchen, National Institute of Nursing, UK, chapter 22 (pp. 244–60) in* International Action Research: a casebook for educational reform, *edited by Sandra Hollingsworth, published by Falmer Press, 1997*

Titchen's chapter presents some specific aspects of the aims, working processes and knowledge outcomes of a three-year action research project sponsored by Oxford Health Authority and the National Institute for Nursing. This is the project to which I have already referred in my personal narrative. The chapter's focus is on the creation of a learning culture in a hospital ward through action research led by Alison Binnie, the ward sister, and Titchen herself as the external researcher working with Binnie and the ward nurses in a highly participatory way. As well as this aim to bring about cultural change, the project aimed 'to generate and test theory about effective change strategies and to theorize the experience of change for those involved in, or affected by it'. There was an explicit intention to generate knowledge that would be of practical use to those responsible for introducing change elsewhere in the system.

The traditional culture of the nursing profession in Britain is described at the beginning of the chapter as having been governed by norms of efficiency, following orders from superiors, carrying out routine procedures, and maintaining professional distance from patients. This had given rise to 'a system of socially-constructed defense mechanisms' that included 'discontinuous care, centralized decision-making and distant nurse–patient relations'. The project deliberately set out to change all this, in line with changes in the culture of society that now gives more emphasis to 'respecting the rights of the individual' and is looking for 'a personalized and individualized nursing service'.

The chapter gives a fascinating account of how Binnie and the nurses on the ward worked towards this change. The first step had to be the establishment of a learning culture within the ward in which open and honest discussion, generated by critical feed-back on practice between one individual and another, was the norm. One strength of the study is the way that it describes the minutiae of the change process. For example, the traditional culture of nursing structured the behaviour of individuals into a deeply embedded set of cultural practices. Although nurses expressed a commitment to the idea of a learning culture and open discussion about practice, their behaviour was governed by two unspoken rules, which Titchen summarizes as: 'needing to get away' and 'seeing criticism as reprimand'. As a result they instinctively and routinely avoided discussing each other's practice in coffee breaks or lunch times and were both defensive when others provided them with feed-back on their practice and extremely hesitant in giving this kind of feed-back to others. The chapter reports on the progress of the action research over two years from this initial position in which embedded cultural traditions blocked the change process to the creation of a genuine learning culture.

The study draws explicitly upon two theoretical frameworks: 'a critical social science perspective' underpinning action research methodology based on the work of Lewin (1946), while 'adopting refinements suggested by' Kemmis and McTaggart (1988) and Elliott (1991); and a phenomenological perspective, which 'informed a simultaneous, parallel observational study …' drawing on the ideas of Schutz (1967; 1970). The references list also indicates that it draws more widely on a knowledge base of more than 60 publications spanning social science research methodology and nursing research. Two key concepts from the action research literature that proved to be particularly useful in the analysis of data were 'making tacit knowledge explicit' and identifying any contradictions between 'espoused theory' and 'theory in use', in both cases through reflection, critical feed-back and discussion between the facilitators and participants. The values embedded in the action research process are expressed in a discourse of 'sensitivity', 'respect', 'self empowerment', 'professionalism', 'collaboration' and 'shared responsibility'. The 'strategy' is 'promoting challenge, openness and debate' through the action research process, but including, crucially, the allocation of 'time-out' to enable nurses to work in pairs and small groups on practical problem-solving projects. Although the work is led by Titchen and Binnie and has a strong social engineering purpose, its impetus is to promote collaboration and encourage nurses to take on responsibility for elements of the action research, which aligns more closely with a social justice/empowerment purpose. We are told exactly the extent to which individual nurses took on these wider roles. One feature of the action research methodology was a demarcation of roles between Titchen and Binnie, which allowed for some overlap between them but used Binnie's time in ways that safeguarded her main job as ward sister: Binnie is predominantly the 'actor' leading the development work; Titchen is predominantly the 'researcher' who observes, carries out interviews with nurses, patients, relatives and other staff and collects, records and organizes the research data.

The chapter is carefully structured to give a succinct overview of the aims, theoretical framework, working practices and analytical procedures relevant to the development of a learning culture. By presenting the project's work as two parallel accounts a careful balance is drawn between giving readers access to the 'lived experience' of the action research and theorizing from it to generate knowledge. The first account is a 'story' presented as a narrative with extended quotations from interview data; the second a 'theorized account.' Both are presented with a combined 'I'/'We' authorial voice interspersed with more formal passages where the authorial voice is left indeterminate; the 'we' always refers to Titchen and Binnie rather than to the whole group of participating nurses.

I have chosen to discuss this chapter because of the way in which it integrates the experiential knowledge of participants with theoretical insights drawn from wider social science literature in order to generate new unique insights that can inform the management and evaluation of other similar change initiatives. It sets out to generate knowledge, grounds the action research meticulously in methodological principles that enable and validate that process and ends with clear statements about the knowledge that has been generated. These include: filling 'a gap' in the literature by identifying and describing 'an effective strategy for creating a learning culture'; developing clear principles for creating such a culture; demonstrating 'that action research can be an effective strategy for achieving cultural change in hospital nursing'; and showing 'how action research itself facilitates the creation of a learning culture' when there is 'an attempt to ensure congruence between the values and processes of the action and the research strategies'.

2 It Comes from the People: community development and local theology by Mary Ann Hinsdale, Helen M Lewis and S Maxine Waller. Philadelphia: Temple University Press (Hinsdale et al. 1995)

This book presents a case study of an extraordinary development process in a small rural community, Ivanhoe Town, in the mountains of Virginia, USA. It is written by two external consultants who carried out participatory research with the community for around eight years – Hinsdale, a sociologist and staff member at the Highlander Center, and Lewis, a Catholic sister whose religious order was already working in the community. Waller is included in the authorship because she led the development work from within the community and is quoted extensively throughout the book. The Epilogue is a 10-page edited transcript of a conversation in which Waller reflects on the draft manuscript and updates Hinsdale and Lewis on recent developments.

The book starts with the history of the community since the early set-tlement period in the eighteenth century, through its development as a thriving mining town in the nineteenth century, and industrial and social decline following the closure of the National Carbide Company in 1966 and New Jersey Zinc in 1981. The experience of sudden large-scale unem-ployment in terms of poverty, disruption to family life and loss of self-esteem is told through the memories of the people, based on interview data and written records. The book is divided into two interdependent sections, the first dealing with community development and the second with local theology. Part One provides an analysis of the processes of community decline, dealing with specific topics such as 'dependency and powerless-ness' and 'fear of failure', and then tracks and analyses the process of com-munity resistance and regeneration in which members of the community engaged in political action to address and overcome problems. These actions included the formation of new structures such as the Ivanhoe Civic League; the affirmation of community culture through poetry and drama, 'parades', special projects such as 'Hands Across Ivanhoe' and – somewhat contentiously – the traditional 'Men's Beauty Contest'; and education to give adults access to essential knowledge such as literacy, numeracy and economics. The focus of Part One is on developing knowledge about effec-tive community action, how to instigate and support it, the role of local culture in sustaining it, the kinds of leadership that emerged through it and their strengths and weaknesses, and the nature of participatory facilitation from an outsider. Part Two tells the story of the development of local theology as a parallel form of action. Through bible study, theological dis-cussions and the development of community rituals – prayer meetings, community 'suppers' and 'hikes' – the community developed and sustained its spiritual energy. Even for those members of the community whose reli-gious beliefs were less formal, these activities were inclusive and served to extend and sustain the vibrant culture of the community.

The ethical values and research methods of this study are primarily concerned with issues of social justice. The authors draw explicitly upon the literature of participatory action research; and emphasize that the par-ticipatory process requires outsiders to work with insiders with considerable sensitivity. This is a large-scale project, involving every aspect of commu-nity life; it is explicitly political and concerned with transformation of local people through giving them the knowledge needed to mount effective resistance to hegemonic bureaucratic structures. For me there is an extraor-dinary sense of equality of esteem in this study, including an intellectual sharing between Hinsdale, Lewis and Waller that begins to overcome the imbalances of power between the professionals and the community partic-ipants. This is particularly noticeable in the discussions of types of leader-ship between Hinsdale and Waller. Waller had attended a Leadership Training Program at Highlander and had discussed her own 'charismatic' leadership style with Myles Horton, so that she was aware of both its strengths and its weaknesses; Hinsdale documents the deep and sometimes painful discussions between herself and Waller about the kind of leadership needed to carry Ivanhoe forward to a new stage of development after its initial break-throughs. She documents the process of negotiation between herself and Waller over the use in the book of a particularly contentious piece of data – a letter written by Waller in which she expressed anger about an aspect of the work. The openness and honesty of the collaboration is clear through the documenting of conflict, and the inclusion of the final 'epilogue' that illustrates the mutual respect between the three women.

In a methodological appendix to the book, Hinsdale and Lewis locate their work within the traditions of participatory research as developed by Fals-Borda. Although they do not use the word 'praxis' their emphasis is on giving the community access to education and assisting them in solving their practical problems through actions informed by knowledge. The research began with 'a series of economic discussions, which were held over a three-month period with fifteen to thirty-five members of the community' (Hinsdale *et al.* 1995: 345); and these were instigated by the Ivanhoe Civic League who invited Hinsdale and two representatives of religious groups (Lutheran and Catholic) to attend. So in all senses the participatory research 'comes from the people'. Another strong influence was the liberation theology of Freire, who developed a strong association with Myles Horton (Horton and Freire 1990) and is shown in a photograph in the book talking to Waller at Highlander Center (Hinsdale *et al.* 1995: 266). Hinsdale and Lewis also draw explicitly upon feminist theories and the 'ritual studies' that had emerged from the work of anthropologists and theologians and acknowledge the influence on their work of John Dewey, George Herbert Mead and Gregory Bateson. *It Comes from the People* is presented as a narrative and includes extensive quotations from data, but it draws on a very wide knowledge base and both sets out to, and is successful in, making a significant contribution to knowledge. This is knowledge that emerges from a process of 'dialogue and discussion … aimed at action and toward solutions of community-defined problems' (Hinsdale *et al.* 1995: 340).

Action research in business settings

A personal narrative

I have worked only very briefly in a business environment, when I was seconded during the 1980s to a group that was taken over by a large publishing house, but I have one very vivid memory of that time that gave me a clear indication of how business culture differs from the culture of educational organizations. I had assumed that my accountability continued to be to the head of the group to which I had been seconded and must have appeared too casual in my dealings with the much more senior Head of The School Books Division. Completely unexpectedly from my point of view, she sent me a memo with an unmistakably sharp tone in which she set out a job she wanted me to do; it was when I noticed that this was copied to a number of very senior people in the company, including the head of my group, that I had a sense of revelation both of my own position vis-à-vis hers in the company hierarchy and my own vulnerability within the bureaucratic power structures.

Seven years later, when working at the University of East Anglia, I found myself responsible for developing a new masters degree in human resource strategy in partnership with a specialist in personnel management, Margaret Woodd, at Suffolk College. The programme included many opportunities for participants, who were combining part-time study with their full-time jobs, to present aspects of their workplace practices and analyse these through discussion. Once again, I was soon conscious of aspects of business culture that came as a surprise to me: for example, the regular annual reviews when employees receive critical feed-back on their 'performance' from their line manager; and even more surprisingly, the 'upward appraisal' that had recently been introduced by the UK branch of a large American company, whereby employees give critical feed-back to their line managers on *their* performance as managers. This certainly clarified for me why many people are impatient of British teachers' deep-seated resistance to appraisal or performance-related pay.

There was a strong movement at the time towards increasing the level of competence of company employees and a university masters degree was seen as an important rite of passage on the path to promotion. In the discourse of the group the word 'strategy' had particular appeal and a joke circulating among the course participants asked, 'What is the difference between a human resource strategist and a personnel manager?' to which the answer was '£20,000 a year'. It was a time when both public bodies and private companies in Britain were undergoing turbulence. We had course participants who worked for central government, several of whom were required to manage the transition from a traditional civil service department to a smaller 'core' department (what was left after making cuts) and a more independent 'agency' (carved out of the former department). Some were working primarily to preserve the conditions of service of former civil servants who had been moved to an agency, others were working primarily to help the agency's chief executive to develop new conditions of service that would reduce the traditional power of civil servants. Bringing these opposite viewpoints together in teaching sessions generated particularly interesting discussions.

The abrasive nature of company culture was clear. Hierarchies and power structures were probably no more constraining than those in educational organizations, but they were certainly more clearly defined. Sometimes, too, company culture demonstrated the cruelties of capitalism and posed huge ethical problems for managers. For example, as HR (or personnel) managers our course participants were responsible for employing new staff and maintaining the conditions of service of existing staff. For all of them this included making all employees aware of the company's 'mission statement', which almost invariably included some variant of: 'our employees are our most important asset'. But during the two years in which I worked with them there was a national movement to increase the efficiency and 'value for money' of organizations and several of our course participants had to go back to their company's employees and tell a large number of them that they were losing their jobs – in one case I remember that the number of jobs to go amounted to 25 per cent of the company's existing workforce.

Theoretical resources for understanding the experience or action research in business settings

How can I make sense of these very limited experiences of the business world in order to better understand action research in these settings? For me the obvious starting point is Kurt Lewin, often credited with inventing action research, whose realist approach to knowledge led him to search for reliable theories that would explain human behaviour very much as knowledge in the natural sciences explains the physical world. Lewin's Field Theory, based on empirical research, explained the behaviour of people in organizations through the formula: $B = f(p,e)$ where 'B' stands for behaviour, 'p' for personality and 'e' for environment (Lewin 1951). In other words, the behaviour of people in organizations is determined not only by their personality (as had been previously thought) but also by the environment. This was an important break-through in management theory because it meant that employees' work practices could be improved by changing the working environment and it was important for managers to take account of psychological factors in planning formal management structures. The tradition of action research in business and management goes back to Lewin's work and also to the work of Trist, Bion and their colleagues (Trist and Murray 1993) at the Tavistock Institute of Human Relations in London. To establish their work formally and publicly, Lewin and Trist founded the journal *Human Relations*, the first issue of which appeared in 1950 and contained two posthumous articles by Lewin.

One of the studies I will focus on in the next section draws on the work of the Tavistock Institute. However, here I have decided to focus on the work of Chris Argyris, himself strongly influenced by Lewin, whose publications span half a century going back to the 1950s. In the second edition of his book *On Organizational Learning* (1999), Argyris reprints a large number of his most important articles. He argues for the importance of going beyond what he calls 'single-loop learning' which seeks solutions to problems to 'double-loop learning' which seeks at the same time to understand the underlying reasons for problems. In particular (Argyris 1999: 19) he argues for the importance of changing 'the values of an organization's theory-in-use for the process of organizational inquiry'. The concept of the organization's theory-in-use provides an explanation for the workplace practices that individuals develop over and above the officially sanctioned practices, and through which they tacitly agree to avoid 'embarrassment' and 'threat'; in effect this is a process of developing 'organizational defences' which function as powerful 'self-reinforcing, anti-learning processes (Argyris 1999: xv). Senge (1993: 182) describes the powerful process of 'reflection in action' he experienced when attending one of Argyris's workshops at MIT. In order to understand the tacit motivations that shaped one's own behaviours, the activity consisted of remembering a recent disagreement with someone in the family, a colleague or a client and recalling 'not only what was said, but what we were thinking and did *not* say'. Such workshops were a regular feature of Argyris' work with organizations.

Argyris argued strongly that research into management processes and organizational change needed to go beyond the purely descriptive and analytical 'to produce knowledge about virtual worlds that provide liberatory alternatives' (Argyris 1999: xv). He advocated an approach to inquiry that involved 'the intertwining of thought and action' (Argyris 1999: 9). He developed a methodology that he called 'action science', which he saw as different from participatory action research because of its focus on investigating theories-in-use (Argyris and Schon 1991). Although this approach differs from PAR in business settings, it is very much in line with the participatory action research tradition developed in 'southern' countries by Fals-Borda (2001) and approaches to action research developed by Elliott in Britain and Altrichter and Posch in Austria. As a student of Elliott, these concepts of Argyris were very much part of my own early action research work. Like Lewin, Argyris believed it was possible to generate knowledge from researching social practices, and saw good theory as pre-eminently 'practical'. In a chapter on making knowledge more relevant to practice he emphasized that his work differed from that of natural science research only in that the criteria of 'objectivity, precision and completeness' should 'take into account the features of the way the human mind works when human beings try to use the knowledge that social scientists produce'. In other words, he aspired to developing generalizable knowledge that met these criteria but rejected the assumption that this would require a remote relationship between the researcher and the participants, since 'one is more likely to reduce distortion and enhance the production of valid information if the individuals see that participating in research will lead to important learning for them' (Argyris 1999: 428–9).

Examples of action research in business settings

I have chosen two published accounts of action research that illustrate somewhat different approaches. The first is an example from the 1970s of action research into organizational change in a coal mine in the USA using the socio-technical tradition developed at the Tavistock Institute in London; the second is a smaller scale study published in 2003 of a consultant carrying out action research with the managers of a small boat-building company in Britain.

1 Action Research in an American Underground Coal Mine by Gerald Susman and Eric Trist (pp. 417–50) in The Social Engagement of Social Science: a Tavistock anthology, edited by Eric Trist and Hugh Murray, vol II, (Susman and Trist 1993)

This account is a revised version of an article first published in 1977 in *Human Relations*. It tells the story of an experimental approach to structuring work practice for workers on one coal face in a coal mine. The initiative originated in an agreement between the president of Rushton Mining Company and the president of the United Mine Workers of America (UMWA) and the aim was to give workers opportunities for autonomy and participation. The company president was motivated to participate by concerns about safety, a history of poor union relations and the need to improve productivity.

The project drew directly on the tradition of *socio-technical research* and the knowledge developed through this approach over the previous 20 years at the Tavistock Institute; as well as upon the work of Lewin and his 'force field' theory (Pasmore 2001). A team of external researchers was commissioned to carry out the work with funding from the National Commission on Productivity and Work Quality and subsequently from a body associated with the Institute of Social Research, University of Michigan. They started by setting up a steering group made up of managers and local union officials and this body developed a written agreement designed to ensure clarity about the work to be carried out and joint ownership of the project by management and the union. This document made four significant changes to the pay and working conditions of those involved in the project (e.g. top rate pay for all involved, freedom to take on new jobs without internal advertising beyond the group). The steering group then called for volunteers to join the 'autonomous work group' and 28 participants were selected. They attended six full-day orientation sessions over a three-week period and this was followed by a six-week period of training and adjustment. One man from each crew and two representatives from the local union leadership were then elected to join five members of management on the joint labour-management steering committee and the group was declared autonomous and took on responsibility for organizing its own work.

The *socio-technical approach* to analysis of work practices is based on the notion that organizations are made up of interlocking social and technical systems. The research team started with a clear knowledge base generated by previous research. For example, that the process of work design involves 'a search for the best solution to a set of conflicting requirements' between the two systems; and that the 'primary task' of both systems should be congruent. The study directly addresses incongruities of this kind between social and technical systems. In a coal mine where a 'continuous miner' machine is used to cut the coal face, this is moved forward incrementally over a period of about 10 days and men focus on collecting, packing and transporting coal rather than cutting it by hand. The journeys to and from the coal face become longer as the machine moves further from the transportation equipment. When the machine has moved the full extent possible, it is pulled back to allow for the roof to be shored up and the supportive pillars of uncut coal removed, before the machine is moved forward to a new position to start the process again. If managers accept that the primary task is a transport system rather than a production system this will bring the technical focus on productivity into harmony with the workers' focus on packing and carrying coal. This in turn makes it possible to re-focus creative energy on the logistical problems of transporting coal from the coal face to the pit head, which are the prime cause of loss of productivity.

The success of the project was measured by comparisons between the experimental 'autonomous' group and other groups, and between this year's and last year's performance. Data were collected on health and safety violations, accidents (those reported only and those leading to 'lost time'), absences, production and maintenance costs and tons of clean coal produced per day. Over a two-year period these figures provided clear evidence that the autonomous working group out-performed the other groups. However, the differences in pay and conditions caused friction with other groups, for example sarcastic taunts from other workers ('Hey, superminer'). To overcome the sense of isolation experienced by the autonomous group the researchers instigated the introduction of a second autonomous group and managers began to suggest moving towards the introduction of this approach throughout the whole mine. Ultimately, however, union members were not prepared to let inequalities in pay and conditions persist for any length of time between workers and this led to rejection by a vote of 79 to 75 of a key proposal put to all workers by the joint labour-management steering committee. As a result, the project was terminated after two years to the great disappointment of those who had taken part.

In some senses this study makes few knowledge claims, other than to confirm that a combined process of socio-technical analysis and action research is very effective in bringing about change. The increased autonomy of the experimental group, and their ability to take on new roles and develop new specialisms to overcome delays formerly caused by lack of specialist workers on every shift, radically changed work culture and provided individuals with the intrinsic rewards of job satisfaction and increased self-esteem. When contacted for a follow-up discussion 12 years later many said that involvement in the project had been a unique opportunity for them and it emerged that a much larger proportion than expected had gone on to promoted, leadership positions, which appears to have been related to their experience of autonomous working.

Susman and Trist (1993) also suggest that the 'failure' of the project to survive long term and roll out to all the teams was due to a basic flaw in the research design, specifically that the sponsors' insistence on a 'control group'/'treatment group' comparison was the root cause of considerable tensions and bad feeling between the two groups of workers. They claim that they adopted this approach very much against their will and felt that the research design was flawed in any case because of inevitable contamination between the control and treatment groups, as individual foremen picked up good ideas from observing the project group and introduced these with their own groups. Reading the account it also seems obvious that the comparative measures adopted were unrelated to two of the fundamental aims of the project, the increased autonomy and better motivation of workers. In Argyris' terms insufficient attention was paid to the theories-in-use of individuals who were subjected to embarrassment and threat and needed to develop alternative working practices in self-defence.

By comparison with the examples of PAR from 'southern' countries or the study of community development by Hinsdale et al. (1995), this approach to action research is more formal, less focused on social justice issues and more on improving efficiency. In this way it conforms with the culture of business as I have experienced it. The researchers remain external; the insiders are not themselves the researchers although the links between the two groups are mutually supportive. The researchers are engaged primarily in setting up procedures rather than participating in the day-to-day complexities of action. The action research process is necessarily different in the business world. Perhaps this led in this case to the researchers implementing strategies based on socio-technical knowledge without paying sufficient attention to the complexities of relationships in the particular local case. The strongly realist epistemology, in line with the work of Lewin, was perhaps a disadvantage for those implementing this study almost 30 years ago.

2 From Measuring Clouds to Active Listening *by K. Alan Rutter, University of Portsmouth Business School, UK (pp. 465–80), in* **Management Learning,** *vol 34, no 4, 2003 (Rutter 2003)*

Rutter's study, written 25 years after the original version of the Susman and Trist chapter, indicates both the continuations and the divergences that have occurred in business research culture. For example, both studies argue for a different approach to research that takes account of social factors in the workplace, rather than relying on rationalist methods; but whereas Susman and Trist were opposing the scientific management theories of Taylor (1992) (known in the management literature as 'Taylorism'), Rutter distinguishes his approach from that of strategic management. From my experiences of working with HR 'strategists' I know how important this approach has been in management literature over the last 15 years. In terms of approaches to knowledge, Rutter, like Susman and Trist, is meticulous in producing a research design that will guard against researcher bias; but unlike their approach, he sees the 'insiders' not himself as the best source of knowledge that will be useful in solving their problems. He uses the metaphor of 'measuring clouds' to explain why strategic management was useless in relation to the extremely volatile, fragmented, unstable nature of the available data.

The action research study was carried out with the Managing Director and the other five managers of a boat-building company with 28 employees. The company was faced with a crisis since it had only enough work to last for another three months and an empty order book. Rutter worked with them as a facilitator to enable them to 'learn to liberate themselves from their own indecision'. He had previously undertaken several studies of the UK boat-building industry using a strategic management approach to analysis, but had come to the conclusion that the findings were meaningless because the industry was too fragmented and varied to be amenable to categorization and the data were therefore spurious, making the outcomes of statistical analysis meaningless. In addition, the company's managers were explicit in saying that they were not looking for a consultant since their previous experience had shown them that this was an expensive option that produced no results that were useful in relation to their own business.

Rutter's approach was to adopt the combined strategy of 'active listening' and 'empathy'. He set up 'strategy sessions' rather than 'workshops' with the five managers so that there would be no implication that he was teaching them. The starting point was a procedure (which I have always known as 'nominal group technique') whereby each participant lists the issues they think are important and then these are read out one at a time, going round the group enough times to allow all the issues to be listed, thereby ensuring that all points of view are given equal consideration. The issue that was mentioned by most people – 'low-priced competitor products' – then became the main focus for discussion. Altogether there were four strategy sessions over a period of six weeks. Rutter's role was to document the discussion by drawing a cognitive map on a flip chart. This was amended and elaborated during the session and later extended and refined from a tape-recording of the session. He then circulated the revised map to participants two days before the next session. In each case, the map was then discussed and amended through discussion that acted as a process of clarification moving towards shared understanding. As Rutter puts it, 'the intention was not to find an absolute truth but a strategic direction'.

Rutter brought to the sessions his own fund of specialist knowledge, but rather than presenting to the group insights drawn from this knowledge, he used it to guide his questioning. Adopting the techniques of active listening, drawn from counselling theory, he used his questions to help the managers 'unravel confusing impressions and conflicting information', develop new scenarios and realistic agendas and both make choices and commit to following them through. Through this process he helped them to probe and understand strategic issues and expose and discuss their own mindsets. Here his approach matches well with Argyris' workshop approach to uncovering tacit theories-in-use and defensive strategies discussed earlier, as it does also with Bion's early work on group therapy at the Tavistock Institute (Bion 1946). Through this process the group was able to come to a decision that took account of the current economic climate and market situation and built directly on the company's strengths, but that initially had been unacceptable to at least one member; because it was a group decision they all committed to it unanimously and it resulted in the company securing a large contract from the Ministry of Defence within a very short period of time.

This is a meticulously executed study in which Rutter makes it clear he was aware of the seriousness of the situation for the group and the need to ensure he did not provide poor advice or in any way make their situation worse. He takes particular care to address three problems relating to facilitation that he has come across in research literature: ensuring ownership by participants rather than the researcher; giving adequate feed-back to enable further reflection on the process; and avoiding researcher bias. To guard against this last he used a colleague who had reservations about the approach as a 'supervisor', discussing the cognitive maps with him after each session and cross-checking his own understandings. Although his research has resonances with that of Susman and Trist in terms of his careful research design, his approach to knowledge construction is very different from theirs. Like them he brings specialist knowledge to the situation but, unlike them, he does not use it to give any advice but only to inform his questioning. He also reaches no firm conclusions about the knowledge outcomes from the study, saying indeed that he 'learnt an important lesson

– that my desire to understand their views, their reasoning, and their interpretations was never achieved'. He claims he provided no more than a cata-
lytic service in helping them to draw upon their own existing knowledge to
make the best decision for themselves. Referring to the work of Kemmis
(2001) and Reason and Brabury (2001), he says his approach is 'emancipatory' and his aim 'liberalization of the individual'.

Reflections on the culturally responsive nature of action research methodology

What initially fascinated me about exploring action research in these three
settings – four in fact since health/social care and community development
are substantially different from each other – was how different they are
from action research as I first experienced it as a teacher in England.

The kind of action research I experienced in the 1980s had developed
to fit the values of an education service in which I counted myself as a 'progressive teacher in a progressive school' dedicated to 'drawing out' (Latin:
educare) the innate knowledge and understanding in the individual child
(Somekh 2000). The liberal–humanist tradition was not, in fact, as egalitar-
ian as our aspirations for it, but during the 1970s and up to 1982 it provided
a culture in England in which funding was available through the Schools
Council for teachers to work in partnership with university-based
researchers, and action research could be the dual mechanism for transforming the curriculum, and for the individual empowerment of teachers.
After the Schools Council was disbanded leaving no formal mechanism for
partnership between teachers, policy makers and university-based
researchers, teachers continued to have the opportunity to become action
researchers in the context of part-time masters degrees. The norm for action
research in Britain became the individual study carried out by the teacher–
researcher under the supervision of an academic tutor for an award-bearing
course. It had a strong orientation towards teacher professional development and reflexivity and was often well grounded in the action research literature because of its location in part-time study for higher degrees. This
work was strongly influenced by the work of Hopkins (1985), McNiff
(1988), Whitehead (1989), Winter (1989), Elliott (1991), Dadds (1995) and
others. Although students were often required to read Carr and Kemmis'
(1983) book, *Becoming Critical: Knowing through Action Research*, very few
studies could be said to be strongly informed by critical theory in terms of
having any purpose of political emancipation.

At the same time, the tradition of action research as a collaborative
endeavour between teachers and university-based researchers, which had
flourished under the Schools Council, was continued in a small number
of funded projects of which my own work provides examples. In these

projects teachers carried out action research as an extension of their normal job with small-scale academic accreditation (at certificate level) as an optional added incentive. This work built on the tradition of action research into curriculum renewal that was established by Stenhouse and Elliott, but in my own case became diversified in both its focus and the educational settings in which it was carried out. Chapters 4–8 of this book give an account of five projects in which I have been engaged in a leadership role.

What is different about the studies reviewed here when compared with teachers' action research in Britain in the 1980s and 1990s? What are the characteristics that make these studies differ from one another and how do these depend on the context in which they were carried out?

First, the values of social justice are predominant in the action research carried out in contexts of colonial oppression or extreme economic disparity between the rich and the poor. In this sense they can be said to be strongly constructed by their positioning in colonial or other oppressive settings where political 'struggle' against oppression is a dominant value. This is very evident in the two 'southern' studies and in the work of Wadsworth in Australia and Hinsdale *et al.* in the USA. This work draws – across three different continents – on the work of Paulo Freire, and his close associates Miles Horton and Fals-Borda, and has a strong emphasis on group participation and collaboration rather than on supporting the efforts of individual action researchers. Walker, Knijnik and Hinsdale *et al.* all carry out work that is meticulously well theorized, yet their assumptions are quite different from those of Titchen and Chiu in a health care setting. Although very different from each other, Titchen and Chiu's studies can both be seen to be strongly constructed by their positioning in hospital settings dominated by the values of the medical model. This is not at all to imply that their work is any greater or lesser in value, but rather to note the sensitivity and flexibility of action research methodology in responding to the needs of different social contexts. Chiu adopts a social engineering rather than a social justice approach; Titchen works to integrate a social change purpose – to improve the care given to patients – with an empowering participatory methodology. The latter is developed with meticulous precision from two extensive theoretical frameworks: the critical theory of Habermas, filtered through the work of Carr and Kemmis, and the phenomenology of Schutz. The extensive grounding of Titchen's study in 'western' philosophical literature makes it very different from the equally carefully theorized studies of Walker, Knijnik and Hinsdale *et al.* Wadsworth is perhaps just as concerned as Titchen and Chiu with considerations of validity, but she draws her authority from establishing the authenticity of participation, the 'we' – as do Hinsdale *et al.* – rather than from more traditional procedures of systematic analysis (Chiu) or comparative reflexivity (Titchen).

The studies carried out in Business settings are distinguished by their positioning vis-à-vis Taylorism or strategic management as structuring 'others'. In a recent article about action research in the journal *Management Learning*, Coghlan (2003: 451) refers to 'insider action research' as 'a relatively neglected form of research in organizations'. This sharply distinguishes the traditions of action research in business settings from action research in schools and university departments of education, illustrating that what is 'neglected' in one setting can be regarded (during the same period of time) as the expected orthodoxy in another. The Susman and Trist (1993) study is an external intervention in a company, severely constrained by the power positioning of the project vis-à-vis the unions and the sponsor, with a 'treatment'/'control group' design externally imposed and in direct conflict with the espoused values of socio-technical research. One hopes that such an internal conflict in the design of this study from 30 years ago would not occur today, but problems in negotiating such matters with external sponsors in the field of business are probably still a distinct possibility. The Rutter study is also an external intervention, but he deliberately distances it from the cultural norm of 'consultancy', by employing the techniques of counselling to ensure ownership remains with the company managers.

The differences between the action research methodology enacted in projects in these different settings – including the educational setting in which the projects described in the following chapters are located – are fundamental rather than cosmetic. They relate to deeply held values underpinning social action, which are constitutive of understandings of being in the world and the nature of knowledge. Each of these traditions is necessarily limited and therefore potentially constraining; each also contains spaces where action research can push against the boundaries and generate knowledge with transformative power; and there are many other traditions that I have not had time to even touch on here. It is useful and empowering for action researchers to explore across the boundaries of action research traditions and guard against constructing constraining regimes of truth.

3 Action Research from the Inside: a Teacher's Experience

What is the experience and possible rewards for a teacher – or any other professional – in becoming an action researcher? How does carrying out action research change the nature of relationships in the workplace, for example between teachers and their pupils? Should teachers enrolled on higher degrees carry out their work on behalf of colleagues as well as for academic accreditation – and, if so, what kind of reporting might meet the needs of both audiences? What ethical issues are raised by such studies? Between 1980 and 1985 I carried out action research while Head of the English Faculty at Parkside Community College in Cambridge. I had already been extremely fortunate in spending a year, seconded from my previous teaching post, studying for an advanced diploma in education with John Elliott at the Cambridge Institute of Education. While at Parkside I participated in the Teacher–Pupil Interaction and the Quality of Learning (TIQL) Project[1] in which participant reachers researched how to improve the quality of learning by changing classroom practices and during 1982–4 undertook a part-time masters degree also at the Cambridge Institute. The advanced diploma had given me experience of carrying out research as an outsider, working on behalf of a teacher (Somekh 1983). Becoming a researcher of my own classroom was at first daunting because of the additional workload involved, but it was also enormously exciting, allowing me to develop a deeper understanding of the process of teaching and learning and to forge new kinds of collaborative relationships with pupils and, later, colleagues. Without question being an action researcher in my own workplace constituted the most powerful professional development of my teaching career. At Parkside, because of my middle management role and the generous support of colleagues I was able to extend my research beyond my classroom to the work of the department and the school as a whole. It was

---

[1] The TIQL project, funded by the Schools Council between 1982 and 1984, was directed by John Elliott at the Cambridge Institute of Education.

an opportunity to try out a range of research methods and explore whether, and if so how, action research carried out by an 'insider' could instigate, support and evaluate educational change.

In this chapter I want to present this work from two points of view, those of my former self when I carried out the work and of my current self looking back upon it in the light of intervening experience. To do this without blurring these two very different voices I have kept them as far as possible separate. The major part of the chapter is made up of a substantial extract from one article and the whole of another article that I wrote at the time. These are reproduced in their original form, written in the present rather than the past tense, which I hope will give my teacher's voice immediacy rather than causing confusion. I have also added brief explanatory introductions to each study to fill gaps in the original versions – about my research methods in one case and the organizational structure of the school, and differences between British and American terminology, in the other. At the end of the chapter I reflect back on these studies, exploring some of the methodological issues they raise and considering how the methods I adopted might be adapted to suit the needs of teachers carrying out similar work in a contemporary context.

A study of teaching and learning in my own classroom

A retrospective introduction

The first study that I carried out in my own classroom when I returned to full-time teaching after doing my advanced diploma was of teaching of poetry (Somekh 1984). It was carried out as a contribution to the work of the TIQL project, to which I was loosely attached although the school as a whole had decided not to take up the invitation to participate. A key question for TIQL was whether it was possible to teach 'for understanding' at the same time as preparing pupils for public examinations. At the time there was no national curriculum and as a secondary school teacher I could choose what to teach to pupils in the first three years (ages 11–14); but in the fourth and fifth years (ages 14–16) teaching focused on preparing pupils for public examinations – either 'O' (ordinary) level of the General Certificate of Education or CSE (the Certificate of Secondary Education) depending on ability – and this necessitated following a prescribed syllabus. However, teachers also had substantial choice in terms of opting to prepare their pupils for different kinds of examinations offered by different exam boards. I decided to undertake a study of my teaching of poetry to pupils entered for the Cambridge 'Plain Text' 'O' level. 'Plain' texts meant that books had no footnotes and pupils were allowed to take them into the examination, so the focus could be more on their responses to the literature and less on their ability to write detailed descriptions of the plot and characters. Poetry was, however, treated differently: there was no set poetry anthology to be studied in preparation for the exam; instead, candidates were invited to respond to an 'unseen' poem printed on the exam paper. In the previous year I had worked as a 'Plain Text' examiner for the Cambridge Board and this had given me insights into how pupils needed to write about a poem in order to gain high marks. Teaching this was not easy, however. I was not satisfied with the way I was teaching poetry, and so I decided to carry out action research to find a new approach that would come nearer to my ideals.

In carrying out this research I worked very much on my own, although I attended occasional TIQL project meetings. At these, we teachers shared our work with one another and were intellectually and emotionally challenged by John Elliott and his team to discuss and investigate the nature of pupils' learning and the kind of teaching that would be most likely to lead to 'understanding' (as opposed to short-term memorizing). To carry out the study I collected data by tape-recording my interactions with the pupils, both in whole class teaching and in group and one-to-one work as I moved around the classroom. I used a radio microphone clipped onto my clothes at the height most likely to pick up pupils' voices, a transmitter slipped into my pocket and a tape-recorder running in an adjoining tiny cupboard. (Very soon this process was to become much easier as small tape-recorders, attached to a lapel microphone, can easily be slipped into a pocket.) I later transcribed these tape-recordings. I also collected documentary data such as worksheets and photocopies of pupils' writing and drawings. On the rare occasions when visitors, such as student teachers, came into my classroom I asked them to help me by observing and making notes for me that I could afterwards discuss with them. The pupils were very much part of the research process. I started by explaining to them that I was interested in the way I was teaching them and how they were learning and that I hoped that by researching what was happening, I might be able to make improvements. I asked their permission to tape-record, making sure they were aware that the radio microphone was linked to the tape-recorder in the cupboard. I also gave them all a small notebook and asked them to make a quick note about *how* they had learnt when they felt they had just learnt something new. Although this last approach produced only a very small quantity of data, it provided me with some crucially important evidence in my interactions with Lup in the extract from the paper quoted here – Lup chose to come and tell me about his learning rather than writing it down, but he only did this because he knew I was investigating the learning process. The pupils' consciousness of my research was clear one day when I was tape-recording a lesson in the school hall and had to stop to talk to the school caretaker who asked me a question as he was passing through. 'Miss, he's spoiled the tape-recording!' one girl said indignantly after he had gone and

I had to explain that it was really not a problem as I was interested in everything that happened while I was teaching.

In the extract that follows the pupils' real names are used, as is the name of the school. This was negotiated with staff and pupils at the time of the original publication. Naming children, with their permission, had become my practice, in response to the huge disappointment that was expressed to me one day by an 11-year-old boy called Adam after he had spent the whole of break time reading a transcript of my interview with him. I wanted his permission to use the transcript in my writing and for Adam, who found reading very difficult, reading this one page of dense text took him the whole 20 minutes. When I came out of the staffroom at the end of break he beamed at me with joy at the wonderful experience of seeing his words in typescript... and then said, 'But why have you called me Benjamin?' in a voice of puzzlement and real hurt. This text contained his words and he was making it very clear (though he could not express it in these terms) that, from his point of view, by taking away his name I was denying him his voice.

Extracts from the paper first published in CARN Bulletin No 6 and reprinted in Elliott and Ebbutt (1986)

TEACHING POETRY FOR UNDERSTANDING FOR THE
'O' LEVEL CAMBRIDGE 'PLAIN TEXT' LITERATURE SYLLABUS

By Bridget Somekh
Parkside Community College

Most English teachers consider teaching poetry to be difficult. I think these are the reasons:

1   Poetry demands a complex response from the reader/listener – a response which is often both emotional and intellectual at the same time.
2   Poems are seldom straightforward and there is seldom a 'right' way of interpreting them. This leads to problems if the teacher is normally used to teaching a received response to literature (or if the pupils expect to be taught a received response).
3   English teachers who love poetry find it disturbing when pupils react badly to it.
4   Poetry has a bad image in this country. It is in the same league as ballet (seen as effeminate) but also seen as 'difficult'.

The poet Anthony Thwaite told me that, whereas in a French cafe strangers will react enthusiastically to being told he is 'un poet', in an English pub it is better to tell strangers he is 'a writer'.

xxxxx

I started with the basic questions:

1   How do you teach someone to respond to poetry?
2   How do you, at the same time, encourage pupils to enjoy poetry?

I believe that these are the central issues in preparing pupils for the 'Plain Text' exam, although I recognize that I must also teach them how to write about poems and this will entail teaching some of the technical terms of literary criticism, such as 'metaphor' and 'alliteration'. I decided to examine my teaching of poetry to my fourth-year class, 29 boys and girls, aged 14–15, all aiming to enter for two 'O' levels in English Literature and English Language. In ability they represent a spread from the top 50% of the ability range in the school (a non-selective school with a favoured catchment area).

The first poetry we looked at in November was given a poor reception. We read some of the poems of Robert Frost. I read them aloud with some brief introduction first. I invited comments from the class. The response was minimal and a student teacher was told later, by one group, that they didn't like Robert Frost. At the end of my lesson, one of the most able boys volunteered the remark that he thought 'people find poetry difficult'. Bearing in mind that I was asking for personal responses to the poems, and that speaking in front of the teacher and the whole class is a public and, for some pupils, a nerve-racking experience, I hypothesized that:

> Class discussions on poetry are counter-productive because the tensions of the discussion situation increase the pupils' perceptions that poetry is 'difficult'.

I decided to work from this hypothesis and try to determine to what extent it is possible to teach pupils how to respond to poetry on a deeper level, by means of work done individually or in groups – there would be no more lessons in which I taught them poetry all together as a class. I believed that they needed to learn how to respond to poetry a) to increase their own enjoyment of it, b) to prepare them for the exam. Could this be done without whole class teaching and with the consequent reduction in teacher contact time for each individual?

In drawing up the programme of work I also took into account two criticisms of my teaching from the evaluation exercise I had conducted, using response sheets, at the end of the Christmas term.
1   There had been too many essays – they would like a greater variety of tasks.
2   There had not been enough opportunities for creative writing.
I drew up the following work sheet, 'Poetry and Writing'.

POETRY AND WRITING

AIMS:
1 That you should read and enjoy as much poetry as possible.
2 That you should look closely at your own responses to poems (your thoughts and feelings).
3 That you should look at the way the poem is written, to understand why you have these responses to it.
4 That you use the poems to give you ideas for writing of your own (poetry or prose).

BOOKS:
Famous Poems of the Twentieth Century and any other poetry books of your own or from the library (Bebbington 1978).

ORAL WORK:
1 Hold a discussion with your group in which each person tells the other about a poem he/she has liked and you discuss the poems together.
2 With your group, make a radio programme about poems of your choice. The completed programme should last between 10 and 20 minutes.
3 Prepare one poem to read aloud to the class. Practise carefully so that your voice and intonation are just right for the poem.

READING:
4 Read as many poems as you can. (You will probably find you always have to read a poem twice. Poems always need to be heard, so read them aloud to yourself if possible.)

cont.

WRITING:
Give each piece of work a heading to make it clear what you are
doing. Include illustrations wherever you wish.

5 Keep a list of all the poems you read, with author's name
   and a very brief comment. The idea is that you come back
   to this list to choose poems to write about more fully.
6 Write in detail about as many poems as possible. What
   you write should fulfil aims 1, 2 and 3 above. Go into as
   much detail as you can without making yourself bored.
   Remember to use the technical terms on the list as tools
   to help you write your ideas.
7 Make a diagram to show which poems seem to you to be
   linked in any way. You could, if you prefer, do a series of
   diagrams to show different kinds of links.
8 Imagine you are talking to one of the poets and write
   down exactly what you would say and what you would
   ask about his/her poem or poems.
9 Write a parody of one of the poems.
10 Make a drawing, painting or collage to show your response
   to a poem or poems.
11 Use a poem for a brainstorming session for ideas for your
   own writing: what memories, hopes, fears, thoughts do
   you have when you read it? See what you come up with
   and then write in any way you like and at any length you
   like.
12 Keep a notebook or a page in your file and jot down notes
   about your everyday experiences, thoughts and feelings.
   Use this as a source for your own writing.

The pupils planned their own work taking the questions in any
order they liked, but with the proviso that they must cover all
three sections: oral work, reading and writing. They had a double
period (80 minutes of class time) and both English homeworks
every week for the first half of the Easter term. A list of technical
terms (some of which had already been taught) was provided to
help them with question 6.

How did the scheme work in practice?

1) How hard did the pupils work?
This varied as one would expect:

- a) 9 pupils completed 10–12 pieces of written work or recordings as well as reading and unrecorded oral work.
- b) 10 pupils produced good work and, in my judgement, were working their hardest although they did not produce 10–12 pieces.
- c) 9 pupils could have produced more work, although the quality of the work they did was quite good. Compared with the previous term, they had 'slacked off'.
- d) 1 pupil responded badly to the freedom and idled away his time (not without friction between us).

2) Did the opportunity to opt for tasks of differing difficulty allow some pupils to follow an easier programme and learn less?
I was quite happy for pupils to select from the questions as they wished. In my judgement all the questions demanded a thoughtful response to the poems (except for no. 12 which, in practice, was not a popular question). I did, however, wish all pupils to attempt question 6, the skill of writing about poems being an important part of the exam course. Only one pupil avoided it altogether (category d above). There was a tendency for some pupils to select 'easy' poems such as *McCavity The Mystery Cat* by T.S.Eliot and *Matilda* by Hilaire Belloc but these poems proved ideal for parodies and were often the right choice for that pupil. In any case, the way they selected poems provided me with a useful insight into the attitudes, self-confidence and level of understanding of different pupils.

3) What about the oral work — was it taken seriously?
Not at first. Some of the first recordings I heard were a waste of time. In the end work for questions I and 2 was nearly all recorded and it improved greatly once pupils realized their recording would be listened to and commented on. No one attempted question 3 except within a small group. It was interesting that this question, the only one which reverted to a whole class situation, was rejected as being too embarrassing: 'Do we have to do question 3?' I was asked.

I would like to look now at the crucial issue of understanding. First of all, is there any evidence in their work, or from tapes of discussions with me, that my pupils developed understanding of the poems they read? Second, is there any evidence here to show what kind of difficulties pupils had with poetry and exactly what they learnt about how to read poems? I will take both of these ques-tions together and attempt to answer them by looking at the work of [one pupil]. [NOTE: In the original publication, I looked at the work of four pupils and also included a selection of work done in answer to questions 5, 8, 9, 10 and 11 as an Appendix.]

Let's look at Lup. He is a thoughtful boy whom I had graded as B (probable 'O' level pass) at the end of the first term. He speaks Chinese at home. At the end of the year he surprised me by coming top in the class in English Literature in the school's annual, inter-nal examinations. His high mark was partly due to a very good answer to the 'unseen' poetry question. Here is a transcript of a conversation I had with him in class on February 5th [about Hal Summer's poem *My Old Cat*].

[The poem is about the poet's feelings when he finds his cat lying dead. It appeared to me on first reading to be fairly conventional in expressing affection for the cat and admiration of what the poet saw as his fierce resistance to death rather than meek acceptance.]

Lup: I don't understand the last four or five lines.
T: *My Old Cat.* Can I read the whole thing a minute . . . . (quite a long pause followed by a laugh). Oh . . . well, down to 'full, of rage, defiance' it's all right, isn't it?
Lup: Yeah.
T: That's just a description of his cat.
Lup: He's saying that the bloke coming in to inspect it, he hated him. The old cat hated the person that's coming in, you know, to look at him. But how can he see that if he's snuffed it, all dead?
T: Well, if anybody dies you tend to think back about them and what they mean to you and their good points and their bad points, don't you?
Lup: Yeah.
T: I think that Hal Summers who wrote this — just those four lines represent one of the things that he thinks was best about his cat, one of the things he admired most about the cat that died.
Lup: Yeah, that he never liked him.
T: What?

Lup: I think that the cat never liked the human — well, you know, these last lines, saying that he didn't pretend that he hated humans but actually showed it.

T: But ...

Lup: Then he goes, 'Well died my old cat', so I think the old bloke here wants the cat to die.

T: Oh look, I've just got an idea, Lup. I don't think I've seen enough in this. Do you see what the cat looked like when he was dead?

Lup: Yes.

T: 'Stiff and . . . His look was a lion's full of rage and defiance.'

Lup: The person who's come to — 'I', whoever 'I' is.

T: Yes or death, maybe.

Lup: Oh yeah (tone of suddenly seeing), I see.

T: I suddenly saw that. It's good, isn't it?

Lup: Yeah, when you put death into it, it really fits in well.

T: And that makes sense of 'Well died my old cat.' In other words, none of this nonsense about, you know, he went gently and it was all for the best.

At first Lup is puzzled because the cat who is dead appears to be having feelings, 'but how can he see that if he's snuffed it?' At this point his reading of the poem is very literal. Next, once again searching for a literal explanation, he presumes that the cat's hatred and anger, at the time of his death, must be directed against the author, the 'I' of the poem, who is the only other 'person' in the poem. In turn this leads Lup to think that the man disliked the cat and wanted him to die. He presumably reasons that it was likely that the feeling of hatred would be reciprocal. This is, of course, a serious misreading of the poem. Up to this point in the conversation, I myself had assumed that the cat's anger was directed against dying in the abstract and the world in general, but Lup's literal approach here gave me a new insight – perhaps it is the approaching figure of death who the cat hates. After I suggest this, Lup says 'Oh yeah' with a tone of voice expressing sudden understanding. He goes on: 'Yeah, when you put death into it, it really fits in well.'

During the conversation, Lup had understood the poem and I, too, had come to a new understanding of it. However, Lup had learnt something more important, he had learnt how to tackle a poem. He explained later in the lesson:

> I just learnt how to understand. I don't know how to put
> it in words … What I'm trying to say … is that … you give
> us an idea … you know, try all the different things, and see
> if the poem actually, you know … see if it fits in with the
> poem – and if it does then it's probably the right answer.

This process of trial and error, of seeing if ideas fit, seems to me to
be very different from the literal approach he had shown earlier.
Following our discussion of *My Old Cat* I suggested to Lup that he
should read *Do Not Go Gentle into that Good Night* by Dylan
Thomas.

xxxxx

[Here is the final verse of the poem and two short extracts from my
article – Lup's response to this verse and the final part of my commentary on his writing.]

> And you, my father, there on the sad height,
> Curse, bless, me now with your fierce tears I pray.
> Do not go gentle into that good night.
> Rage, rage against the dying of the light.
> (From Dylan Thomas' poem, *Do Not Go Gentle into that Good Night*)

[Lup's response to this verse]:
The poet is now talking to his dying father and begging him not to
go gentle into that good night. The 'fierce tears' just adds to the
picture of some one putting up a hard fight. Tears can't really be
fierce but you can be fierce when crying.

[My commentary]:
Here Lup understands everything, but makes clear what his initial
difficulty was by explaining: 'Tears can't really be fierce.' As with
the cat poem, his first approach has been literal, but he has now
been able to go on and find the suggested 'hidden' meaning.

Lup did not ask me for any help with this poem as he had with *My
Old Cat*. My own interpretation of what happened is that he used
the method which he said he had learnt from me: 'try all the different things' and 'see if it fits in with the poem'. On the whole this
method seems to have worked well.

xxxxx

Undertaking this work has certainly provided me with some insights into the particular difficulties of my pupils. I believe the teaching method was fairly successful, certainly much more successful than my previous attempts at 'whole class' teaching of poetry. When it came to the end of year exams there were no disasters in the answering of the compulsory poetry question (i.e. on average pupils performed as well on that question as they did on the questions on Dickens' *Great Expectations*, which we studied in the summer term). I feel optimistic that it is possible to teach poetry for understanding and for enjoyment for the Cambridge 'Plain Texts' 'O' level English Literature examination.

A study of power and decision making in our school conducted in collaboration with colleagues

A retrospective introduction

In this section I reproduce the whole of a published paper in which I reported on some of my masters degree research carried out at the same school (Somekh 1987). Readers not familiar with the British education system need to know some differences between US and British terminology because the British terms are used frequently in this paper. The term 'management' is used in Britain rather than 'administration' for organizational and leadership functions; the term 'staff' rather than 'faculty' for the whole body of teachers and their colleagues; and the terms 'head' and 'deputy head' rather than 'principal' and 'vice-principal' for those with the top responsibilities. Secondary schools in Britain are commonly divided into subject groupings known as 'faculties': at this school there were seven faculties: maths, science, English, modern languages, humanities, physical education and art and design. The faculty heads were overseen by the deputy head (curriculum), and a second deputy head (pastoral) oversaw the work of a parallel group of pastoral managers: the head of upper school (14–16 age group) and three heads of year to cover the age groups (11–14). Pay scales at the time were highest for the head and higher for deputy heads than for other teachers. The majority of teachers were on scale 1 or 2, with promoted posts at scale 3 and 4 for those with middle management responsibility. Most (but not all) faculty heads at Parkside, including myself, were on scale 4.

Readers also need to know that I was a relative newcomer to the school, having been appointed in 1980 whereas the majority of staff had been in post since the school was 'reorganized' as a comprehensive school in 1974. Comprehensive schools take pupils of all abilities, whereas the previous grammar school had selected pupils on the basis of national tests at age 11.

The full paper, first published in CARN Bulletin No 8 (Somekh 1987)

'THE EYES OF A FLY':
AN EXPERIMENT IN COLLABORATIVE RESEARCH

Bridget Somekh
Parkside Community College

Parkside Community College is an 11–16 comprehensive school of 600 pupils situated on Parker's Piece, a pleasant grass area, in the middle of Cambridge. It has a broad intake ranging from the children of academics to the children of those who live in some of the poorest council estates in the city. The school enjoys the reputation of being fairly progressive: a great deal of class grouping in the school is mixed ability and relationships between staff and pupils are frequently informal. The school prides itself on its examination results: in 1983, 39% of the 5th year obtained 5 or more 'O' levels at grades A to C (or CSE 1s).[2] This paper is based on work I undertook during my fourth year as head of English at the school, as part of an MA degree course in applied research in education.

At Parkside there is a tradition of school-based research, four members of staff, including myself, having had quite a lot of experience through connections with the Cambridge Institute of Education and the Open University. In many ways Parkside is a very open school: for example, a large number of student teachers come in each year, for small group teaching as well as for more formal teaching practices. This openness probably makes it receptive to research and projects.

Nevertheless, there has also been some opposition to research in the school. For example, in 1981 it rejected an invitation to take part in the Teacher–Pupil Interaction and the Quality of Learning (TIQL) project based at the Cambridge Institute. At the time some

---

[2]   At the time the pass rates at grades A to C for pupils in similar schools would have been around 32 per cent.

staff, including the Head of Maths, felt that the school would not benefit by this project, but would merely be made use of by academics eager to gain credit from writing a book (ironically when one knows the aims of this particular project); the view was expressed that it would be better for staff to undertake research that would benefit the school and to do this without outside interference.

From the start of my MA course I decided that I would place emphasis on carrying out my research projects *for* the school. I was influenced by the staff's response to the TIQL Project, but had also become interested over several years in fostering action research in schools. In particular, I had learnt from my experience of working with teachers in the school teams in the TIQL Project (in which I was involved as an associated teacher). It was my aim to involve as many members of staff as possible in my research, drawn from across the faculties: in this way I hoped to make the staff as a whole interested in what I was doing, so that it could be of practical use to the school. I believe that this was the best approach, although there were some problems for me in writing for a dual audience: on the one hand, my colleagues in school, on the other, my tutors at the Cambridge Institute.

My first study was of 'Curriculum at Parkside for Children with Special Needs'. It was carried out after consultation with the faculty heads, head and deputy head (curriculum) specifically for the Special Needs Department and with the active support and help of the two members of that department. This study was almost purely descriptive, mainly because I was nervous about the reactions I would get from colleagues.

My second study was of 'The Way in which Experienced Teachers Evaluate their Teaching' and involved my making video films of four colleagues: the Head of Maths, the Head of Humanities who teaches geography, the Head of Physical Education and a teacher of French.

Having been encouraged by the reaction given to my first study by my school audience and criticized by my academic audience for making it purely descriptive, I was much more adventurous with this second study and gave a full account of my analysis of the data I had collected. Once again my colleagues reacted very positively, although two used their right of reply[3] to defend themselves on

---

[3] This was an agreement made in advance that they could insert a response into the text of any of my assignments if they wished to disagree with my analysis.

specific issues and the Head of Maths, having asked me to explain one point to him, declared he could understand perfectly well what I said but had not been able to understand the same point in my study (perhaps because it involved a quotation from a paper by a philosopher of education!). Needless to say, he was critical of what he considered useless 'jargon'. I was surprised and pleased to find that all four teachers found the video-films of their classes very interesting, particularly the three who had never previously been video-filmed.

The major part of the present paper describes my third study, on 'Power and Decision-making in the School', which I carried out during the Easter term of 1984. At the time the Head was on secondment to British Telecom and his absence highlighted the management structures of the school in a way that I believe was particularly useful to my study. Specific permission to investigate this topic was, therefore, obtained from the Acting Head whose usual role is Deputy Head (pastoral).

The report, entitled 'The Eyes of a Fly', was presented to the Head (on his return) and any staff who wished to read it as four separate documents:
1.   INTRODUCTION – CHOOSING THE TOPIC AND AN APPROPRIATE RESEARCH METHOD
2.   CREATING YOUR OWN JOB – AN ANALYSIS OF STAFF ROLES AT PARKSIDE
3.   THE ROLE OF THE HEAD OF UPPER SCHOOL
4.   THE ROLE OF THE FACULTY HEADS

It was written in this form to enable my colleagues at Parkside to read only the sections which interested them. My difficulty with the dual audience was eased by including a great deal of the theory in the first section, although, in practice, several colleagues borrowed it with the other sections. Four short documents seemed to be more acceptable to busy people than one single long one would have been.

I am presenting here the whole of the first document followed by a brief indication of some of the main issues which are explored in the other three documents. Finally, there is a short section on the effect my work has had on the school, as I see it.

THE EYES OF A FLY

A STUDY OF THE ORGANIZATION OF PARKSIDE COMMUNITY COLLEGE IN TERMS OF STAFF ROLES

'We're like the eyes of a fly, aren't we? Everybody sees a different facet of things.'

Head of Science, Parkside Community College

1   INTRODUCTION – CHOOSING THE TOPIC AND AN APROPRIATE RESEARCH METHOD

It is not easy to decide on a research topic relating to the organization and management of your own school, particularly if you hope your study will be of use to the school and of interest to your colleagues. I began by discussing possible topics informally and made one formal proposal to the Pastoral Committee for a study of relationships between the school and parents: for various reasons, this was abandoned. In the end, the one topic that seemed to interest everyone I consulted was 'Power and Decision-making'.

I was very aware of the problems of conducting research on such a wide topic, involving so many individuals who together comprise a complex institution. Philosophically, I subscribe to the phenomenological view of reality as described by Greenfield (1981). As I see it, this leaves the researcher of an institution with two related problems:

(1) The institution has no objective reality: its reality exits only in the interpretations of its members.

(2) The researcher cannot make any inquiries without affecting the reality of the institution: any questions or discussions will cause all the different interpretations of reality to shift and change; even the knowledge that the research is being undertaken will have an effect on the actions and perceptions of the participants.

Researching within one's own school, the metaphor of the eye of the fly seems particularly apt: every individual (single facet of the eye) has a different perspective and the researcher is herself only one of these facets; the true picture is perceived by the eye as a whole from the combined perceptions of all the individual facets;

if the researcher begins to interpret the data by imposing an overview the whole delicate balance of the eye will be destroyed and the study will fail to perceive the reality.

To some extent I could overcome these problems by using the 'grounded theory' approach described by Glaser and Strauss (1967), and by adopting a technique of 'progressive focussing' as described by Dearden and Laurillard (1976). In this way I could hope to ensure that the focus of my study arose from the real concerns of my colleagues rather than being imposed by my own interests. However, I also had to find a way of giving validity to my interpretations of the data, as well as ensuring that I did not do violence to the delicate balances of power and relationships within the institution.

The problem was stated most succinctly by the Head of Maths at a later stage of the study when I hoped I had already identified a way of coping with it:

> I've mixed feelings about this being for any purpose other than your research. It is interesting and *might well* be useful to bring it into Parkside, rather than just keeping it to yourself but it is biased. By bringing it to the faculty heads as you have done it has now become a piece of Parkside. (He questions the rightness of this.)

I explained the precautions I was taking but I do not think I satisfied his anxieties, mainly because to preclude bias he was looking for a piece of research which could be replicated as in the scientific paradigm. Within the parameters of qualitative research, a solution did, however, seem possible. It lay in Habermas's linked concepts of the 'ideal speech situation' and the 'communicative community' as described by Winter (1984). If I could allow staff members to participate in analysing my data, so that I and they became 'active partners' in 'authenticating' the interpretations, then my study would have a validity in terms of the reality of the fly's eyes. In other words, I wanted a method of achieving the 'communicative validation' described by Terhart (1982), in which 'a research result can be regarded as being valid, if a consensus is reached among the participants in the research process'. I was not, however, interested in a study that was purely descriptive, and I was aware of the danger of producing a piece of very dull research if I allowed the search for consensus to guide my research methods from an early stage. These are the procedures I adopted:

I began with a series of 13 interviews with members of staff at all levels in the school's formal structure, from the caretaker to the Acting Head. I used the following schedule of open ended questions:

QUESTIONS FOR INTERVIEW
1   How has your job been different this term because of the absence of the Head?
    Supplementary question: Any small changes?
2   Have you noticed any changes in the organization of the school this term?
3   How do you think decisions are made in this school? I would like you to back up what you say with an example if possible.
    Supplementary questions:
    a)   who can you remember initiating a change?
    b)   who can you remember preventing a change?
    c)   who can you remember being influential in bringing about a change?
4   Do you think you personally have any say in the running of the school? Please give examples.
5   Any other comments?

During all the interviews I took extensive notes, largely made up of chunks of direct quotation. These were typed on to a word processor and returned to the interviewees as soon as possible for checking, alterations and additions. I gained permission at this stage to use the notes for my study, but guaranteed to ask specific permission for any direct quotations identified by name.

Using the techniques of 'progressive focusing' I identified two or three issues of particular Interest to me which arose out of the body of interview notes:
(1)   The role of the head of upper school was selected because the interviews revealed that after four years at the school I had a very different perception of his role from that held by those who had been in the school since it was reorganized in 1974.
(2)   The role of the faculty heads was selected because a minority of those interviewed criticized faculty heads strongly.
(3)   Democracy was selected because it was an issue that came up in almost every interview.

To gather information on the history of decision making and its present patterns, I examined the minutes of faculty heads' meetings from March 1974 to the present day and staff meetings from September 1980 to the present day.

At this stage I wrote two confidential documents in which I described and analysed the roles of the head of upper school and the faculty heads. Bias was knowingly included in these documents, in that minority views were quoted, as were my own subjective interpretations of the data. By including this kind of material in preliminary documents at this stage I hoped to avoid producing a final document that was merely descriptive or, at best, bland.

These documents were then given to the people they most nearly concerned: 'The Role of the Head of Upper School' went only to the head of upper school himself; 'The Role of the Faculty Heads' went to all those who attend the faculty heads' meetings with the exception of the head of the school and the two deputies.

These confidential documents were intended to be provocative in order that they should stimulate a response. I carried out a supplementary series of interviews with all but one of those concerned (the Head of PE was too busy to see me on the day arranged and illness, together with industrial action, prevented our making an alternative appointment). In all these interviews I was talking to people of comparable standing to my own in the school. In all of them we were discussing a topic of importance to the interviewee in the knowledge that my document was confidential and would not be seen by other members of staff without the interviewee's permission. In all of them I explained that I was going to 'substantially rewrite' the document to incorporate the views of those I was interviewing. As far as possible, therefore, there was the 'symmetrical distribution of control by dialogue participants', which Winter (1984) identifies as being essential for Habermas's 'ideal speech situation'.

Notes from this second round of interviews were typed and, as planned, were used to rewrite the two documents. The intention was to make these new documents almost collaborative in authorship, while still preserving the opinions of other members of staff who had only been involved in the first stage of interviews.

At this stage, further analysis of both sets of interview notes revealed that the vast topic of democracy could not be dealt with in the scope of the present study, but that the data on democracy included some fascinating insights into the roles of many members of staff. The study as a whole finally focused on the issue of staff roles at Parkside. The rewritten papers on the roles of the head of upper school and the faculty heads became detailed examples of the general theory that emerged about staff roles in the school as a whole.

It was difficult to decide who should be consulted in order to give validity to that part of the study concerned with staff roles in general. Since it was largely a matter of management style it could be said to affect the Head most nearly, but there was another sense in which, because it was related to the staff as a whole, it should have been validated by discussions with the staff as a whole. Practicalities meant that time was running out and I needed clearance of the study in order to meet my deadline. Even without this pressure, however, I doubt whether it would have been possible to set up ideal speech situations with every member of staff: the operation would have taken time out of proportion to its value and, further to that, it is doubtful whether 'symmetrical distribution of control' could have been achieved even supposing all my colleagues had been equally interested in discussing the issues. Therefore, once the faculty heads and the head of upper school had given permission for the collaborative sections to go to other members of staff, the study as a whole was given to the Head (newly returned from his period of secondment to British Telecom). Final revisions were made in line with his comments and the study was then made available to any member of staff interested in reading it.

A SUMMARY OF HYPOTHESES AND ISSUES FROM SECTIONS TWO, THREE AND FOUR

2 CREATING YOUR OWN JOB – AN ANALYSIS OF STAFF ROLES AT PARKSIDE

This section looks at the issues of institutional change, motivation and accountability and develops a theory to explain the way the school functions. It presents evidence for that theory and examines some of its implications.

Here is the theory:
(1) At Parkside nobody's role is very precisely defined; instead, a substantial portion of everybody's job is what the individual wishes to make it. Thus, the hierarchical structure of organization bears little relation to the actual power structures of the school.

(2) The effect of this great flexibility of roles is that each individual has a constant incentive to spread his/her net a little wider. It is not so much that everyone is empire-building, although there are elements of that: it is more that no one higher up is seen to have authority as a right, and every decision and accepted practice is therefore open to question.

(3) There seem to be two main ways in which this affects the organization and ethos of the school:

    (a) Staff at all levels are constantly coming up with ideas or responding actively to the ideas of others (either by criticizing them, adapting them or suggesting alternatives).

    (b) All are being held accountable by the rest of the staff for the jobs they do. Depending on the personality of the individual this accountability can be more open or more hidden, but options about the wisdom or otherwise of people's actions and practices are expressed much more openly than in most other institutions.

3   THE ROLE OF THE HEAD OF UPPER SCHOOL

This section focuses on one person who has a key role in the school. It also offers some comments on the particular difficulties of this role.

(1) The head of upper school is the only member of the Head's 'inner cabinet' group who is paid on a scale 4 (rather than at Deputy Head level). This anomaly exists because there has been a change in the structure of the hierarchy since the school was established in 1974: specifically, year heads have replaced the former post of head of lower school. Members of staff appointed to the school more recently are not at all aware of his status as a member of this group. This places the head of upper school in a slightly difficult position.

(2) The head of upper school has a very large work load and in the opinion of some staff is doing the job of Deputy Head. He is responsible for: discipline and pastoral care in the Upper School; 3rd Year Option Choices; 5th Year Collegiate Board applications; Careers Teaching in the school; and 16 periods of History teaching each week.

(3) The head of upper school fills an important authority role within a democracy. His role is much more clearly defined

than that of any other member of staff (see 2). He opts out of the democratic processes of the school to a large extent and, by carrying an enormous work load, enables everyone else to have sufficient time for those slow-moving processes.

(4) Parkside is a school which is primarily 'child-centred' and relationships between many members of staff and their pupils are very informal: on the whole this works well, but there are occasions when some pupils overstep the dividing line between friendliness and familiarity and this leads to discipline problems. Within this framework, the head of upper school is an authoritarian teacher who makes it very clear to pupils exactly where they stand. The staff as a whole probably relies on this strong disciplinarian presence in the upper school.

4   THE ROLE OF FACULTY HEADS AT PARKSIDE

This section examines the role of the faculty heads and looks at some of the criticisms made by other members of staff of the Faculty Heads Committee.

(1) There is great variation in the roles of the different faculty heads, depending partly on their personalities and partly on the make-up of their faculties. These differences indicate two quite different concepts of the role of faculty head:
   a)   On the one hand there are those who see it as primarily consisting in being an expert teacher of a subject and taking responsibility for the subject curriculum.
   b)   On the other hand there are those who see the role of faculty head as a managerial and organizational one.
(2) The heads of faculties have a vital role in forming a link between their faculty members and the head. As part of this, everyone is agreed that at faculty heads' meetings each individual should be representing the views of his/her faculty. This kind of liaison may not be easy, however:
   a)   Sometimes a faculty head may genuinely forget to report back to the faculty some apparently small decision that is later seen to be crucial.
   b)   Discussion at the faculty heads' meetings will often enforce a compromise decision and individual faculty members may then feel that their views have not been put sufficiently strongly by their representative.
   c)   Because some faculty heads put their views more forcefully and even dominate the meetings, others who

are by nature more retiring may not feel that they have taken much part in the decisions made. If this is so, they will not see it as their role to support those decisions if members of their faculty criticize them: instead they may join their faculty in criticizing decisions made by 'them'.

(3) Some individual staff members have made forceful criticisms of the faculty heads. The way in which I have dealt with these is explained in the first section of the study. There was no sense in which my study proved the validity of these criticisms, it simply provided a vehicle for discussing them formally and publicly.

THE EFFECT OF MY WORK ON THE SCHOOL

What can I claim? Well, first, I have not alienated the staff. I believe many people have found it interesting to be consulted and to take part in a dialogue on professional matters. I believe this is a tribute to the staff at Parkside who are very committed to their work. In February 1984 I was asked by the Cambridge Institute of Education to act as a co-ordinator at Parkside during the International Seminar on Action Research. I believe that my experience of carrying out research for my colleagues made it easier for me to do this. Several of those teachers who took part were experienced researchers, but some of the most interesting work was carried out by the Head of Maths, who had no previous experience, working with a visiting inspector from another LEA. (Unfortunately the inspector did not follow up his connection with the school as he promised and this was seen as an example of a 'researcher' coming in and making use of the school for his own ends.)

Looking back on my study of the curriculum for children with special needs, I know that the Head of the Remedial Department made use of my 'findings' to bring about several immediate changes to the option scheme in the upper school. She and I were to put forward forceful arguments for change, drawing on the evidence of my study. The Head of Maths told me he supported my general points although he did not consider that my study really provided any evidence because my sample was too small to have any statistical validity. I was subsequently asked by the Head to chair a forward planning group (one of several) looking into this particular issue, and the report from this group to the staff spelled out the implications of my study as well as following up some new issues.

The day when I presented the first piece of the 'Eyes of a Fly' (section 2, 'Creating your own Job') to the Head at lunch time, he came over to my classroom during the afternoon and asked me to see him after school. I went with a measure of anxiety and spent half an hour discussing with him a wide range of topics relating to the study. Among other things he speculated on the proportion of deliberate planning that had gone into the flexible role system I described; and the extent to which it had emerged as a consequence of the developing ethos of the school; he also confided his reluctance to write very precise job descriptions despite some pressure from the council's education office to do so.

The Head of Upper School said, in response to my preliminary document on his role, that he found it a 'flattering portrait' although he couldn't recognize it as being himself. Much later he told me that the Head had said he thought it was an accurate portrait. At the end of term his *final* comment was: 'It was an interesting experience, but one I would not wish to repeat.' The Head himself said that it had come at a good moment just when he was about to appoint a new deputy head of upper school: he had decided to redefine the role of the deputy head of upper school and would find my study helpful. The member of staff appointed to this job subsequently asked if she could read my study and told me that the Head had repeated this remark to her. I put a notice on the staffroom board offering to lend 'The Eyes of a Fly' to anyone who was interested. A small number of senior staff asked to borrow it. The Head of Maths read the whole thing and said (only half in jest) that he could understand it all. 'You're improving,' he added. All faculty heads had a copy of section four and at least one of these passed it around his faculty.

Looking back: a retrospective commentary

Rereading these studies I carried out as a teacher researcher reminds me of the passion and excitement of the experience. I became fascinated by what I was researching, first, by the process of teacher–pupil interactions and how much I could learn from pupils when I really listened to them and treated them with respect, second, by the dynamics of inter-relationships and change processes in the school as a whole and, third, by my own developing sense of agency through drawing colleagues into participation in action research. At the time I had few doubts about the value of my work, certainly for myself and my teaching and I hoped also for my colleagues and the school. I saw no distinction in value between the research I was conducting as a teacher and the research that others were conducting based in universities. Perhaps this may seem very arrogant, but I still hold onto it as a truth. It is not the researcher's location that affects the quality of action research, it is careful research design, ethical sensitivity and growing expertise, as a result of reflexive inquiry into the research process rather than the application of formulaic methods. This confidence in what I was doing was inspired to a considerable extent by John Elliott's inclusive practices in working with teacher–researchers – helping us to present our work at conferences and then get it published, inviting us to teach part time with him on evening courses at the Cambridge Institute, and involving us as partners in leading workshops in exciting places like Klagenfurt and Malaga. It was not until 1983 that I overheard two teacher educators talking about teacher–researchers in the bar at a CARN conference and was surprised – and I must say angry – to hear them saying that teacher research was mainly a process of 'empowering teachers' rather than having any value in terms of generating knowledge. I still find this proposition deeply patronizing and without foundation.

Looking back I can see that a rather simple model of change was embedded in this research I carried out as a teacher, linked closely to Lewin's original model of action research as a process of developing and testing hypotheses. Nevertheless, the theories that I drew on to inform my research, particularly the ideas of Habermas filtered to me through the work of Winter, were extremely powerful as tools for some complexity of research design. 'The Eyes of a Fly' study in particular is certainly not atheoretical, but the language of both studies is simple, with a clear sense that theories drawn from the literature are integral to understanding the complexities of practice, including the practice of carrying out research, rather than something separate to be called upon at a later stage to bolster the importance of the study. It is also very pleasing to realize that the knowledge generated by this research, both about the process of teacher–student interaction in my poetry study and the way that organizations are shaped and controlled by individuals and relationships in 'The Eyes of a Fly', has remained influential in my thinking ever since. Parkside was a school where it was easy to exercise agency and creativity and from the experience of working there I have been better able to identify patterns of leadership and relationships in other institutions which are likely to create similar energy and drive development.

I am interested, too, to recognize that the assurance of some of my claims, despite relatively light evidence, is something that I have since found common in other teachers' research. Recognizing this in my writing, and reflecting back on my own experience, I think it derives from the enormous amount of evidence embedded in day-on-day experience, which is available to the teacher – or any other professional – to confirm the findings emerging from action research. This breadth of evidence is never available to the researcher coming in from outside; but its usefulness to 'insiders' in terms of knowledge generation is relatively low until some involvement in systematic research provides key leads and markers to make its meanings visible.

Partnership seems the critically important feature of action research. Indeed, partnership seems an inevitable result of engaging in action research, in the sense that it fundamentally changes all one's relationships. Initially, it is true, my study of poetry was very much a lone venture, but it resulted in very fundamental changes in my relationships with my pupils. By the end of the study it would be much truer to call them partners in the research rather than informants. Ethically, I think that the time I spent on research while I was teaching them was well justified, because as I learnt more about the pedagogical process I was able to feed back this new knowledge immediately into changes designed to bring about improvements in their learning experiences. In terms of my deliberate intention to intervene in the processes of power and decision making in the school as a whole, I am a little less certain in claiming ethical justification. When the Head of Maths said he was uneasy about my research because it 'has become a piece of Parkside' he was pointing to something I had intended to happen. I had negotiated what I was doing with colleague at every stage, sought permission from the appropriate committees and, in effect, managed to put myself in the position of carrying out research semi-'commissioned' by the school. Nevertheless, as the work evolved I found that, by undertaking this kind of participatory action research, I had much more potential power to affect change than I had anticipated and I was aware of an increasing responsibility to ensure that the intervention brought about benefits and caused no harm.

I was very fortunate that I had already had some research training before I carried out this work, through studying full time for a year for an advanced diploma at the Cambridge Institute of Education. Such opportunities are no longer available to teachers today. Otherwise, however, there are many similarities between my experience of carrying out action research as a teacher and those of teachers and other professionals I know who are currently carrying out action research. It is not important to collect large amounts of data – what is important is to read, reread and interrogate two or three small bodies of data related to the same events and to use them to develop alternative explanatory theories that can be tested out in practice. My study of poetry was based, from memory, on two or three tape-recordings of lessons (80-minute periods), at most, and photocopies of pupils' writing carried out as part of their normal school work. Once the recordings are on tape and the photocopies made, the time-consuming task of transcribing can be carried out over a period of time. It is not necessary to transcribe everything, indeed often it is better to listen to the tapes several times and select three or four 10-minute sections for transcription and in-depth analysis. Whether you are a teacher, a nurse, a teacher educator, a senior manager, a social worker, a police officer or any other professional, the rewards of working in this way are personally high and the value to the profession of knowledge generated by professionals, from the inside, is invaluable. For me, there was an outlet for publication in the *CARN Bulletins*, and for others carrying out similar work today there are journals like *Educational Action Research* (www.triangle.co.uk/ear/). There is an urgent need for more work of this kind to be published.

4 Action Research and Radical Change in Schools[1]

How do schools respond to the challenge of new educational policies? In the 1980s desktop computers, called 'microcomputers' at the time, arrived in schools as the result of initiatives such as the Microelectronics Education Programme, the Technical and Vocational Education Initiative and the Department of Trade and Industry's Micros in School Scheme. (See the end of this chapter for some further information on these three initiatives.) During this period I was working at the Cambridge Institute of Education on a project funded by Norfolk and Suffolk LEAs, called the Support for Innovation Project, which supported senior managers of large secondary schools in providing school-based professional development for their staff to help them cope with the challenges and stress of a multiplicity of new initiatives.

The arrival of computers was just one of these. While a teacher myself I had become an action researcher as a participant in the TIQL Project (see Chapter 3) and had later focused my masters dissertation on experimental work with word processors with my 'first year' English class (11 year olds). I had since, as part of a secondment to Netherhall Software, a co-operative group of teachers and computer programmers (staff and ex-pupils of the Netherhall School), worked alongside the Cambridgeshire LEA team that trained two teachers from each primary school in how to use the new computer acquired through the DTI scheme. I saw the stress computers caused vividly one day when I sat beside an experienced teacher who jumped with anxiety and uttered a startled cry because the computer gave a loud 'bleep' when she pressed a key. Knowing the difficulty for teachers and schools in adopting new initiatives; the excitement and professional growth I had experienced through carrying out action research in my own classroom and school; the stress that computers were causing many teachers but also the

[1] I would like to thank Bob Davidson, Jon Pratt, Erica Brown and Lorna Tickner, and all the teachers who worked on the PALM project, for their enormous contribution to the ideas contained in this chapter.

way in which my own computer was already transforming my own working practices; I wrote a proposal to the newly established Microelectronics Support Unit (MESU) for an action research project to be called Pupil Autonomy in Learning with Microcomputers – the PALM Project.

This chapter reflects back on the PALM project, telling its story, celebrating the achievements of the participants and noting its shortcomings and the reasons for them. The chapter is written from my own point of view, but PALM was a project that was personally experienced and owned by a large number of teachers and by the LEA inspectors and my colleagues in the project team. It had powerful impacts at many different levels. The aim of the chapter is to give readers some of the excitement of taking part in such a project and suggest how a similar initiative could take place today – including what would have to be done differently. Although PALM focused upon the specific innovation of using computers for teaching, the final section provides a commentary that is relevant to all large-scale action research projects set up in a similar way with external funding and leadership from a university-based central team.

PALM: an inter-LEA project to investigate effective use of computers in schools

The aims of the PALM project were:

1   To work in partnership with teachers to research the role of information technology in developing pupil autonomy in learning.
2   To investigate the effectiveness of action research as a means of teacher professional development in the information technology innovation.

The reason for the focus on autonomy in learning needs some explanation. Through my work with Netherhall Software and the Cambridgeshire support team for computers in schools, I was very familiar with the claims being made for computers in education. Then, as now, the claims were visionary but many teachers, teacher educators and educational researchers believed they were hyped up and unrealistic. Since the technology was much less powerful than today the case against its usefulness was much more persuasive. My desire in setting up the PALM project was to work with teachers to investigate whether any real benefits to children's learning were possible from using computers. My background as an action researcher and involvement in the process of software development at Netherhall – including observations of classrooms in which teachers trialled early versions – had convinced me that teachers' pedagogic skills were the crucial element. Apparently poor software could be used powerfully in the classroom of a creative teacher and software that was generally acclaimed as good could be used for nothing but low-level tasks in the classrooms of teachers who did not understand its possibilities. I wanted to ask teachers to carry out research into how to use computers effectively, to develop pedagogical knowledge that could be made available to other teachers to inspire them to try similar methods and I wanted teachers to be free to choose what software to use, when to use it and how to use it, so that they remained in control of their research. But naturally enough a project without a focus, without apparently clear direction and without a visionary 'selling point', was unattractive to the sponsors. The project I was suggesting had to be about something. So I chose one of the biggest buzz-phrases of the time, which had a clear pedagogic rather than subject-specific or software-specific focus – autonomy in learning. 'Pupil autonomy in learning with microcomputers' gave us an acronym of PALM and the opportunity for a palm tree logo – something living and growing rather than technical, which was also important to me since, as a former English teacher, I thought that the technical aura that surrounded computers was one of the major barriers for teachers with a language or humanities background.

PALM was sponsored by the National Council for Educational Technology (NCET, formerly MESU) in collaboration with the local education authorities of Cambridgeshire, Essex and Norfolk, and was based at the Centre for Applied Research in Education, University of East Anglia, where I moved to work shortly after its funding had been secured. It ran for two years from September 1988–August 1990 and was led by a full-time team of myself as co-ordinator, three project officers, Jon Pratt, Bob Davison and Erica Brown, and a secretary, Laura Tickner. My colleague and mentor John Elliott took on the role of director to champion the project and defend me when my inexperience led me into difficulties. PALM was modelled on the TIQL project in which I had worked with John as a teacher–researcher, making his advice and support particularly valuable.

There were 24 PALM schools. In Essex the eight schools were clustered around two large secondary schools; in Cambridgeshire there was some clustering of the six participating schools, although it was entirely informal; in Norfolk the nine schools were widely spread so that all the divisional areas of the LEA were represented. Geographically, the project covered a rough square, 85 miles as the crow flies between schools at the extreme north–south and east–west boundaries.

In each school there was a team of teacher–researchers (or a number of research pairings or groupings), in the majority of cases led by an inschool co-ordinator. Selection of the schools was on a different basis in each of the three LEAs, providing the project with a varied clientele. Schools were deliberately not selected on the basis of high levels of equipment. The project had a small budget to fill gaps in provision of software, disks and peripherals, and in addition all three LEAs were generous in providing some extra hardware and software. A second small budget supported research expenses and in-service training, including some replacement cover to free teachers during the school day.

Around 100 teachers undertook action research in PALM. They contributed to different extents depending on the demands of their full-time job and characteristically they all had periods of greater or lesser activity. In each school, the nature of the team was different. In some there was a whole school approach co-ordinated by senior staff. In others a group of teachers worked more autonomously, relating directly to their project officer and the PALM central team. Both kinds of organization brought their own benefits. It was very important for PALM to work with the kind of structure that best fitted the culture of each individual school.

Developing an action research methodology to fit participants' values and needs

PALM collaborated with teachers to research the impact of using a computer on pupils' learning. To an extent this entailed teachers researching their own practice and making informed decisions about necessary changes, but the emphasis was not on the improvement of teachers' practice. To me – then and now – the notion of a project setting out to 'improve' teachers' practice has authoritarian connotations, so the PALM focus was rather on exploring teacher–pupil interactions to understand and improve the necessarily complex process of pupils' learning. Learning, not improvement, was the focus of PALM – autonomy in learning for the children, the teacher–researcher, central team members, head teachers and their deputies. The project was also testing the hypothesis that professional development in ICT would result naturally from involvement in research into learning *while using* ICT and that this would be more effective than specialist courses on ICT skills.

We deliberately chose not to define action research closely in PALM. At the beginning I was the only member of the team who had prior experience of action research, although once we began working with schools some of the teachers brought experience with them from masters study at UEA or the Cambridge Institute. I saw my task as being to work alongside the three project officers and helping them to pass on research skills to the teacher–researchers. We developed a form of action research that focused on the three-way interactions between teachers, pupils and computer-related tasks.

PALM was a collaboration of teachers with a university-based research team, of whom the three project officers were, themselves, teachers on secondment and I myself had only been out of the classroom for three years. It was strongly embedded in teachers' culture and able to establish greater equality of esteem between all members of the extended team than is often possible in collaborations between schools and universities. We drew up a code of confidentiality at the start which was agreed at the steering group with the inspectors of the three LEAs and the chair, Ralph Tabberer, from NCET. The introductory paragraphs included this statement:

> The heart of PALM's work lies in teachers' investigations of the way microcomputers can help to build a context favourable to autonomous learning. It is assumed that teaching is a complex professional activity and that project teachers are likely to want to experiment with changes in their classroom organization and their teaching style. PALM, therefore, needs to establish ground rules for its day to day work which will ensure honest engagement with, and open sharing of, problems.

It included guarantees for both teachers and pupils of control over the way that data relating to their work were made public; of anonymity for pupils unless they or 'where appropriate' their parents had given permission otherwise; of full recognition of teachers' authorship of writing and publication of their work. It also gave head teachers and the LEAs final control of publications relating to their organization and clarified that the central team would be reporting formally and informally to MESU and the LEA advisory teams but 'these reports will not infringe the ground rules outlined above'. In terms of outcomes there was a clause stating that 'wherever possible' PALM teachers would communicate the outcomes of their investigations with their school and cluster teams, the central team and the participating LEAs 'and more widely where appropriate'. This document was important as a contract between the central team and the teacher–researchers, clarifying what was expected, safeguarding teachers' and children's rights and giving the sponsoring LEAs and MESU guarantees of access to information about work in progress while safeguarding against the project being unintentionally co-opted into a covert form of inspection.

My own experience in the TIQL project led to the initial structuring of the project's work in two strands: research into autonomy in learning to be carried out by teachers; and research into how best to facilitate this process by the central team. This was the classic division into first- and second-order action research which Elliott (1988) advocated to prevent teachers' role in action research projects being subverted to that of research assistants to university researchers. As PALM developed, however, it became clear that this role was not sustainable. Teachers looked to the project officers to work alongside them as co-researchers rather than merely acting as administrators; Bob, Jon and Erica were scarcely out of the classroom and had had no experience of action research other than what I could provide in a two-week induction course, so it made much better sense for them to learn to be action researchers alongside the teachers. The development of a co-researcher, rather than a facilitator, relationship was a key part of PALM's work in year two. We came to see collaborative research between teachers and a university-based team in terms of 'inhabiting each other's castles' – an inherently energizing and liberating process, which is at the same time problematic, in which individuals move between the 'constructed realities' of the school and the university and learn to understand and respect each other's values and criteria for truth testing. Like all other aspects of PALM, this was to be confronted most clearly when we came to the stage of writing up the project's work, because we were working in an education system in which both school and university cultures harboured hostility for each other's writing and this necessarily had an impact on how individual members of the extended PALM team viewed the purpose and form of their writing (Somekh 1994).

Getting teachers involved

The most important first step was to build a research team by seeking volunteer teachers and establishing relationships. All were uncertain when first approached: the project was complex and we had to explain its purposes clearly and what would be expected of participants. At its most basic we said: 'You've got a computer in your classroom for at least some of the time. Is it making any positive impact on pupils' learning? Would you like to join us to carry out research to find out? If you end up thinking that it is not having any positive impact we would expect you to want to get rid of it. But we don't think it's a professional response for you to reject it without exploring its possibilities.' Towards the end of PALM we asked teachers why they had decided to join and several reasons emerged. The professional relationship with the project officer and opportunity for dialogue was an important factor; linked to this, the opportunity to engage more deeply with their practice as teachers was another; the opportunity to get some help with using computers which most would have to use anyway, sooner or later, was a third; the encouragement of senior managers was a fourth, especially in schools where there was strong leadership that encouraged exploration and risk taking; finally there were some who said they had been coerced into participating by the head teacher but, unsurprisingly, few of these became fully involved. Later many teachers took up the opportunity to present their action research reports for accreditation with the Cambridge Institute of Education and this was undoubtedly an important factor in extending and deepening their research activities.

Developing support strategies

One of the first difficulties we confronted was the multi-layered nature of the innovation we were asking teachers to engage with. Our primary focus on the use of computers in teaching was greatly complicated for the teachers by the concept of autonomy in learning. What did it mean? How would they need to change their teaching to enable it? Without the advantage of the knowledge and experience I had gained from working with Stenhouse's notion from the humanities project of the 'neutral chairperson', using the materials developed by John Elliott's Ford teaching project to promote 'discovery learning' and working as a teacher–researcher on his TIQL project, the concept of autonomy in learning was initially very challenging for many PALM teacher–researchers. And added to these two innovations they were also being asked to learn how to be researchers. We had to find a way of helping them to come to terms with three innovations, not one.

Through working with the teachers, we tried things out and developed strategies that seemed to work. This process was then consolidated in team meetings at which we brainstormed problems on a flip chart and used various strategies to promote shared reflexivity. The 'triple innovation' problem was identified through these discussions and we decided to deal with it by taking the innovations one at a time, starting by providing teachers with simple research techniques and asking them to start an inquiry into their pupils' current learning and then moving gradually to focusing on the changes needed to give pupils autonomy in learning and the ways that computers could help them to do that. However, we also started from the beginning providing them with support in experimenting with computer use. The strategy was to find one piece of software that caught their imagination and provide them with a hands-on session to try it out with our help and plan a lesson using it. PALM started working before the advent of the national curriculum so teachers were able to plan their work within their school's agreed learning framework and they expected to take this kind of decision as part of their professional responsibility.

To take the research innovation forward we developed materials to use with teachers at twilight meetings. Although they were later put together as a pack, their real strength lay in being introduced one or two at a time, through a practical research session involving a group of teachers and their project officer planning data collection or analysing a selected piece of data (for example, part of a transcript of children talking from a tape-recording made of group work in a normal lesson with the children's permission). We produced these materials as single sheets using desktop publishing and an Apple Mac computer that produced a quality of design that, at that time, was impressive. We also provided cream cakes and chocolate biscuits because we could remember how exhausted we ourselves had felt at the end of a school day. We tailored the project officer's support to working with individual teachers on particular days, collecting data agreed at a meeting in advance. What proved to be important was the three-stage group process of the project officer explaining the purpose of the session (with the handout as backup), everyone engaging in silent planning (or analysis of data as the research progressed) and individuals explaining ideas to each other/engaging in dialogue. I was often present at these meetings and found them enormously exciting because there was a real sense of mutual inquiry rather than any idea of us 'teaching' the teachers. At the end, when we left, the handout remained behind as an aide-mémoire.

Another support strategy that proved really helpful was the notion of *bounded time*, which we developed from an idea described by Almond (1982). This is a very simple technique whereby teachers (or any busy people) review their diaries over a period of time looking for the naturally occurring peaks and troughs of activity. Research activities can then be planned in advance for periods when a 'trough' is predicted, and by making preparations in advance, booking rooms and planning to collect two or three kinds of data about the same lesson, the bounded time can be marked out and protected and the research can be time effective by enabling comparative analysis of data about the same event (triangulation of a kind). Another important aspect of 'bounded time' was the setting of deadlines for the completion of work. The three project officers adopted different strategies in this respect and they needed to vary their approach to suit the needs of individuals, but it emerged very clearly that it was easier for teachers if they were given definite deadlines to complete planned research activity, particularly writing. This was a strategy that allowed teachers to 'give themselves permission' to give the research work a high priority, an essential psychological component of teachers' research in view of their deep acculturation to the ethic of always putting the children first.

Research issues for the PALM central team

Once the project was well underway, some major issues emerged related to the process of teachers becoming researchers. These issues became a particular focus of our attention and led to the development of action research practice and knowledge.

Research issue one: negotiating a research question

A problem of large-scale action research projects such as PALM is that the original impetus comes not from the teachers themselves but from outside instigators. The project had a firm focus on *autonomy in learning* but this still did not help teachers to develop any research questions of their own. In some ways, this is not so different from any other research. Most researchers are in the position of negotiating their research question in relation to circumstances, opportunities and the predilections of funding sponsors. Nevertheless, this is not an easy thing for teachers to do without previous research experience. If PALM had been a project whose focus was on the participating teachers' professional development rather than research this would not have mattered very much; but PALM set out to generate knowledge about the kind of pedagogy with IT that would enable pupils to become autonomous learners. Within this broad frame teachers needed to be able to focus down on some particular aspect.

We did not suggest or impose any questions, which meant there was a problem in identifying a question from a position of inexperience, so we suggested starting with a broad area of interest such as the use of a piece of software, the interactions of a particular group of pupils, or a particular lesson. Research for many teachers began, therefore, without a research question, the project's theoretical position being that the question would emerge for each teacher as a result of *progressive focusing* as described by McCormick and James (1988: 219). For many, this was, in fact, the case. The analysis of data brought into focus issues of real concern that could be followed up and explored. The project officers played a crucial role by sharing in the analysis and discussions from which these issues emerged. However, an issue or focus is still not a research question. There remained the difficulty that a focus needs to be turned into a question, or made problematic, before it becomes a fruitful field for research. Without this, research can easily degenerate into a bland process of confirming the already known.

At the beginning of our third term, after six months' work, some teachers had identified research questions to which they genuinely wanted to find some answers; others had identified a research focus of broad interest, but had yet to uncover its problematic nature in order to give their research real direction; and a few remained unquestioning and unfocused. Our role was increasingly one of injecting ideas into the debate, stimulating reflection and indicating possible problems. One strategy was to raise teachers' awareness of the problematic nature of learning by putting forward questions drawn from the literature relating to autonomy in learning. Most were now familiar with research techniques and confident in the use of computers, so that the issue of autonomy could now come to the forefront without constituting a third innovation. The implications of autonomy in learning, challenging many traditional notions of good practice, were of sufficient intellectual interest to raise many questions relating to practical action.

Research issue two: the analysis of data

Analysis of data proved much more difficult for the PALM teacher– researchers than we had anticipated. The first few times we returned transcripts of tape-recordings of children's group work to their teacher we were disappointed to see how quickly they were scanned through and how little they appeared to interest the teacher. Reading data is not like reading any other text: it requires slow, careful reading, clearing the mind of any prior assumptions and a conscious effort to adopt a questioning mind-set. The analysis of a transcript begins with a process of reading, rereading – and rereading, subjecting the text to interrogation, identifying themes, searching for patterns, and then standing back to view the text again and engage in the creative process of answering the question, 'So what?' Meanings are generated out of the meeting of one's mind with the text.

We had already developed several sheets of practical advice on data analysis (see strategy two above), some based on techniques such as 'pattern analysis' (Ireland and Russell 1978) and 'metaphor analysis' (Winter 1982) developed through the work of the Classroom Action Research Network. What we now realized was that it was essential to hold practical data analysis sessions in which teachers shared their data with colleagues, rather than expecting them to be able to embark on analysis alone.

Typically, a teacher who had some data s/he wanted to discuss would sit down with a small number of colleagues and the PALM project officer and a big pack of different coloured highlight pens. Sometimes I would also be present. Let's say on this occasion the data consist of a transcript of children talking as they work together around a computer on a collaborative task. It includes some sections when the teacher interacts with them briefly. After some brief discussion of the analysis method (in this case pattern analysis) members of the group work for about 20 minutes reading the transcript and highlighting any recurrences of any kind – either of phraseology, ideas or behaviour. During this individual, focused activity everyone is comfortably engaged in marking up pieces of text with their highlighter – a quiet but not silent, 'busy' activity that seems to play a part in relaxing everyone. Next comes a sharing and listing of 'patterns' with discussion to ensure that at this stage no judgements are made – as far as possible the 'patterns' are recorded as statements of fact about the events/talk in the transcripts. Finally there is time for some discussion of the implications of the patterns in terms of the children's learning experiences – although the final tentative hypotheses (statements of possible cause and effect) will be left to the teacher who 'owns' the data.

It was common in sessions like this for teachers to experience the intense engagement known as 'flow' (Csikszentmihalyi 1996), indicated by them saying things like 'Goodness is that really the time? I had no idea it was so late.' They also expressed strong feelings of surprise and fascination, for example: 'I feel I have seen my classroom with new eyes,' and, 'I never expected so much to come out of that. When I read the transcript through beforehand I didn't see any of those things.' Other remarks indicated that they felt a strong sense of professional satisfaction, for example: 'That's the best professional discussion I ever remember having with colleagues.'

It seemed that the combination of formality and professional sharing in this approach to analysis – its 'otherness' on both counts from normal teaching experiences – was important in helping teachers to distance themselves from their own data sufficiently to see what was in them. We came to compare the process of data analysis with the breaking up of light into colours when it passes through a prism.

Research issue three: writing

Writing requires a very different state of mind from the kind of continuous action under pressure that is characteristic of any form of teaching. We always made it clear to teachers in PALM that they were expected to write, and although this could take the form of keeping a research journal, we encouraged them to write a research report for publication that we produced in-house using the new facility of desktop publishing.

Teachers certainly did not initially show enthusiasm for writing. Writing is not a simple matter of transferring spoken words onto the page. It is usually differentiated from spoken language by far greater precision of expression, a wider range of vocabulary, more complex syntax and an absence of repetition. In writing down ideas we clarify and develop them, so that this process of writing is often characterized by intense thought and concentration. Although this adds to the difficulty of writing it also constitutes another important reason why action researchers need to write: through writing their research is enriched.

PALM developed a number of strategies to help teachers write. Perhaps the most important was to view writing as an on-going process rather than a finished product. By adopting this approach we encouraged teachers to carry over to their own writing some important ideas about the teaching of writing to children. The work of the National Writing Project in England, during the 1980s, built upon the work of Graves (1983) and others to present writing to children as a process of drafting rough ideas that might or might not be later edited into a finished product. The advantage to PALM of viewing writing in this way was that it began at once rather than being left to the end of the project's life. This enabled the central team to discuss issues relating to writing with teachers at an early stage. We found that writing not only helped to clarify teachers' thinking, but also gave direction to their collection and analysis of further data. We also believed that beginning writing early would reduce the pressure on teachers towards the end of the project – which to a certain extent it did. Nevertheless, we were aware that it could be counter-productive for too much energy to be spent on writing up early work that might not have reached the depth and quality of what would come later – if early writing became product oriented it could be stultifying.

We, of course, also encouraged teachers to use a word processor. This was not immediately easy for all, as few teachers at that time owned their own computers at home, but we were sometimes able to lend a teacher a computer for a short period. We also used tape-recorders: some teachers found it helpful to dictate their ideas; others found it useful if we recorded an interview with them. These tapes could later be transcribed and given back on disk: although the text required quite skilled editing to give the flavour of written as opposed to spoken language, for many teachers it was the way to get over the barrier of the blank page. We also experimented with *Thinksheet*, a software package that allowed ideas to be entered on individual 'cards' and then grouped and sorted in related hierarchies. Where possible we also provided teachers with supply cover to get away from the classroom for the purpose of writing. However, in the end quality writing depended on the expenditure of considerable energy on the part of the teachers.

A lot depended on the skill of the project officers in discussing rough drafts and providing positive critique: most professional researchers rely on trusted colleagues to fulfil this function, so we did not see it as taking any-thing away from the teachers' own work. To reinforce our notion of writing as a process of thinking and shaping ideas PALM produced a regular newsletter, *Palmleaves*, which was primarily a means for the project's inter-nal communication, for 'thinking aloud in print'. We also began very early to produce the *Teachers' Voices* series of action research reports, the first of which was published in early 1989. The aim was to experiment with differ-ent forms and language registers to give freedom to teachers and ensure variety and readability. A good deal of skill is involved in forms of writing that incorporate a combination of narrative, analysis and reference to data and such writing was not always appropriate: the series title, *Teachers' Voices*, allowed for a range of forms. It was important to PALM that our writing should be readable across a wide audience: reaching practising teachers as well as academics, administrators and policy makers. This remained a challenge to the end and placed on some of our more specialist readers the onus to set aside preconceptions.

Generating knowledge from PALM action research

PALM did not start out with a blueprint of stages through which its work would move towards the production of outcomes. Instead, it moved from an exploratory starting point through stages that developed in response to emerging needs, towards a goal of multiple publications that would reflect different aspects of its work for different audiences. These stages were paced and directed by the central team according to needs, on the basis of reflec-tion and dialogue. Once teachers had decided on their specific research focus the main energy during the first year went into carrying out this work. A few teachers completed their study and wrote a *Teachers' Voices* report within the first year. Many wrote short pieces that were published in the *Palmleaves*. Others produced working drafts and fragments. At the end of the first year around 50 teachers attended a weekend conference at a hotel in Swaffham, a Norfolk town with a thriving Saturday market which lent a buoyant atmosphere to the lunch and coffee breaks. This was an occasion for teachers and project officers to get to know those from other LEAs; for sharing ideas; and for embarking on the development of a more coherent focus. Teachers worked in groups to reflect back on the first year of their research, identify issues emerging from analysis and project forward to how they could build on this work in the second year. To ensure that empirical work was informed by previous research, they were also asked to discuss a pack of 'readings' on autonomy in learning selected from the work of writers such as Mills, Sheffler, Papert, Rogers, Elliott, Dearden and HMI (1989, Gabriel Goldstein's 'raspberry ripple' curriculum document on IT). The plenary session in which the groups reported back to each other was tape-recorded and, from analysis of the transcript, the central team identified seven questions relating to autonomy in learning. The first incorporated a working definition:

> It's been suggested that autonomous learning consists in some combination of these characteristics amongst others: Choice; Confidence; Responsibility for one's own learning; Creativity. How can these be encouraged and how can the computer help?

The other questions developed related issues. Each was filled out with subquestions to make the key idea clearer but, in brief, questions two to six covered: Is structure necessary? Can individuals within groups be autonomous? What differences does a computer in the classroom make to the teacher's role? Is autonomy influenced by age, ability, gender or culture? What kinds of context/environment support autonomous learning? The seventh question related to the national curriculum, which was due to be introduced for pupils in Years 1 and 7 during the project's second year: How can computers be used to create opportunities for autonomous learning within the national curriculum?

These seven questions were published in *Palmleaves* and proved useful in the second year, as an anchor to which teachers could link their continuing research and a checklist against which to plan their writing. Altogether 35 studies were published by CARE/UEA in the PALM *Teachers' Voices* series and sold quite widely to those who heard about the project through conference presentations or NCET's network of contacts. Many of these were LEA advisers or inspectors, in particular from the five LEAs who participated in the seven-month PALM Extension Project funded by NCET from September 1990 to March 1991.[2] In 1988, the then Department for

Education and Science had appointed around 700 advisory teachers (subject rather than IT specialists) to support teachers introducing IT to their classrooms and PALM published an Advisory Teachers' Pack, made up of the 'practical materials' introducing research methods, which was used by the extension project LEAs (PALM 1990). Later these materials were placed on the ICT Educational Research Forum website funded by Becta and hosted by Exeter University (http://telematics3.ex.ac.uk/erf/).

At the second PALM conference in March 1990, teacher–researchers worked in groups reading the complete set of draft *Teachers' Voices* reports in the light of one of the seven focusing questions. Their task was to develop hypotheses relating to their group's question, some of which were revelatory, even prophetic. For example:

- in relation to changes that IT brings about in the teacher's role one of the hypotheses was '*The computers may remove teachers' access to process which may mask problems in learning*', something which has emerged as an issue in a recent evaluation study of young people using digital photography to produce AS-level course work (Somekh *et al.* 2005a and b: 40).
- And in relation to the context of use, one of the hypotheses was: '*Autonomy can be encouraged if a school adopts a holistic view, attempts to cross all boundaries and tries to establish a consensus among as many staff as possible*', something that has also emerged as imperative in a recent project looking at innovative pedagogies with e-learning resources (see Chapter 8).

As an illustration of the knowledge generated from the research of an individual teacher, here is most of the final section of Marlies Marshall's study (Marshall 1990) on the effect of using *Image* on child autonomy. *Image*, produced by Fred Daley's group at Homerton College, Cambridge, was at the time the most innovative software available for art, widely used in both primary and secondary schools in the UK.

The Children's Role
In autonomy the children pass on their knowledge. This knowledge is the sum of trial and error. It comes from deep inside. The experience is intense, therefore the impact is such that it is stored and ready for re-call. Children's learning is based on imitation and

---

2   The LEAs that participated in the Palm Extension Project were: Croydon, Dorset, Hampshire, Nottinghamshire and Sheffield.

experience. A peer is a powerful teacher especially if he or she is much admired. Autonomy uses this powerful influence to make the child self-sufficient and confident. Dialogue stimulates wider communication and the sharing of experience, the desire to achieve the same as someone else is strong in the young. The co-operation among children is at times quite touching. There are other moments of fierce competitiveness as well, these too can lead to achievement, although the motive is less positive. In encouraging autonomy we are changing the roles of pupil and teachers. I can't help thinking that autonomy in its purest form will alter our whole concept of school.

The Role of the Teacher
How does autonomy of pupils affect the teachers? I am not ready to answer this, but I know what happened during our research in working with the microcomputer. I became a pupil with my pupils, we no longer stood apart. We were experimenting, we were sharing our experiences and we were brought together by a common interest. My role had changed to a friend, an adviser, an interested party – who at this stage could only make suggestions, comments, and give encouragement – but no answers. The children saw that even teachers have to learn – and that teachers too can make mistakes before they learn. This changed the atmosphere in class. The change of emphasis from pupil/teacher relations to that of a team radiated into all areas of the curriculum. The children showed more interest, I felt myself becoming more accessible. Our relationship became more open and trusting, it was more relaxed and our mutual respect was growing.

(Marshall 1990)

As the culmination of a narrative account of her research, Marshall's final statement both sums up what she has discovered about children's autonomy in learning and asserts its importance in terms of her own beliefs about teaching. Writing shortly before she retired after many years teaching, she describes a radical change in her relationship with children as they become autonomous learners. It is clear that the computer has played an important role in this, both empowering the children and preventing herself, as a novice with computers, from playing the traditional teacher's role as 'fount of all knowledge'. The language is clear and compelling, written from the heart to speak directly to other teachers. It is a fine example of the best of PALM's writing from 'the castle of the school'.

The knowledge that emerged from the writing of PALM teachers has profoundly influenced my work as a researcher and evaluator ever since. Although PALM was set up to research the impact that IT could have on learning, its specific focus on autonomy rendered the concept of learning problematic for teachers, even for those with many years' experience. Hence, they were able to shed many of their prior assumptions and look at learning with fresh eyes. The research process helped, providing them with what many teachers described as 'a third eye', giving them distance from the overwhelming barrage of activity and interactions that was the key factor in their daily lives.

This knowledge from the PALM teachers' writing was used to produce a PALM working document called *Shared Perspectives*, written by my colleague Richard Davies. It became the basis for an article in which he and I presented PALM's *Dynamic Model for a Transforming Pedagogy for Information Technology* (Somekh and Davies 1991). This presented both general and computer-related competences, first for pupils and then for teachers, followed by a commentary under the headings of the first six questions used to plan and structure the second year of PALM's work. The seventh question on application of the ideas to the newly introduced national curriculum is perhaps one that can only be – and arguably urgently needs to be – properly addressed now, 15 years after its introduction. Since Marshall's work quoted above deals with questions one and four, I will focus briefly here on questions two and three. In terms of structure, PALM teachers' research showed clearly that the extent and nature of the structure that teachers give to the tasks pupils undertake has a direct impact on the extent to which they can work autonomously. They developed the metaphors of 'the walled garden' and 'stepping stones' for two kinds of structure that encourage autonomy in different ways. In the walled garden[3] the teacher creates 'a safe environment within which pupils have freedom to explore learning opportunities and control the pace and direction of their own learning'; when there are stepping stones 'a route planned by the teacher through a particular learning task provides staged opportunities for freedom and exploration' (Somekh and Davies 1991: 160). Teachers who want to enable autonomy in learning need to provide different levels of structure for different tasks, always individualizing (personalizing we might say today) the task as much as possible, and as far as possible minimizing structure to encourage learners' exploration. In terms of group work, PALM teachers' research showed that working with others enables individual pupils to develop self-confidence and become more autonomous of the teacher. The group can become an autonomous unit. Nevertheless, group dynamics are complex and often allow some individuals to become autonomous at the

---

[3]   This should not be confused with the way that this term has since been used to describe computer environments in which screening software is used to limit children's access to the internet.

expense of making others subservient. Key findings are that when pupils work in groups this 'calls for some careful observation by the teachers' and that teachers' assumptions from cursory observations are often counter to what is actually happening in groups: 'For example, an individual may dominate the group while showing little overt sign of activity' (Somekh and Davies 1991: 160).

As is clear from reading Marlies Marshall's writing about the changes that came about in her own role, PALM work had a profound impact on the professional development of the participating teachers. The point was not that we neglected this second project aim, but that we focused on both aims through one continuous, holistic process. An important part of the cross-case analysis was to identify the key features of teachers' practice that enabled pupil autonomy in learning and these were fully reported in the teachers' competences section of the pedagogical framework. In addition, the extensive field notes kept by the project officers and myself throughout the two years of PALM enabled us to identify the stages of professional development that teachers went through to become confident, skilled and creative users of IT in their classrooms. They resulted from three very different assumptions about the role a computer would play in pupils' learning:

a   The computer as tutor
b   The computer as neutral tool
c   The computer as cognitive tool.

The computer as tutor

Many teachers assumed when they first began working with PALM that computers were a kind of teaching machine. For example, at the end of a lesson using simulation software that allowed pupils to explore aspects of the First World War battlefields, a history teacher told me that he was disappointed because he felt that the pupils had not learned much from the software. Having watched other teachers using the same software I knew that everything depended on how the teacher 'framed' the software-based task in other activities, the interest he or she showed in the pupils' progress, opportunities they were given to feed back what they had done to other pupils and discuss the implications of the experience. Tactful questions and suggestions from the project officer were the first step in moving teachers forward from this kind of misunderstanding.

The computer as neutral tool

Many other teachers assumed initially that the computer was simply another tool that would take the place of pens or pencils or worksheets. Sometimes they actually set the same task to be done on and off the computer – a piece of writing, for example – and compared the pupils' products in terms of the amount of writing produced in a given time. These comparisons seldom showed the computer in a good light since the pupils were slow keyboard users, so often teachers quickly assumed that the computer's usefulness was mainly as a presentational tool that could turn a messy piece of handwriting into a smartly designed piece to be displayed on the classroom wall. This led them to give pupils the arguably senseless task of copying up on the computer what they had already written by hand. Action research into the nature of pupils' learning when undertaking such tasks proved a very good way of challenging their value and getting teachers to begin thinking about alternative kinds of tasks.

The computer as cognitive tool

When teachers became confident and experienced and especially when they worked very collaboratively with their pupils and allowed them to become more autonomous, they moved forward to a higher level of computer use in which new kinds of tasks could be undertaken. Drawing graphs on a computer, for example, is far quicker than drawing them on paper, so instead of taking a whole lesson on the drawing of one graph and the last few minutes on its interpretation pupils could be asked to produce a number of computer-generated graphs in the first half of the lesson and then spend time on interpreting their meaning in the second half. This is, of course, a more cognitively challenging task and teachers need to radically change the way they teach the lesson once they can no longer rely on keeping everyone occupied for most of the time with the pleasant 'busyness' of drawing a graph. Action research into pupils' learning clearly showed teachers that this kind of computer use created exciting new opportunities for learning in much greater depth.

Most PALM teachers began by assuming one of the two lower models of computer use, but by the second year the majority had developed an understanding of its potential power and were experimenting with much more interesting ways of using it.

Looking back: a retrospective commentary

In the PALM project I learnt to work in research partnerships with teachers in a new role as a university-based researcher, rather than carrying out teacher research myself. But I remained close to teachers' thinking and found it easy to understand the intensity of their experiences in becoming researchers and the tensions for them in integrating research with teaching. I embarked on PALM at a time when my commitment to action research was passionate but my understandings were relatively naïve. A major factor in the changes that subsequently took place in my thinking has been the opportunity to read much more widely over the intervening years. Reading interactively and creatively is, for me, an important part of action research.

In this short section I have the luxury of reflecting back on PALM to draw out what can be learnt to inform a similar project starting work today. The key focus of this section is on action research as a means of supporting change: although IT was centrally important to PALM itself, it is not the focus here.

The first response of most readers is likely to be that PALM was a lavishly funded project that provided an unusually high degree of support for the teachers' action research. While that is true, there are some factors not present 15 years ago that would be particularly helpful in mounting such a project today. The most obvious is that educational policy since the mid-1990s has re-branded teaching as a research-based, or evidence-based profession. Teachers are encouraged to engage in research, to present their work at conferences and to read the research of others and build on it. Even though PALM took place in East Anglia, which had a fine tradition of teacher research fostered by the Cambridge Institute of Education and UEA from the mid-1970s onwards, many teachers saw research as something esoteric and 'hard' and research publications were often characterized as 'full of jargon' and 'irrelevant' to practice. For this reason, I believe that a less lavishly funded project could thrive today provided participating teachers were fully supported by their heads and senior management teams. Indeed, a good example of a recent action research project in primary schools, which generated a considerable body of actionable knowledge, is reported by Torrance and Pryor (2001).

A key factor is how schools come into a project. PALM was not able to select its schools independently of the three LEAs and this had some unintended, unfortunate consequences, which are worth rehearsing here as I have since discovered that they are very common in projects of this kind. The central issue is the extent to which motivation to participate comes from teachers themselves or from managers at school or LEA level. Several of the primary schools found themselves coerced into taking part in the project because the nearby secondary school had already more or less agreed to bring them in as part of a cluster, so in this case neither the head nor the teachers had opted to join voluntarily. In other cases, the main motivation for schools being 'volunteered' by their LEA and head was their perceived need for IT professional development. Whereas we were explicitly seeking schools where staff already had reasonable levels of competence and confidence in using IT, some schools came into PALM because their staff did *not* have these qualities.

The support of the LEAs, and their existing culture and relationships with schools, are crucially important in large-scale action research projects of this kind. Although the three LEA inspectors' perceptions of the purposes of PALM were necessarily different from my own, and there was some variation between them, much of the success of the project was due to their energy and commitment. However, the start-up phase of the project was tricky. I had developed a good working relationship with one of the inspectors who helped in developing the proposal; but the other two LEAs were brought in a little later and a fourth LEA, which was involved in negotiations, dropped out at this stage. My problem was my inexperience and low status as a researcher because I had so recently been a teacher. In this sense one of the great strengths I had with PALM teachers was a weakness in setting the project up. The extensive rereading of the PALM data that I have undertaken in order to write this chapter makes it very clear that I owed a great deal to Ralph Tabberer in bringing the support of MESU to back my vision at a formal meeting with the LEAs to discuss possibilities; and to Lesley Kant, a senior adviser in Norfolk who had a strong belief in action research, having worked with me on the Support for Innovation Project, and offered to pay for the PALM project officer out of central LEA funds rather than it coming out of the IT adviser's budget. Once I moved to CARE/UEA John Elliott brought the experience and gravitas I needed to enable the project to maintain a leadership role and carry the three LEAs with it, but the original negotiations were carried out while I was at the Cambridge Institute of Education and my inexperience made it difficult for me to take the strong line needed over some key issues such as the choice of schools and selection of project officers. It would clearly have been a huge advantage to the project officers and the project if they had had prior experience of action research, but the LEA inspectors had almost no understanding of what action research involved before we started work and they chose the project officers according to other criteria such as availability and prior experience of working with LEA support services. The three project officers proved to be excellent, but they had a very steep learning curve in the early months of PALM.

Perhaps because of the level of its funding, PALM expected a great deal of the participating teachers – possibly too much, in retrospect. They identified their own research focus, collected data, analysed them, wrote a report and took a lead in the process of cross-case analysis at the second PALM conference. We saw the teachers' research as the core of PALM's work and very much 'their' research. This gave them status and respect but it also constituted a heavy work load. Although it is true that teachers had far less paperwork to do before the days of the national curriculum they also took on many more responsibilities in those days. For example, secondary teachers collaborated to write the syllabus and set and mark the examinations if they opted like my former school for the 'mode 3' Certificate of Secondary Education. There were many after-school meetings at teachers' centres, very large numbers of new initiatives which called on teachers' energy and creativity and with all but examination classes (14–18 year olds) both primary and secondary teachers shouldered the responsibility for drawing up the curriculum, planning what to teach and deciding how to teach it in order to fit the needs of their pupils. It would probably be wrong, therefore, to assume that PALM teachers found it easier to take on this additional work load than teachers would today.

I think that today I would want to develop a different kind of research partnership in an action research project such as PALM where teachers participate while continuing to carry out their full-time job. In the second year, PALM moved away from the idea of a clear demarcation between teachers who researched learning and the central team who facilitated them; were I to start again today I would adopt a co-researcher stance from the start and attempt to share out the work load more fairly between all participants. Ironically, this would not necessarily make the jobs of the project officers more onerous as supporting from the sidelines can be just as time demanding as working in partnership. It might also have the advantage of helping to ensure that teachers would not become dependent on the project officers. Bob, Jon and Erica provided marvellous support for the PALM teachers, but the inevitable result was that the teachers became dependent on them to varying degrees and this clearly influenced the nature of their research.

The focus on knowledge generation was crucially important to PALM and this is still my priority for any large-scale action research project today. Professional development is always an important outcome of teachers participating in action research but that is dependent on the inquiry process, because it is through collecting data, looking for patterns and emerging themes, finding possible meanings and testing them out, that the process of teaching re-engages our curiosity and we get the buzz of mental stimulation. I use 'we' and 'our' here because it does not make sense to speak about teachers as 'they' and 'them' when writing about action research partnerships. Successful classroom innovation depends on acquiring knowledge and understanding of the theories underpinning the changes, in order to go beyond the merely cosmetic changes of classroom organization that Bussis *et al.* (1976) called 'the surface curriculum'.

LEAs may see such a project as having benefits mainly in the professional development of participants, but it is hard to justify the expense of a large-scale project of this kind on the grounds of teacher professional development only. The justification has to be that its primary purpose is the generation of knowledge and understanding to inform the profession as a whole. It is possible that we would have generated more knowledge by having a more coherent focus for the teachers' research from the start, rather than giving them freedom to choose their own focus and research questions. However, rereading the data and publications I have come to think not, since the focus on autonomy in learning was central to all aspects of teaching and learning, no matter what the identified topic. The problematic nature of this focus was also extremely important in ensuring that no one made easy assumptions about the project's purposes: any large-scale project of this kind needs to make everyone think freshly about its focus from the start and the word autonomy, which was new and strange to most teachers, proved to be an excellent strategy for making this happen.

PALM's biggest disappointment was probably that it did not have much impact on the development of future policy. When I wrote the proposal and secured funding the national curriculum had not been mentioned in any government policy document and both I – and I believe the sponsors – saw PALM as a curriculum development project.

However, the development and launch of the national curriculum, during its lifetime, effectively closed the door on any fresh thinking about the curriculum and pedagogy for some years to come. PALM was not without an impact on the system, through the PALM Extension Project and the future work of many of its participants, but without the shadow of a newly established mandated curriculum, and with a more extensive network of contacts among policy makers, a similar large-scale project today could expect to give the outcomes of the teachers' research much greater prominence, particularly since teachers' research is given much higher status by policy makers today.

A project with such major funding over two years should have had a more substantial outcome, however, such as a book. Presenting at academic conferences, writing articles in academic journals and the *Times Educational Supplement* and publishing the *Teachers' Voices* series and the Advisory Teachers' Pack in-house were all important, but to be widely disseminated a large-scale action research project of this kind should have its work put together in the easily accessible form of a book. Today of course there would be a website, but this might still not be sufficient. The truth is, I simply ran out of time. I was employed on a new project funded by NCET immediately PALM came to an end and my energies were directed elsewhere (see Chapter 5), which leads to another point – those who lead large-scale action research projects of this kind should not expect the writing up to be completed during the funded period. I was working on short-term research contracts at the time and had to move straight to another project, but I continued to write about PALM in many forms over many years. However, to maximize the opportunities for publications resulting from work of this kind universities should find ways of bridging researchers for at least three months between contracts.

Note: further information on three initiatives

The Microelectronics Education Programme (MEP) received £23m from the Department of Education and Science from 1980–86 to introduce computers into schools through initiatives such as developing software and training materials.

The Technical and Vocational Education Initiative (TVEI) received £140m from the Employment Department's Manpower Service Division between 1983 and 1987 to fund schools to develop students' technical skills and bring about radical changes in teaching and learning styles through IT use.

The Department of Trade and Industry's (DTI) Micros in Schools Scheme funded half the cost of purchasing computers if parents and schools raised the money to pay for the other half. It ran from 1981–85 at a cost of £15m.

5 Action Research for Organizational Development in Higher Education[1]

What are the processes for managing change in higher education? How does an organization with traditions of academic freedom respond to a new government policy for teacher education? Can action research support the processes of change more effectively if senior managers and professors carry out action research into their own role as change agents? In 1989, while I was still working on the PALM Project but aware that my contract would be coming to an end the following year, I heard about the newly published Trotter Report on Information Technology in Initial Teacher Education (DES 1989a) at the Association for IT in Teacher Education (ITTE) conference. The Trotter committee had been set up after an education minister had been embarrassed by roars of laughter when he announced at a conference that newly qualified teachers, skilled in using information technology (IT), would be able to take the lead when they took up their first teaching posts in schools. The report confirmed suspicions that the provision of training in how to use IT for pre-service teachers was generally poor, 'patchy' at best. Reading the report in detail I found that it included a recommendation that 'NCET should take steps to expand and broaden the advice and assistance that it offers to initial teacher education institutions, especially in the area of staff development' (DES 1989a: 22). Knowing a lot about the challenges and possibilities that the IT innovation was posing for schools, I was interested in looking at the same innovation in the very different context of teacher education. I went home and wrote a proposal to NCET outlining an action research project to explore how to support the development of IT in teacher education. I received no response for several months. The Trotter report attracted considerable interest among policy makers however, and as a result, new guidelines for teacher education produced by the Council for Accreditation in Teacher Education (CATE) included requirements for all newly qualified teachers to be able to:

[1]   I would like to thank the 14 members of the Project INTENT team with whom I worked for their enormous contribution to the ideas contained in this chapter.

i   make confident personal use of a range of software packages and IT devices appropriate to their subject specialism and age range;

ii   review critically the relevance of software packages and IT devices to their subject specialism and age range and judge the potential value of these in classroom use;

iii make constructive use of IT in their teaching and in particular prepare and put into effect schemes of work incorporating appropriate uses of IT; and

iv   evaluate the ways in which the use of IT changes the nature of teaching and learning.

(DES 1989b: Circular 24/89)

Then, in the spring of 1990, NCET advertised the post of co-ordinator for a project that had considerable similarities with the proposal I had sent them the previous year. The person employed could either be based in Coventry or remain in their current institution. I applied for the job and was appointed, opting to remain based at CARE/UEA.

The project was to be called Initial Teacher Education and New Technology (INTENT). As originally specified by NCET, five participating teacher education institutions (TEIs) would each be given half the funding to release a tutor from teaching for a year, provided they matched this to release the tutor full time. The idea was that the tutor would support colleagues in beginning to use IT in their teaching by working alongside them very much in the way that the newly appointed subject specialist advisory teachers were working with teachers in schools (see Chapter 4: 101). There was to be support from a national co-ordinator and project secretary with a budget to provide low-level additional funding for specific initiatives in the TEIs, and NCET had a further budget to fund regular meetings of the project team and publications arising from the work. The project would run for two years and the co-ordinator, according to the original plan, would provide support in year one and evaluate the impact of the initiative in year two.

In the fortnight or so after my appointment I worked with NCET to develop and refine the research design, making changes which significantly shaped the future project's methodology and working practices. A key feature of the re-designed project was that very senior managers would become active participants, carrying out action research into their own role in supporting change. The project would adopt 'a research approach to development', continuing to carry out development work over two years rather than one, led by a partnership of a staff development tutor (SDT, funded in year one) and senior manager (without external funding) in each TEI, who would both attend the residential project meetings; as co-ordinator I was to work more holistically, combining support for development in the TEIs with evaluation over the whole period. The participating institutions were selected through a competitive tendering process in which, from

24 original applications, 12 TEIs were short-listed. This surprisingly large number of applications, given the low level of funding, perhaps indicated the perceived timeliness of the initiative. Over a period of three weeks, during glorious summer weather, I drove around the country spending a day in each TEI, interviewing those identified to lead the project if they were selected, asking to know who exactly would be making up the 'active team' of colleagues, outlining the proposed roles of the lead staff development tutor and senior manager, and ending by asking, notebook in hand, if they would both be available to attend the planning week in early September. Five TEIs were selected: Chester College of HE, Goldsmiths' College at the University of London University, Liverpool Polytechnic, Worcester College of HE and the University of Exeter.

Designing a collaborative action research project to lead innovation

The design of the project was strongly influenced by my experience of working on the Support for Innovation Project in schools (see Introduction: 3) where a senior manager had worked with a group of teachers in each school to give the advantages of both 'top-down' and 'bottom-up' leadership. I was also able to draw on the research literature on innovation, in particular the first edition of Fullan's book *The Meaning of Educational Change* (Fullan 1982) and a number of papers by my colleague, John Elliott, that were later published in his book *Action Research for Educational Change* (Elliott 1991). These ideas underpinned the design of the programme for the planning week when the project team met for the first time. Another important factor was the make-up of the team. Its members were Charles Desforges, Niki Davis and Chris Taylor from Exeter; Geoff Whitty, Graham Byrne Hill and John Jessel from Goldsmiths'; Rod Coveney and Gay Vaughan from Worcester; Wendy Nuttall and Katrina Blythe from Chester; David Clemson and Maureen Blackmore from Liverpool; and myself and the project secretary, Laura Tickner.[2] I was a senior research associate at CARE/UEA and my role as the national co-ordinator gave me a certain status; I had a strong background in IT in schools but far less experience of teacher education than any other member of the team. Charles and Geoff by comparison were professors in their TEIs and already at that time among the leading researchers in educational psychology and sociology, respectively, in the UK. Rod was about to be appointed Assistant Dean at Worcester

---

[2] During the second year of INTENT Wendy Nuttall left Chester College and Katrina Blythe took over the 'senior manager' role, with Andrew Hamill and Malcolm Glover sharing the role of SDT.

and Niki and Katrina were both nationally known for their innovative work in IT. The other members of the team all contributed specialist knowledge that fitted the needs of their own institutions. Within a higher education culture which valued academic freedom, but also had a tradition of strongly differentiated roles in terms of status, I needed to share ownership of Project INTENT to make it work at all. To try to force through a particular programme of work would, arguably, have been suicidal on my part: on the other hand, such a diverse team with so many strong-willed individuals needed strong leadership. I am not surprised that Geoff asked me two years later if I had felt trepidation at the beginning (not his exact word, but certainly I think his meaning).

Reading again the programme for the planning week, the transcript of the first session, the written outcomes from group planning sessions and my own research journal, the attempt to build a collaborative project giving equal voice to all team members is clear. We were lucky to have glorious weather and a beautiful venue at Dyffryn House Conference Centre just outside Cardiff. Over the next two years, all the meetings of Project INTENT were held there because we liked it so much:

On the first day:

- The week began with an introductory session at 11.30, led by myself, 'to discuss the programme and make any necessary changes – plus brief introductions' (quotes from programme).
- After lunch, from 1.30 – 6.00 with a half hour tea break, there were two 'artifacts sessions to explore together the question, "who are we as professionals?" – thus to understand each other's needs and purposes and find out more about each other'. This involved each of us in turn having 'seven minutes to present three or four objects which represented significant elements of our lives as a professional, followed by seven minutes of questions from the group to clarify and explore the account'.
- After dinner there was the first of three 'reading and discussion sessions' for silent reading of a selection of books and articles I had provided on innovation and IT, followed by a 20-minute plenary to exchange ideas.

The intention was to build a strong collaborative team. At the start of the introductory session I had the opportunity to explain my thinking about the project's work. The aims of Project INTENT, defined by NCET and the DES were:

- to develop the quality of teaching and learning with IT (both in HEIs themselves and the schools where their students carried out 'teaching placement');

- to provide support for tutors integrating IT across the curriculum for initial teacher education;
- to develop management strategies to support these developments;
- to monitor the processes for institutional change.

The project would have 'an educational not a technological focus' and it would integrate research with development to keep it on track. I explained:

> There is a lot of research into innovation that already exists, but we're also looking at an innovation in schools in this country which has been put in without much reference to that research. If we simply go into development work, get into action and we just develop things, just write about what we've done, and we don't have a research aspect to what we're doing, then I think that would be a rather crazy way of going about it, but it would be possibly something that nobody would question if we did it. But I don't think it is what is suited to our knowledge, as people in HE, of the need to think carefully.
>
> (transcript of session: lines 36–41)

When I had visited them all to select participant TEIs many people had mentioned action research because they knew something of my previous work. I explained:

> I don't know whether I want to call it action research, but I see a kind of continuing formative, evaluative process, which you can call action research or you can call it implementing, monitoring and then changing ... that's what I mean by a research approach to development, that it would be development work but that research is going to go hand in hand with that.
>
> (transcript of session: lines 46–50)

In terms of who would be carrying out the research activity, I explained that in addition to myself and other the members of the team:

> I think that writing papers and carrying out research is linked for a lot of our colleagues to promotion and that therefore one way of bringing people into the project would be to support them in research projects that they want to do, whatever methodology they want to use. I certainly wouldn't want to impose a particular kind of methodology on anybody, even if our basic framework for the team is one of looking at what we're doing and action research type development.
>
> (transcript of session: lines 51–7)

The roles of the staff development co-ordinator (SDC) and senior manager would be flexible – two of the participant TEIs had already decided to share the role of the SDC between two people and another, where the SDC already had significant release from teaching, would be giving some release to the senior manager. I explained:

> Your role is jointly to lead a team of your colleagues and therefore to get as much participation (as possible) ... the name of the game is getting people involved ... (getting them) to participate ... to do bits of writing with you ... bits of research.
>
> (transcript of session: lines 86–8)

Everyone had agreed, as a condition of taking part, that the project would last for two years although funding for the SDC's release from teaching would only be for year one. I explained:

> There are some benefits to the fact that the injection of funds has come in the first year, because often, as you know, when you withdraw the money everything stops. The second year is an opportunity to make sure that it's fully integrated and that you don't lose what it is you've developed.
>
> (transcript of session: lines 101–4)

In terms of outcomes there would be case studies (as specified in the invitation to tender), research reports, including those written by colleagues in the TEIs, and dialogue about our work with other TEIs through establishing a network to include all the original applicants and others funded in other ways to carry out similar work.

Most of the major decisions about INTENT's work were made during the planning week. Collaborative decision making was built into the programme that included a strong emphasis on group work and sharing of ideas intended to make the work personally meaningful and provide mutual support. My strategy was to present a strong framework of suggested project activities – such as my regular visits to each TEI, an all-day symposium at the CAL91 conference, a regular slot in the ITTE newsletter, and a series of peer-reviewed publications – and to invite open discussion on whether or not to take them forward. By building a discussion of the programme and 'making of necessary changes' into the opening session I hoped to set the tone of collaboration and also guard against any build-up of hostility later in the week. Initially it seemed like a challenge. My research journal records: 'It was very stiff when people arrived. Probably everybody very nervous.' In retrospect, I wonder if there was also quite a lot of resentment at having to return to work early from the summer vacation and/or precious reading and writing time. The first afternoon's two 'artifacts' sessions proved to be crucially important. Devoting four hours to working in this way on the first afternoon was clearly risky, and its value was questioned in the introductory session; however, once I had explained its purpose more fully, it was agreed to go ahead with it and everyone participated with full commitment. We learnt a great deal about each other's values, aspirations and reasons for wanting to be involved in INTENT. It was important I think that we worked outside, on the terrace in the shade of a huge tree, because this helped to establish a culture of informality and gave a strong feel-good factor; early in the week we took a photograph of the whole team under the tree and everyone had one of these to keep – mine is still on my office wall as I write this chapter.

- The week also included sessions on 'Project INTENT aims and purposes', 'Finding out about each other's institutions', 'Roles and the team: developing working procedures' 'Personal and institutional planning', 'Dissemination issues' and 'A writing morning'.

We were joined for part of the week by Peter Seaborne, then senior HMI (Her Majesty's Inspector) with responsibilities for IT in teacher education, and Andrea Tapsfield, our manager from NCET. I remember that Peter, arriving mid-week, was not entirely happy about the programme. Speaking to me privately he queried the value of the artifacts sessions (which he had not attended) and, in retrospect, I am sure he must have been worried by the programme notes for the two sessions on aims and purposes (which he had also not attended) because of the suggested expansion of INTENT's work beyond what had been specified by the DES:

- The purpose of these two sessions was 'to begin developing a coherent philosophy for the project – within which each individual and institution can see how our own needs and purposes fit and make sense – leading to drawing up an internal confidential draft document for team members only'.
- During the first session we 'worked in four cross-institutional groups (threes and fours) to begin identifying the project's aims and purposes – taking into account the existing parameters (CATE, Trotter, Project INTENT's brief and discussions with other colleagues during Bridget's preliminary visits) – notes to be kept'.
- In the second we worked as one large group 'to draw up a statement of INTENT's aims and purposes. (Reports back from each group recorded on flip chart and discussed – and any agreed statements listed.)'

The emphasis on building collegiality and making the project personally meaningful meant that during the week as a whole a large proportion of the work was focused on deepening understanding of processes and developing working procedures, rather than discussing specific aspects of the use of IT in teacher education and how its use could be improved:

- One of the activities in the session on developing working procedures was group work to develop 'a Code of Confidentiality within which all participants in INTENT can work creatively (be able to experiment and "risk-take" etc.).'

As in all other sessions, written outcomes were collected and points put forward in the plenary discussion were recorded on a flip chart. By collating and editing this material I developed a draft code, which was circulated to the team before the end of the week. It opened with this statement:

DRAFT PRODUCED FROM THE GROUP PAPERS – EDITED AND ADDED TO BY BRIDGET – FOR PULLING APART AND INTO SHAPE ETC.

A code of confidentiality enables a positive, frank and productive climate to be maintained and ensures security of the parties involved. This is essential to allow the necessary experimentation and risk-taking to take place within a collaborative framework. The central idea is the ownership of data (of all kinds) and ideas. The Code is intended to facilitate the research and development process and enable the project to adopt an 'open' approach to dissemination of ideas. If these procedures become too cumbersome and impede this process they should be renegotiated – BUT they cannot be changed without the unanimous agreement of the central inter-institutional team.

The code had four clauses which dealt with: procedures to ensure confidentiality of data at different levels (children, teachers in schools, students, staff in each TEI, the project team members); sharing of materials, research instruments and literature reviews; a commitment to publicizing the project's work; and procedures to govern publications so that all the team members, their institutions and NCET would be given credit for their work.

The final two days were strongly focused on planning. Thursday began with a session led by Peter Seaborne in which he outlined the problems we had been set up to address, as identified from HMI reports of both schools and TEIs. Thursday afternoon from 1.30–6.00 was for 'Personal and Institutional Planning' and Friday from 9.00–12.30 was 'a writing morning: to produce some documents for immediate use – as nearly finished as possible'.

The planning week came to an end and we all returned to our own institutions to start work. The staff development tutors, supported by the senior managers, had to publicize the work of the project, build teams of colleagues to work with them, and begin to move their institution forward in its use of IT in teacher education. I myself was soon embarked on a round of visits, spending one or two days in each TEI, interviewing, observing and engaging in dialogue, filling as far as I could the role of 'a trusted outsider/insider in the institution' rather than that of an external evaluator. Laura was engaged in sending out information, answering queries, managing the project's finances, and furiously typing up notes dictated by me in the car on my way back from these visits. Having attended the planning week and spent three hours in the car with me on the drive back from Cardiff to Norwich, Laura (with whom I had already worked on PALM) was also invaluable as my colleague and confidante.

Working tensions in Project INTENT and how we addressed them

Collaboration is a difficult process. When it is supported by action research the main advantage is that tensions emerge into the open and can be discussed and addressed by the group. They may not be entirely overcome, but they will never be as destructive as they probably would have been had they remained covert. To illustrate this process I will deal with three examples here and explain how we dealt with them.

The balance between INTENT's development work and its research activities

Project INTENT meetings took place twice a term, involving three days and two nights at Dyffryn House. The staff development co-ordinators attended all these meetings and the senior managers attended half of them, although in view of some blurring of roles between the partners at Liverpool, David opted to attend them all. When the team arrived on Friday evenings they were tired after driving long distances. The after dinner session on Friday was, therefore, potentially a stressful one.

At the December meeting at the end of the first term's work, half-way through the Friday evening session at which we were discussing, as I remember, some issues relating to IT in education, Katrina made a strong statement to the effect that she felt we were wasting time on far too much talk. She felt that there was an enormous amount of work to be done, a lot of materials and resources to be produced, and that far more time at meetings should be spent on practical tasks rather than discussions. Immediately, Charles responded with an equally strong statement that far too little was known about the actual value of using IT in education, saying that he would be extremely disturbed if we simply implemented this innovation without first inquiring fully into its nature and purposes, to ensure that what we implemented was of genuine value. This strong difference of view which we addressed as honestly as we could, was symptomatic of a deep cultural divide. The balance between INTENT's development work and its research activities was a difficult one to get right, especially as the cultures of the participating TEIs and the past experience of the individual team members was sharply divided in terms of attitudes to research and the relative value consequently to be placed on theory. The two university departments had strong traditions of research and cultures that valued inquiry; the two HE colleges and the polytechnic were strongly embedded in the culture of teaching and had traditions that gave priority to careful planning and implementation of initiatives rather than inquiry into their purposes. Another important point was that the team members had vastly different levels of expertise in IT so that for some, like Katrina, discussions of the purposes of using IT in education were covering old ground, while for others, like Charles, these were relatively new discussions.

To a considerable extent the tension between these two views remained at the core of INTENT's activities. Action research was particularly helpful as a methodology that brought action and theory into the closest possible alignment, but this was a tension that was embedded too fundamentally in two different cultures to be easily resolved. The strength of INTENT was that it was working with representatives of the whole community of IT in teacher education and, because it could draw on strong team members who held opposing views, it was better able to respond to the needs of both kinds of institution.

Different assumptions about evidence for learning

Arising directly from the previous point, we also found ourselves confronting different definitions of learning and, in particular, very different notions of what counts as evidence of learning. Charles challenged us to give him evidence of IT having made a difference in children's learning. Niki, myself and others replied in terms of children's high levels of motivation and greatly increased time on task. 'But,' Charles was quick to reply, 'that's not evidence of learning – they may be staying longer on task, but suppose they are just practising mistakes!' He had plenty more to say in a similar vein. That particular discussion lasted for most of a session (and really continued for the whole of the project): eventually Charles was interrupted, while he was giving us evidence of learning from an experimental study of pairs of children undertaking a task, by Geoff who said something like, 'Come on, Charles, you're talking about an ideal situation with just two learners working in isolation. This project is about looking at learning with IT in classrooms, which is very significantly different.' The paper that many of us went on to write, to address Charles' question with his help, drew on recent research from both psychology and sociology (Davis *et al.* 1997). In this way, project INTENT benefited enormously from the specialist knowledge of psychology and sociology that Charles and Geoff brought to the group. I remember saying this to Geoff some time during the second year and he replied, 'But that's not what we are here for!' However, for me, right from the start, the opportunity of having their expertise in traditional research knowledge to inform our action research was central to why I had wanted their institutions to participate in INTENT.

Evidence of success and approaches to evaluation

In May 1991 I was called to a meeting with HMIs Peter Seaborne and Gabriel Goldstein at the DES at Elizabeth House, accompanied by Peter Avis who was by then the Director of the Schools' Division of NCET. No doubt the anxiety that Peter Seaborne had felt when he attended the planning week eight months earlier – which can be seen as very similar to the concern Katrina later expressed that the team spent too much time on discussion at the expense of action – was a factor in determining the tone of the meeting. Pressure from senior officers at the DES to ensure that there was clear evidence of the impact of the INTENT spending was clearly another important factor. Questioning briefly became confrontational. For example, early in the meeting, I was asked a question relating to students' experiences of using IT on teaching placements and I had scarcely begun my reply when I was cut short by a further question, which included the phrases: 'I'm disappointed to hear … I do hope that you are not …'. Later, when I was giving an account of staff development work being undertaken by project team members, I was pressed for information on the kinds of evidence by which I would be measuring achievement. The performance indicator of 'numbers of staff attending courses' was suggested and my instinctive (unspoken) reaction was that this indicated their misunderstanding of INTENT's approach to staff development, of which training courses were only a very small part. Pressure was being brought to bear on me relating to two points that I would have difficulty in meeting. First, the provision of successful experiences for students using IT on teaching placements was certainly the most difficult challenge that the project faced, and our research (despite its action orientation) was leading to the conclusion that a closer partnership with schools would be necessary to bring it about. It was very unlikely that the project would be able to meet this expectation adequately in the short term. Second, it was difficult to think of what performance indicators we could use to evaluate our work across all five TEIs, since our concern to embed development work in the culture of each institution and, beyond that, our concern to work one to one with individuals to suit their particular needs, meant that we had multiple foci rather than a small number and certainly nothing that we could easily quantify.

The tension that arose from this was initially within me, since I found myself thinking I would need to impose a new set of activities on the team members in order to generate the kind of evidence that HMI were expecting, but knew that this would rupture our collaborative relationship and be disruptive of on-going work which had already been planned. At first I worried about trying to develop performance indicators. Then, I realized that the only way of dealing with this problem was to share it with the team by consulting them about how we should respond as a group. The strain was shared between us, showing the strength of the collaborative team we had built up. The action we took was a fine compromise. With the agreement and assistance of the team, I developed questionnaires for staff and students in the institutions and we issued these at the end of 1991 and again at the end of 1992 (although Katrina was not prepared to administer them to staff at Chester College because of the additional work load it would bring). From these we were able to quantify changes in staff and student perceptions of their competence and confidence in using IT, as well as students' perceptions of the barriers that had prevented them from using IT and the extent of their use of IT on teaching placements. With regard to 'performance indicators', these were discussed at a meeting of the INTENT Principals, at which Charles and Geoff deputized for their heads of school. Geoff made a strong case for PIs being an inappropriate evaluation instrument for project INTENT since they can only be successfully applied if they are determined in advance: as we had not been told in advance of the requirement to have PIs we had not developed them and it would be methodologically unreliable to try to impose them at this late stage. The meeting, which was attended by Peter Seaborne and another HMI, as well as Peter Avis, was persuaded by this argument and the requirement for PIs was dropped.

[Additional information, presenting this series of events to me from another point of view, was provided by Gabriel Goldstein and Peter Seaborne in discussions of the draft of this chapter. I have included this as part of a retrospective analysis of how I handled relationships with policy people during Project INTENT in the final section of this chapter.]

Knowledge outcomes from Project INTENT

The dissemination of outcomes from Project INTENT was carefully designed and I believe as effective as it could have been. There was a range of different kinds of publications:

- *Project INTENT: The Final Report*, published by NCET (Somekh 1992).
- *Five INTENT Strategy Cards* to be used to lead discussion with different groupings of staff in TEIs in order to get development work going.

- The *DITTE* series (*Developing IT in Teacher Education*) of five journal-style booklets, containing in all 31 articles by INTENT team members and colleagues, encompassing research into all aspects of the project's work.
- The book, *Using IT Effectively in Teaching and Learning*, edited by myself and Niki, which contained two jointly authored papers on key aspects of INTENT's work – learning with IT and the management of change – and 16 other chapters of which 10 were written by members of the project team and two by participants in the PALM project (Somekh and Davis 1997).

An important outcome of INTENT was that it played a role in establishing a research literature on IT in teacher education. The DITTE series was set up as a mini-journal with a board of reviewers who provided critical feed back on draft articles so that authors could improve them with further work. Prior to this process, it was a major part of my role as co-ordinator to read drafts and give advice to inexperienced authors – of whom there were many in those days when research was only beginning to be a requirement for many teacher educators. DITTE was provided free by NCET to all TEIs and was widely read. It provided a model for carrying out research into practice in order to support development. After the project came to an end the *Journal for IT in Teacher Education* (*JITTE*) was founded and, together with the *Journal of Teaching and Technology in Education* (*JTATE*) published in the USA, embarked on the long-term business of establishing a research literature in the field.

Key findings in relation to the specific innovation of IT in teacher education

From the combined outcomes of INTENT the following findings emerge clearly:

- The strategy of appointing a staff development tutor and a senior manager to work in partnership to promote development had been proved to be very effective.
- It had been demonstrated that it is important to use a range of strategies for staff development in order to engage the motivation and commitment of a wide range of staff. From this range, some strategies are likely to be more effective: for example, one-to-one support alongside a tutor is generally of great value. Although this approach appears at first sight to be expensive, its long-term value and the potential for setting up a 'supported cascade' of similar support for colleagues, makes it excellent value for money.

- Appropriate provision of hardware and software, including easy access for all staff and students, had been shown to be a necessary but insufficient condition for effective development.
- Technicians had been shown to be most useful when their role was broadened to include a support role for staff and students using new hardware and software as well as a technical role in making sure that equipment works.
- It had been shown that students can only learn to use IT effectively in their teaching placements if tutors in the TEI and teachers in the school are already familiar with IT and – crucially – are prepared to support its exploratory use with children, rather than expecting the student to be an expert.

Key findings in relation to the management of change

Overall, INTENT's action research generated considerable knowledge and understanding of the process of managing change. This is fully explored in a chapter Geoff, Rod and I wrote in the book Niki and I edited (Somekh and Davis 1997). It ends with a summary of 'useful ideas for the management of change across a whole institution', which is quoted here in full:

- *Setting up a 'project', especially if it has links with other institutions, enables special priority to be given to an initiative so that management can provide it with extra resources in the short term without being perceived to be unfair.*
- *Nevertheless, the 'project' needs to be sufficiently integrated with existing institutional management structures to ensure that its work continues after the special funding comes to an end.*
- *A change initiative or 'project' needs to strike a balance between fitting the existing culture of an institution ('the way things are done around here') and challenging that culture.*
- *A change initiative or 'project' needs to identify and build upon the key factors which motivate individuals at this time, in this institution.*
- *A change initiative or 'project' needs to identify and make use of existing 'spaces' or ambiguities in the institutional structure, or in the informal power structures.*
- *The key to the process of change is the hearts and minds of the individuals who have the power to make it happen. One good way of engaging their hearts and minds is by involving them in some way – however small – in researching the effectiveness of the innovation with the aim of improving its implementation.*
- *The two-pronged strategy of a staff development tutor working closely with a senior manager is very effective. This is because it provides support for colleagues on a one-to-one basis as needed,*

while simultaneously making it possible to put into place supportive structures, to allocate essential resources, and to highlight the importance of the initiative to the institution as a whole.

- *This partnership between 'coal face' and senior management (assuming it involves regular discussions) always uncovers surprising misconceptions on both sides. This new mutual understanding of the perspectives of 'them and us' can reduce tensions and enable a genuine cross-fertilization of ideas.*

(Somekh *et al.* 1997: 204–5)

Some of the unexpected features that emerged en route to these findings were particularly interesting. For example, the extent of misunderstanding between individuals at different levels in the hierarchy of the organization was a real surprise: typically, staff development tutors thought that managers were much more powerful than they actually were and interpreted lack of financial support as intentionally obstructive; and typically managers had very little idea of the potential value of IT for teaching and learning across the curriculum, seeing it instead as yet another expensive technological fashion that would be of value to the IT department but not to other colleagues. A feature of this was the difficulty that managers had in giving large-scale support to a single initiative when everyone in the institution was competing for resources and quick to perceive and condemn favouritism. These two features of organizational relationships, which generalized across all five participating TEIs, are likely to be significant in the management of change generally.

Other features came as no surprise. For example, the importance of attending to the micro-political processes that give some individuals much more power than others, regardless of their formal position in the hierarchy was already well known in the literature (Malen 1994) and confirmed many times over by INTENT. Likewise, the huge importance of institutional culture in shaping the responses of individuals to innovation was confirmed yet again by INTENT.

Looking back: a retrospective commentary

Project INTENT enabled me to bring together what I had learnt from SIP and the PALM project and greatly increased my knowledge and understanding of the processes of managing change in organizations. It is also valuable as an example of action research in which senior managers in an organization were actively involved in research into their own practice as leaders of change, working in partnership with grass-roots colleagues. It was a huge pleasure to lead a collaborative action research team made up of teachers and researchers in higher education, who brought with them a wide range of knowledge and experience. At the end of my time co-ordinating INTENT and its extended network, I found myself part of a broad network of researchers in the field of IT in teacher education who have been an important support group in the development of my work ever since.

Reflecting on INTENT now, I think one of its main strengths was in broadening conceptions of action research. It showed that action research can be powerfully adapted to fit different contexts. Although very different from the focused work that an individual, or partnership of insider and outsider, can achieve in a contained setting, such as a classroom, action research across a whole organization can provide a broad structure for large-scale collaborative effort while also embracing and supporting many small and diverse action research mini-projects. The key is to allow those who wish to participate to make research contributions that fit their own values and needs, rather than constraining colleagues to fit into a tightly defined template. Another key is to involve individuals at different levels in the organizational hierarchy working in partnership, *each carrying out action research at their own level*, so that barriers to innovation identified at 'grass-roots' or middle management level can be addressed by exploring possibilities for changes to structures (e.g. role designation, room allocation and designated time-frames) at senior management level. INTENT also reinforced my understanding of management as a moral activity involving decision making that affects the lives of many people (staff and students in this case). The core values of action research, which include respect for all participants, sensitivity to culture, support for risk taking, honesty and openness, and intellectual engagement to try to understand human and social processes, ensure that managers remain morally vigilant and resist the temptation to exercise power thoughtlessly in order to get things done quickly.

Looking back, it is also possible to identify things that went less well and that I would want to manage differently if I were to work on a similar project today. I think that, despite INTENT's rhetoric of taking into account organizational culture, I did not fully understand the implications of this for the way the project was managed. I focused on the way in which organizational culture influenced the relationships between the five TEIs and their willingness or not to engage in research. It is only when returning now to read much of the data again that I realize that organizational culture also strongly influenced the way in which organizations worked with me as co-ordinator. It has become very clear in the intervening years that the way in which universities and further education colleges use IT in teaching is significantly different from the way in which it is used in schools. In retrospect, I think that Liverpool, as a polytechnic, embarked on INTENT with more of an 'HE-focused' than a 'school-focused' approach. An important purpose for effective use of IT at Liverpool was the development of learning resources to be used by students independently, and accordingly the Head of Learning Resource was appointed as the staff development tutor. She had never been a teacher herself so was not able to work alongside teacher–educators to assist them in preparing student teachers to use IT in schools. Liverpool's contribution to the project's research was not through action research but through surveys of students' attitudes to IT (which were, of course, extremely useful). Much of the development work they were carrying out was focused on the production of resources for self-study. It is a real pity that I did not realize the significance of this at the time since it might have been extremely interesting to evaluate the effectiveness of this different approach in terms of student teachers' learning, as a comparison with the project's main strategy of supporting tutors' professional development through action research. Instead, I never fully understood the radical difference in their approach to INTENT and persisted in expecting evidence of collaborative development work with colleagues that had probably never been on their agenda.

The other thing that, in retrospect, I realize was not very well handled, was the interface between the project and policy makers. Partly this was as a result of being distanced from the latter by middle management from NCET. The decision to fund INTENT was initially taken by NCET and the DES who negotiated the brief contained in the invitation to tender. The re-negotiation of the brief with NCET, following my appointment as co-ordinator, was probably never formally agreed with the DES and then, relatively soon after INTENT started work both Ralph Tabberer and Andrea Tapsfield left NCET. Thinking of myself as working for NCET, I paid far too little attention to the concerns that HMI Peter Seaborne expressed to me during the planning week and yet even so he had probably not really grasped the changes made to the project's design. At the meeting with him and Gabriel Goldstein eight months later it now seems likely that the two HMIs were expecting to discuss a project with a clear and separate evaluation phase in its second year rather than the re-designed project I had come to tell them about. This meeting must have been as difficult for Peter Avis as it was for me.

[Fascinating further insights have been shed on this analysis by discussing the draft of this chapter with Gabriel, with whom I have continued to work in recent years. It appears that I had forgotten that HMIs were at the time carrying out an internal evaluation of Project INTENT, involving visits to three of the five TEIs and the preparation of a paper by Peter Avis and myself, which was to be discussed at the meeting at Elizabeth House. The visits and the contents of our paper had indicated some drift in the project's work away from the direct support for the CATE criteria set out at the beginning of this chapter, hence there were already concerns before the meeting began. Discussion of the draft with Peter Seaborne also clarified for me the extent of the pressure that HMI felt under at that time to ensure that

Project INTENT, as a project managed by NCET, should deliver what it had promised.]

While I think that we went on to deal credibly and fairly comprehensively with the requirements for a formal evaluation of Project INTENT, it would have been much better if I had not been caught by surprise at their expectations at this meeting. My somewhat strained relationships with HMI also did little to help my pursuit of follow-up funding to roll out to all other TEIs the INTENT model for IT development. Peter Avis and I spent a considerable amount of time writing proposals to the DES for this 'daughter of INTENT' but they were all finally rejected. However, knowing more of policy making now than I did then, its rejection probably had more to do with the then government's desire to come up with a new eye-catching, small-scale initiative as a vote winner (of exactly the type that INTENT had been) rather than to fund the much larger expense of rolling out a tried and tested model to all the TEIs in the country.

Project INTENT was funded because it was timely, capitalizing on a recommendation in the Trotter Report that NCET should provide ITTEs with support for staff development in IT, and catching the moment when CATE had made IT a top priority in initial teacher education. A follow-up project would not, by the same token, have been timely because it was seeking funding just at the moment when CATE criteria for newly qualified teachers had been changed, yet again, to remove the explicit focus on developing competence in IT. An important lesson to be learnt from this is that however potentially important a funded project may be it will only be funded if it appears timely to the sponsors.

6 Action Research in a Partnership between Regional Companies and a University[1]

Can individuals in an organization use action research as a means of bringing about organizational change? Is action research an effective strategy for supporting collaboration across the cultures of a university and local businesses to develop work-based learning for academic accreditation? This chapter is about a project called 'From Competence to Excellence' (COMEX, 1994–95), which adopted an action research approach to developing work-based degree programmes at undergraduate and masters levels. Leading COMEX was demanding because of the institutional politics that shaped and constrained all its activities, both in the university and the partner companies. In this context action research could only be effective through the formation of strategic alliances and constant interpersonal manoeuvring to overcome blocks to development.

During the previous academic year I had been involved in developing a new masters degree programme in human resource strategy at UEA, in collaboration with Tony Brown, the newly appointed Director of Management Education. This was the background which led the Dean of EDU, John Elliott, to ask me in November 1993 to write a proposal with Tony for the Employment Department's (ED) work-based learning programme. This was the second phase of an initiative to integrate work-based learning within academic programmes in higher education, the first cohort of 10 projects having completed work in 1992 (ED 1992). We were informed just before Christmas that our proposal had been successful and Dave Ebbutt, with whom I had worked closely when he co-ordinated the TIQL project with John Elliott (see Chapter 3), was appointed as senior research associate to work with me from January 1994.

[1] The research reported in this chapter was carried out jointly by myself and Dave Ebbutt. I would like to thank Dave for his enormous contribution to the ideas contained here. I would also like to thank Barbara Zamorski, from whose excellent evaluation study I have quoted extensively.

This chapter looks back on the COMEX initiative, its challenges and achievements and my own work-based learning in attempting to drive it forward. COMEX moved forward at hectic speed and encountered many barriers as a result of the successful proposal having committed the university to meet what at first seemed to be impossible targets. Dave's extensive experience in action research and meticulous attention to detail, and our mutual close – if sometimes challenging – relationship with the Dean of EDU, John Elliott, as well as the support of Barry MacDonald, Director of CARE, gave us a secure base from which we set out to negotiate the complexities of the university's systems and procedures.

From competence to excellence: an initiative in multi-level, inter-cultural, organizational change

We were told that COMEX was awarded funding by the ED because it offered an innovative approach to work-based learning, radically different from the approach taken by previous projects that started with the specification of learning outcomes and engaged learners in building up portfolios of evidence to demonstrate these had been achieved. Instead, COMEX engaged students in carrying out action-oriented research in their workplace, working as 'insider consultants' commissioned by senior managers to implement some aspect of organizational change, supported jointly by a workplace tutor and academic supervisor and assessed by a combination of written assignments for the university and workplace presentations to peers. The proposal, which became the basis for our contract with the ED, stated that students' work would be 'designed to contribute to the company's development as well as meeting the requirements of academic accreditation'. The university submitted the proposal in collaboration with nine East Anglian employers.[2] 'Other course elements [were to be] developed by both participating employers and the university to enable maximum flexibility in meeting individual needs.' We promised to develop accreditation at a range of levels and 'where possible to dove-tail [them] with existing national, professional and vocational qualifications'. We began work in January 1994 (although the contract with the ED was delayed and not signed until March) and we were committed to enrolling 40 students to the new courses in September of the same year.

---

[2] COMEX partners were: Her Majesty's Stationery Office, AMEC Offshore Development, Norfolk Constabulary, Norfolk Mental Health Care NHS Trust, Birds Eye Walls Ltd, Norfolk and Waveney Training and Education Council, King's Lynn Borough Council and Norfolk County Council.

COMEX built upon the experience of cross-professional masters degree courses at CARE/UEA, which had catered for police officers and health professionals for some years, and on the MA in human resources management (HRS) in which I continued to work with personnel managers from both private and public companies, including the civil service. Further, drawing on the experience of Project INTENT (see Chapter 5) I hoped that students would be able to be effective as change agents in their organization by working in partnership with a senior manager who would 'commission' and thereafter support their project work. This was where I imagined that the core of the action research activity would take place. As soon as we started work, however, it became clear that we were simultaneously engaged in two further levels of action research, one with employers that focused on the development of a collaborative programme that would fit their needs and the other with the university that focused on the development of a radically new kind of award. COMEX was itself 'a bridge between the university and industry' challenging the established cultures of both while trying to deliver the new courses it had promised within a very short time-frame. To support us in the complexities of this tripartite action research we fortunately had an internal evaluation strand built into the COMEX funding. This was led by our colleague, David Bridges, who attended several key meetings between January and June of 1994 and gave us important feed-back and advice. His long experience of university management as a professor and former vice-principal of Homerton College Cambridge proved invaluable, and the probing curiosity and *simpatico* sensitivity of Barbara Zamorski, who carried out an interview study in October–November 1994, resulted in a report containing a number of fascinating insights (Zamorski *et al.* 1995). This small-scale internal evaluation proved to be essential to our action research, making us aware of problems and their possible causes, and sustaining our own reflexive questioning.

COMEX development work was planned as one continuous process, but in terms of the focus of the team's activities its first year fell into four phases. These phases were not distinct but overlapping and each of the three phase shifts took place because the momentum of the work demanded us to move on before we were ready. This chapter focuses only on the first year because in February 1995 I moved to a new post at the Scottish Council for Research in Education. I left just as COMEX was moving into its fifth phase of preparations for year two.

The first phase of COMEX's work, between January and June 1994, focused upon building relationships with our employer partners. When we were writing the proposal we held one meeting with as many partners as possible and talked drafts through with others on the telephone. Inevitably, this process had been strongly led by the director of management education and myself, so now Dave and I had to work hard to engage all partners collaboratively in developing the programme. Our intention was to do this through action research to identify their needs, negotiate our working methods and procedures and incorporate their contributions in the teaching (drawing on their in-house trainers). But first we had to explain the purposes of the COMEX initiative, its underpinning action research philosophy and our vision for how it would meet the needs of both students and the company that employed them. In this sense we were a very unequal partnership – the university team was already committed to a model of experiential learning embedded in an inquiry process and had in mind a number of roles and responsibilities to translate this vision into action; the companies' representatives may not always have been easy to persuade, but their starting point was an assumption that the university would lead and they would follow. Very real power was retained by the companies, however, because we were dependent on them to fund the students who would make up the first year's cohort. We could only meet our recruitment targets if they made a substantial financial contribution in terms of students' fees. In this first phase we established the Consortium Group, made up of representatives from the companies and the project team and negotiated with each company variations in how the three roles of student/insider consultant, commissioning manager and workplace tutor would be concretized. We also set up a workplace awareness programme for the university-based team, involving a whole day's visit to one or two of the companies, learning about its business, meeting senior managers to explain what COMEX was offering the company and its employees and talking to potential students. My own visit to AMEX, which serviced oil rigs in the North Sea, was memorable for a visit to the submersion pool in which technicians were taught how to escape from a ditched helicopter.

The second phase of COMEX's work, between March and July 1994, focused on finding a way to fit our vision of work-based learning into the university's established frameworks for teaching, assessment and the award of credit. At the same time we had to carry our employer partners along with us and bring them to the point of committing financial support to enrolling some of their employees on the new courses. We proceeded in a state of tension, increasingly distracted by the imperatives of phase two from the continuing need to consolidate the gains of phase one. As one Consortium Group member told the formative evaluation:

> I felt it was a partnership until June, and then the meetings dried up – it felt remote then. Things were going on, I know they were because students were ringing me up and asking me things, but I couldn't help them because I didn't have as much information as they did at this point.
>
> (Zamorski *et al.* 1995: 21)

There were a number of sticking points. The ED was very keen for us to offer accreditation at five levels, but the university was resistant to offering qualifications below first degree level. This was a point of agreement with the employers, it turned out, for whom 'the gold standard' of a UEA degree was significantly attractive; they did not see the university as the provider of choice for sub-degree level courses. We decided to develop two programmes, masters and undergraduate; the former fitted well with our previous experience but the latter took us into new territory where we had to call on the advice and expertise of colleagues outside EDU. The dean of EDU was explicit in not wanting to reintroduce undergraduate teaching that had been abandoned seven years earlier. It seemed for a while that we would have to locate the COMEX undergraduate programme within another school. Neither would it be possible to develop an undergraduate degree based entirely on workplace learning since there were regulations governing the proportion of project work permissible in an undergraduate degree. Often as we pushed against a problem a solution would emerge and in this case we found out that the university had just completed the move to a common course structure (CCS) in which undergraduate degrees across all the schools had been sub-divided into modules and given a credit rating. So far no one had found the need to make use of CCS, however, which meant that while COMEX was seen by senior academics as providing an ideal opportunity to implement and test out the new system, we soon found ourselves in the role of 'calling the bluff' of departments that had gone through the motions of modularizing and credit rating their courses but had no mechanisms in place to open them up to students wanting – as ours would – to 'pick and mix' in consultation with an academic adviser.

This phase of COMEX required Dave and myself to operate with a combination of obstinate determination, strategic opportunism and tactful diplomacy. Neither of us had all of these qualities but we could draw on each other's strengths in partnership. We were schooled by powerful allies such as John Elliott and we had the great advantage of having the contract with the ED to provide leverage in our negotiations with powerful people. The first strategy was to set up the steering group required by the ED and use this as the opportunity to involve several key people as members of it. Using the traditional participatory structures of a university, decisions at UEA were made by a hierarchy of committees, through a process of presenting proposals for discussion and adoption at one, prior to the proposal being passed up to the next. At any stage, failure to get agreement from a committee had the potential to delay the whole process while a revised proposal was prepared for presentation to its next meeting, although it was possible for committees to set up 'working groups' to take matters forward on 'chair's action'. The chairs of the university's two most powerful committees, the Teaching Committee (TC) and the Board of Graduate Studies (known jokingly as BOGS), were persuaded to become members of the

COMEX steering group, as was the Dean of EDU, John Elliott. To bring in a highly respected authority in work-based learning at the national level, we invited Norman Evans, Director of the Learning from Experience Trust and an old friend of John's, to chair the SG. David Pearce from the ED was also a member and saw the SG as the mechanism for monitoring the project's progress and calling the project team – and the university – to account. The establishment of a steering group with such powerful members was a key strategic action that involved individual lobbying of each of these people to persuade them of why their contribution was needed. These meetings with individuals were very important in themselves as opportunities for explaining COMEX's purposes and the challenges we faced. For example, when we met the chair of the Teaching Committee he advised us of key actions, warned us of potential barriers and mapped out the procedures for taking COMEX through the chain of committees. He also made us aware of the need to lobby right at the top by making an appointment to go and discuss COMEX and its importance to the university with the vice-chancellor, since he alone, as chair of the university Senate (the very top committee), would have the authority to drive through the necessary decisions if we met real opposition. The extent to which COMEX was radical in 1994 – and the distance that English universities have come in diversifying their core business in the intervening years – is clear from this quotation from a senior academic taken from the formative evaluation:

> If COMEX succeeds, and why shouldn't it, then it will just show us that we can take our blinkers off and do very strange new things. This is an extremely useful lesson to have learnt. The classic way of running a smallish high standard university is not going to suffice. We've got to find a way of running a much more diverse university at high standards.
>
> (Zamorski *et al.* 1995: 36)

During this second phase we several times reached points where what we were striving to achieve was shown to be impossible – if we stuck to the correct procedures. However, many of these key people were able to suggest ways of 'botching things' by using creative strategies to let us meet our targets. The most important of these strategies was to cast the whole of the first year of COMEX's teaching programmes as 'pilots' so that nothing that was decided was irrevocably embedded in the university's infrastructures. This was a strategy, suggested to us by senior academics, that acted to circumvent the procedures implemented by senior administrators as the guardians of quality assurance in the university. The inherent tension between academics and administrators was a feature of the university territory through whose undergrowth we were pushing and we were able to use this tension to gain leverage. Another important strategy was to append the

COMEX masters award to the existing masters-level awards (MLAs) in EDU. This required only minor paperwork to set up a new pathway to the award for the pilot programme, in which we were greatly assisted by the EDU administrator. We were still required to convince the Senate that the proposed award would meet the university's requirements for high standards, by providing additional information to a joint working group established as a sub-committee of the TC and BOGS to ensure the quality of the COMEX award. This WG was also entrusted with reviewing the procedures and quality assurance processes for the COMEX undergraduate route that would be located within the division of management education (under Tony Brown's purview) rather than EDU but would draw on modules from a number of schools by means of the CCS. A contentious issue, which was not resolved until after teaching began, was whether or not this degree should have 'honours' status.

The third phase of COMEX work (August–September 1994) focused on the recruitment of students. During the summer vacation, before we received the working group's request, dated August 26, for further documentation in response to specific questions, we were producing a publicity brochure for the COMEX programme, the first COMEX newsletter and a range of materials giving answers to frequently asked questions. The newsletter, dated September, included the following boxed sections:

What will employers gain from COMEX?	What will individuals gain from COMEX?
• Better qualified staff • Better motivated staff • Tailor-made consultancy from an insider • A better knowledge base for developing policy • Improvements to functional efficiency and effectiveness • Accreditation for in-house training	• The confidence to take on complex tasks and new responsibilities • The opportunity to fulfil their potential as individuals • The opportunity to enjoy different sorts of mental stimulation • The opportunity to prove to themselves (and their employers) that they're cleverer than they thought they were • The opportunity to make further, faster progress in their careers

We were also engaged in sorting out final fee structures (confirmed by the registrar's office on 8 September), negotiating with consortium members and making visits to our partner companies to meet potential students. A major problem in recruitment was that we had not had time to develop a procedure for accrediting students' prior learning in advance of their enrolment. APL (accreditation of prior learning from courses) and APEL (accreditation of prior experiential learning) were always intended to be key components of the COMEX programmes, but the machinations of negotiating our way through university regulations and committees had meant that we had no time to develop this strand of COMEX work. This was a major discouragement for some who were reluctant to enrol as a student without a significant amount of APL/APEL credit to shorten the period of study. Another major problem was that we had not had time to develop and deliver an induction programme for workplace tutors prior to the commencement of teaching. Since these people were in nearly every case not the same as the company's Consortium Group member, they took on this new role without any real idea of what it entailed. A third problem was that recruitment in this first year was limited to COMEX partner companies and the delays in sorting out the exact fees to be paid to the university made it difficult for the company representatives to decide on the number of students they could support. Unfortunately, it was only at the stage when we had gained approval 'in principle' for the courses that we were able to begin our negotiations with the registrar's office over fees; and the general shortage of funds across the whole university made the registrar keen to set the level as high as possible, while we were keen to set it as low as possible in order to reach our recruitment targets. To complicate matters further the question of overheads on the COMEX budget was raised by an acting manager in EDU, which got us into a minefield on how that budget broke down into research and development component parts. The decision on the name of the degrees (BA and MA in professional development) was not made until the COMEX steering group meeting on 28 September, but was ratified on the same day by the chair of the Teaching Committee who was present at the meeting.

The fourth stage of COMEX, from October 1994, was the commencement of the teaching programme with two cohorts of students, at masters and undergraduate level. Each course began with a three-day residential teaching block in which:

- We focused on the key principles and practices of action research methodology and methods, and supported students in planning their first action-oriented research in their company.
- We engaged students in discussions of interpersonal relations and ethics and they drafted codes of practice to negotiate with company colleagues.

- We worked with them to write the first entry of their research journals 'focusing on a recent incident which was problematic and aroused strong feelings' and then debriefed this exercise 'to construct a list of factors which cause stress in the workplace'.
- Students interviewed each other 'with the aim of collecting their current perceptions of the issue which [would] be the focus of their investigation' and tape-recorded these interviews as base-line data for their inquiry.
- There was also time set aside for questionnaire design and planning
  (quotations are taken from the programmes for the teaching blocks)

Each block was taught partly over a weekend and partly in work time as employers were keen to provide support but also to be seen to require employees to demonstrate their commitment. We did not meet our target of 40 students but, given the pilot status of the programmes and the limited field for recruitment to the pilot (from only COMEX partner companies), felt that we did well to recruit 18. The feed-back from students to the evaluators on these first teaching blocks was very positive. The formative evaluation report recorded:

> All the people interviewed said that they had enjoyed the first three-day courses. They thought they were stimulating and that they had learnt from them. A couple of people believed too much time had been spent on administrative matters at the beginning; that these should have been sorted out beforehand and 'not wasted precious teaching time'. Some people said they were not used to this style of teaching (echoes of traditional chalk and talk in memories) and were pleasantly surprised by the informal, intensive and participative style of the sessions.
>
> (Zamorski *et al.* 1995: 25)

For me, one of the most memorable and treasured moments in my whole career came in the bar on the university campus on that first weekend when a team leader from Birds Eye Walls who had enrolled on the undergraduate programme smiled excitedly and said that he would never have believed that he would one day have the opportunity of attending a university. This man was one of so many who had reached the age of 18 at a time when university education was available to less than 10 per cent of the age cohort. He went on to complete the course and be awarded the BA (hons) in professional development.

Research issues for the COMEX central team

The methodological issues arising from the COMEX action research were both challenging and fascinating. They emerge strongly from a rereading of the extensive data, including the project proposal, official documents of EDU and the university, notes between Dave and myself, records of our interviews with senior academics (cross-checked with each other), notes of discussions with the evaluators, official memos from administrators, informal hand-written notes from the chairs of committees, minutes of Consortium Group and steering group meetings, responses to draft documents from Consortium members and indeed numerous iterations of a set of core documents in which the COMEX degree programmes were defined and codified and created as a 'product.' I will deal with three of these issues here.

The cultural divide between the university and the partner companies

We knew there would be cultural differences between ourselves and our company partners, but the extent of the divide we uncovered was unexpected. At a surface level it seemed to be a matter of language: we valued 'education' and they valued 'training'; we wanted to explore all possible factors in detail before reaching a decision, they found our language in discussions complicated and 'woolly'. At the second steering group meeting in September, our manager from the ED queried why we were using the word 'research' for the students' work-based inquiries; to him 'research' suggested something 'airy-fairy' and 'academic' (intended pejoratively) – he wanted to know 'what's wrong with calling [the students' work] "studies"?' David Bridges recorded in notes on the meeting: 'John Elliott replied that we don't want to collude in this view of research – we are committed to the view that people can and should research their own workplaces and that research can be close to the workplace and has the capacity to inform practice.' Language, therefore, in the Foucauldian sense of discourse, was revealing regimes of truth that constructed the relationship between us and those, like our ED manager, whose identities had been formed in company cultures:

> Each society has its regimes of truth, its 'general policies' of truth; that is, the types of discourse which it accepts and makes function as true; the mechanisms and instances which enable one to distinguish true and false statements, the means by which each is sanctioned; the techniques and procedures accorded value in the acquisition of truth; the status of those who are charged with saying what counts as true.
>
> (Foucault 1972: 131)

Just as John Elliott revealed in his response the extensive body of values and beliefs that underpinned our use of the word 'research', so the very different values of our partners were revealed in their assumption that this, and other words we used, made unnecessary claims of status and power that they distrusted as part of 'the ivory tower' and detached from 'the real world'. Yet the divide was not simple as they valued highly the status of a university degree; several showed themselves to be as keen as the university to ensure that the COMEX degrees were high quality and in no way 'second class'; they wanted what they called 'the gold standard' of the university. The level of possible misunderstandings was immense. I remember that over a conversation at the end of one of the teaching blocks a police officer remarked to me that he envied me my unpressured job. Queried, he further explained: 'Well, you spend all day just sitting around talking.' This was how, as a participant in the programme, he observed me as a teacher, apparently without any awareness that I had had to make huge efforts to clear my desk of all other commitments in order to focus my whole attention on teaching for three days. Because he saw me behaving in this way during the teaching block he assumed that this was what I did every day. He was also probably unaware that informal teaching requires the same amount of prior preparation as the highly structured teaching that he was accustomed to. David Bridges pointed out that one problem was the length and wordiness of the documents we produced for discussion at meetings. Company people were used to far fewer words and were impatient of lengthy documents that they expected to find 'difficult'. This problem, he felt, was rooted in our very different cultural norms, in which those of us in the university expected to have to persuade colleagues through marshalling a rational argument and covering all possible eventualities; whereas those from the companies expected to be given succinct instructions on what to do and how to do it. Their line management systems made them unused to the process of negotiation; while for us this process was a core value in establishing a socially just partnership. The matter was further complicated by our need to negotiate documents on two fronts: with both the university committees and the Consortium Group. Documents that were written in draft for the latter were rejected as insufficiently explicit by the former and vice versa. A strategy we adopted to make the lengthy documents agreed with the university more palatable to the Consortium was to produce a summary on overhead transparencies and present this orally. Another strategy we adopted to ensure that Consortium members made an input to the development of COMEX's practice was what David Bridges called 'Bridget's approach to "enforced participation"', in which during one meeting I asked them to commit their responses to paper. This he felt had several advantages:

It did gently but firmly commit everyone to making a contribution; they made their contributions privately and independently;
it meant (I think) that you got something in answer to every question from everyone; you got it in written form – so it did not get
lost in the discussion; people did start to talk around their writing.
(evaluator's reflections on COMEX Consortium meeting, June 27)

Transitions in training and challenges to the status quo

COMEX was funded as part of a long-term government strategy for putting
pressure on universities to introduce new kinds of awards that would have
more immediate relevance to business and industry. When our ED manager
pushed us to introduce sub-degree level qualifications and the Dean of EDU
told Dave and me that, were we to do this, we would be 'threatening the
whole basis of a university', the conflict between policy aspirations and traditions of academic excellence became clear rather than hidden. However,
the university had already begun to move down this path before COMEX
was established through introducing the common course structure; moreover EDU, particularly through the tradition of action research established
in the Centre for Applied Research in Education by Stenhouse (1981),
Elliott (1985) and others, was already well advanced in supporting the
development of professional knowledge generated through enquiries into
students' own practices, in multi-professional contexts. COMEX was, therefore, seen as a timely project by many in the university, but the challenges
its new degree programmes posed to the university's traditional assumptions about the nature of knowledge were so extreme that they sharpened
up points of conflict: in the words of the chair of the EDU Continuing
Professional Development Committee, COMEX's interest in making active
use of the new CCS system was risky, as this was 'a hot topic'. A common
course structure and credit-rating system were both notionally in place, but
many academics and most administrators were taken aback when their
implications were clarified through COMEX's attempt to mix these 'uni-
versity-led elements' with 'employer-led elements', 'prior learning elements' and 'core elements' of workplace enquiry to make up its undergraduate programme. Meanwhile, companies were also experiencing changes
that challenged traditional approaches to 'training'. There was an emphasis
on becoming 'a learning organization' at a time when Senge's book (1993),
newly published, was very influential. The evaluators found evidence in
their interviews of 'a new discourse and concept of training' in the companies. As one interviewee put it, 'the language of training is changing so fast,
and the understanding is falling behind the language learning'. He identified resistance to COMEX in his company, but saw this as 'resistance in
understanding rather than pure resistance'. He saw many of his colleagues

as 'task-driven ... driven hard ... and having to deliver fast on specific objectives' (Zamorski *et al.* 1995: 14).

COMEX was, therefore, attempting to bridge between two distinct systems concerned with learning – universities and companies – both of which were already in transition as a result of external pressures to change their assumptions and practices. The university itself was an employer partner as well as leading the COMEX initiative, since two of its staff enrolled as COMEX students. All of the company partners, including the university, were under pressure at the time to become more efficient and Peters and Waterman's book (1982), as well as Senge's (1993) had established a climate for seeing successful companies as those where employees were given opportunities for learning and participation. Yet those same companies were also engaged in 'downsizing', 'restructuring', 'rightsizing', 'rationalizing' and (for public companies) 'privatizing the service', which were all euphemisms for making staff redundant. Whatever their level in the company, staff were all living with a sense of threat. Dissatisfied with their own in-house training, but wary of investing in traditional degree programmes for their managers, some of the COMEX partners bought into the COMEX vision because they saw it as offering a way forward in an area where they had great need of radical solutions. These comments taken from the evaluation present two commonly held views:

> COMEX is tailored to our needs, unlike some other forms of institutional training which usually come in pre-prepared packages.

> COMEX will help to produce 'hybrid managers', that is, those with 'multi-talents, multi-skills, multi-disciplines, people who can help our organizations move forward, and perhaps even, keep us existing'.
>
> (Zamorski *et al.* 1995: 16)

Nevertheless, the deeper level learning offered by COMEX, embedded in educational rather than training values, was seen as a huge gamble by some, as this extract from the transcript of the Consortium Group meeting on 23 May makes clear:

> There is the issue which came up in our group which is: Would an employer anyway, want to fund an employee on what you described as a generic or holistic upgrading (...) programme where the employer isn't going to get their employee coming back with the specific competence-based skills that they would like to see them upgrading on? – which are very much more focused than your generic more general skills – which are very useful to the

person but not necessarily economically viable for the employer, possibly …

At the heart of this confused debate was the contested nature of knowledge, seen by the university as its core business and source of its claim for prestige – indeed the justification for its very existence. This was at the heart of the continuing debates with the Teaching Committee about the quality and standards of the COMEX degree programmes and the extended checks made within the university before confirming the honours status of the COMEX undergraduate programme. For employers too, although they did not use the term knowledge, the focus was in fact the same: for them the key was relevance and likely impact of the knowledge gains and, schooled in the new discourse of 'learning outcomes' and 'portfolios of evidence' rapidly developing in previous ED projects and some post-1992 universities, COMEX appeared to them dangerously unfocused and 'academic'. New understandings of the nature of knowledge were important outcomes of COMEX (see below).

Tensions arising from the custodial role of the administrative arm of the university

> Custodial: sb. a vessel for preserving sacred objects, as the host, relics etc.
>
> (Oxford Shorter English Dictionary)

The university's administrators were not people I had come across much in my first five years of employment at UEA. I had been located in CARE/EDU, reaching out to schools, local education authorities, government departments and their agencies and other academic institutions. While I was beginning to build national and international networks in the policy and academic communities, the functions and power of the administrative engine of the university had remained unknown territory for me. In the first months of COMEX my attention widened to take in the powerful academic figures in the university: the vice-chancellor, chairs of university committees and the Dean of EDU. At that time, the attendance of a senior administrative assistant and the university's validation officer at the COMEX steering group meetings appeared to be a device for providing us with support. Summaries of things that Dave and I needed to do, which they sent us after SG meetings, were seen by me as useful checklists rather than mechanisms of control. The EDU school administrator was always immensely supportive, sometimes taking off our hands tedious jobs like the drafting of programme regulations. It therefore came as a great surprise to receive, on 14 July, a memo from the academic registrar that adopted a punitive and threatening tone:

- The first paragraph contained the sentence: 'I am writing to express my serious concerns about the production of the leaflet advertising Comex [sic] and to suggest a way forward to meet my concerns.'
- The memo went on to accuse us of failing to comply with the requirements of the Senate at its meeting on 15 June, and instruct us to take specific actions ('I would be grateful if the Comex project team would address these issues and liaise with x and y to ...').
- It informed us that he had 'stopped the print run' of our publicity leaflet.
- And went on to provide 'a series of suggested modifications to the leaflet which I would be grateful if you would implement'.
- Finally, it reprimanded us for 'the lack of clear communication between the project team and the academic division'.

The authoritative tone of the memo and its impact on the Dean of EDU to whom it was copied and to whom Dave immediately wrote a detailed response, signalled that here was a coercive force of which I had previously been unaware. What is interesting about this story is the way that it illustrates the function of the administrative arm of a university. Subsidiary to senior academics in terms of their service role, they are nevertheless the guardians of quality, upon whom the vice-chancellor relies to make sure that regulations are solid and procedures are followed to the letter. The most senior administrators are like sleeping lions that you disturb at your peril. COMEX was a potentially revolutionary force, seen as a threat to the sacred relics of quality and for this reason we must have attracted the anxious attention of the most senior administrator in the university over many months, which boiled into fury when he saw our leaflet apparently confirming his worst suspicions. His required changes to our leaflet all reduced the product 'offer' while clouding it in imprecise language ('woolly' as our partners would call it). For example:

Page 3, final para
Replace 'COMEX will give credit for what you have already achieved'
With
'Via COMEX you may be able to claim credit for previous study and learning undertaken at work'.

As one senior academic put it in interview with the evaluation:

> But what the project does suffer from is, and this in a sense shows how sensitive the project is … Normally we do lots and lot of projects, and, we just go ahead and do them. It'll be only once in a blue moon that anyone from over there in the Registry would say, yeah, don't like what you've doing. But with COMEX, it's regarded as highly sensitive in the University. We keep getting messages from the Registry that say, you can't say that, you mustn't say that, you must do this, you mustn't do that.
>
> (Zamorski *et al.* 1995: 33)

But perhaps I learnt most from the way that Barry MacDonald, as Director of CARE, responded to this memo on his return from holiday. Dave had gone carefully through each point and provided evidence that we had already covered all the requirements of the senate and held extensive negotiations with the working group set up to advise the Teaching Committee and BOGS. The problem appeared to be that the senior administrative assistant, on holiday at the time our leaflet crossed the desk of the academic registrar, had failed to keep him informed. On his return Barry, who was undoubtedly annoyed that the memo had been copied to the Dean but not to him, replied as follows:

> Thanks for the (belated) copy of your memorandum of 14 July. I do like, as you do, to keep in touch with critique of projects for which I am accountable. In this case I understand that the communication problem to which you refer in your memo has since been traced to a source nearer home than you initially assumed. Personally I put it down to the World Cup – yet another yellow card that failed to survive the video replay. Not to worry. It's been a long hot summer.
>
> Barry MacDonald
> 22 July 1994

The apparently light touch, the barbed innuendos, the 'boys' club' appeal to camaraderie in the reference to the World Cup, and the final put down of academic to administrator embedded in 'not to worry' were clever, clever. But, of course, as an example of discourse this would have counted for nothing in the world of the COMEX partner companies.

The knowledge outcomes of COMEX[3]

The most obvious outcomes of COMEX were the BA and MA in professional development. These programmes were formally established in the university during 1995–96 and recruited more students in following years. The masters programme was offered for several years to come, but the bachelors programme, which was by far the more radical of the two, ceased to recruit new students after 1997–98. The university was at that time unable to offer the kind of supermarket of courses, with flexible time slots, that would have given part-time students genuine access to modules in the common course structure; distance learning modules in 'Theories of professional development' and 'The history of and central ideas underpinning the market' had been specially developed by COMEX for the BA but the programme did not offer a sufficient range of options to attract large numbers of students.

However, at its core COMEX was engaged in an exploration of the nature of knowledge, specifically what should count as knowledge in the award of a university degree. UEA, founded only 30 years previously, was proud of the high quality of its degree programmes that offered what might be called 'traditional academic knowledge'. EDU, founded later than the rest of the university, had introduced courses with teaching placement elements for its students, but few other schools had similar programmes. There was at that time no business school, no medical school and no school of nursing. COMEX introduced, into this very traditional university, degree programmes that were grounded in a very different epistemology. CARE/EDU had been involved for 20 years in curriculum development work that conceived of children's learning as an active process of constructing meaning from engagement and discovery (Stenhouse, The Humanities Curriculum Project; Elliott and Adelman, The Ford Teaching Project; Somekh, the PALM Project). COMEX attempted to transfer this approach from schools to the university and develop degree programmes in which university students would construct knowledge through engagement and discovery (action research) in the workplace.

Assessment in COMEX was grounded in an epistemology of professional knowledge that conceived of the two elements – coming to know and improving one's practice – as occurring in one holistic process. The assessment of work-based learning should acknowledge and celebrate the value and uniqueness of practitioner knowledge. The starting point was an

---

3 Some of the writing in this section draws on an unpublished paper by Dave Ebbutt and myself entitled, 'The development of a procedure for the accreditation of prior experiential learning (APEL) for academic accreditation at bachelors and masters levels'.

acceptance of Elliott's insight (1980: 315) that: 'There are some kinds of human action which can only be described from a phenomenological perspective, i.e. by adopting the point of view of the agent', and hence that knowledge of human endeavours that excludes the practitioner's perspective is incomplete knowledge. Another key component was a recognition that practitioners' knowledge develops through exploration and analysis of their tacit understandings (Polanyi 1958). Experience per se is insufficient; the habits of practice need to be informed and transformed by reflection-on-action and reflection-in-action (Schön 1983).

The APEL procedures developed in September 1994 and used during November to decide on the award of credit to 16 of the 18 students who had already enrolled were grounded in the concept that expert professional practice is characterized by generic competences that can be identified from close examination of that practice. Behavioural event interviews, based on the work carried out by McBer and Co (McClellend 1978) had already been used by John Elliott to identify the characteristics of good practice in experienced police officers (Elliott undated). To award credit for APEL in COMEX, we conducted 90-minute interviews with candidates, focused on two 'key learning experiences', each summarized in advance by the student in a short piece of writing. Behavioural event interviewing focuses on the informants' detailed recall of their behaviours during the event – in other words what they did, said, thought, felt and why. If the informant starts lapsing into more generalized statements the interviewer must break in and redirect attention back to the specific event. The COMEX APEL interviews were tape-recorded and double-assessed by the interviewer and an observer against each of nine statements of generic competence. Based on work carried out by Elliott and other colleagues at CARE/EDU (Maclure and Norris 1990), these generic competence attributes were divided into three types: conceptual, interpersonal and impacting.

Conceptual

1 The ability to synthesize diverse and complex information in terms of thematic consistencies (patterns of meaning) that link parts to wholes and to communicate these insights to others.

2 The ability to understand different sides of a controversial issue.

3 The ability to learn from experience by reflecting upon observations of one's own and others' performances in the work situation and inductively translating them into practical theory of how such performances can be improved.

cont.

Interpersonal

4   The ability to empathize accurately with the thoughts, feelings and other mental states of individuals.

5   The ability to promote feelings of efficacy in another person.

Impacting

6   The ability to learn interpersonal networks and use them in performing occupational tasks.

7   The ability to discern and develop a shared set of values and goals with the individuals one wishes to influence.

8   The ability to identify coalitions within the workforce at all levels of the hierarchy and assess their value in achieving organizational goals.

9   The ability to think of oneself as proactive – a determiner or cause of events – rather than reactive – a passive victim of circumstances over which one has no control.

These nine attributes clarify the radical epistemology that underpinned the work of COMEX. Knowledge was extended beyond theories and concepts acquired through the exercise of reason in the course of study (reading, memorizing, critically reviewing, conceptualizing new possibilities) to include knowledge-in-action, knowledge sensitive to contexts, emotional knowledge, the capacity to position the self socially and politically so that knowledge can have impact and the capacity to enact appropriate behaviours and exercise agency.

In developing this radical framework for assessing students' knowledge in COMEX, we were influenced by the work of Dreyfus (1981). According to Dreyfus, 'situational understanding' develops through stages (from 'novice' through 'advanced beginners', 'competent', proficient' to 'expert') and it is, therefore, possible to assess an individual's progress through these stages. As understood within COMEX, situational understanding is characterized by knowledge which underpins the ability to handle ambiguity and 'remain open to the situation's backtalk' (Schön 1983: 269). In a professional context this is knowledge that incorporates Aristotle's *phronesis*, in other words knowledge with a moral purpose (Elliott 1989: 83–5; Aristotle 1955: 209) (see Chapter 1).

Of particular interest, for me, were the factors that enabled some managers to build up greater abilities to make judgements in situations of ambiguity and uncertainty than others. The APEL interviews provided a rich body of evidence on their thoughts and feelings linked to specific actions. It was clear that these managers had not merely learnt from experience, but from repeatedly subjecting experience to immediate and continuing reflection, including such behaviours as: observation of others' responses, mental 'replays' with imagined variations, analysis of structural implications, observation of follow-up actions. COMEX was set up on the assumption that these behaviours can be taught and can become embedded in practice through engaging in action research. What we were centrally engaged in teaching becomes clear from what Aristotle had to say about the process of knowledge acquisition:

> Let us assume that there are five ways in which the soul arrives at truth by affirmation or denial, viz. art, science, prudence, wisdom and intuition. Judgement and opinion are liable to be quite mistaken.
>
> (Aristotle 1955: 206)

In the Greek, these five kinds of knowledge acquisition are *episteme* (what is known, believed to be universally true), *techne* (the reasoned process of creating something), *phronesis* (the reasoned process of moral action), *nous* (the state of mind that 'apprehends first principles' – an unreasoned state of knowing) and *sophia* (overarching wisdom). Much has been written about *techne* and *phronesis* in the literature on action research, particularly about the concept of praxis which incorporates critical reflection with moral action (Noffke and Stevenson 1995: 1). What COMEX enabled me to understand was the crucial importance in the acquisition of knowledge of taking the basis for action beyond what Aristotle's translator called 'judgement and opinion', and which I believe is much better understood as 'common sense', to intuitive understanding (*nous*), which incorporates an understanding of underlying principles that govern human action. *Nous*, acquired through the long habit of in-depth reflection on experience, is the set of generic competences that enable managers (and other professionals) to take well-judged action intuitively under the pressure of the moment, despite partial information and ambiguity (Somekh and Thaler 1997).

The work of COMEX served to illuminate, but only partially to resolve the fundamental disagreement between the world of companies and the world of the academy on what counts as credit-worthy knowledge. On the first occasion of awarding credit for APEL the Teaching Committee recommended that the three conceptual competencies should in future be the dominant ones, on the basis that these are outcomes that could reasonably be expected from an academic programme. In the revised criteria, this meant that if candidates registered highly in terms of the 'interpersonal' and 'impacting' competencies but very low on the 'conceptual' categories they would be recommended for little, if any, credit under APEL. However, within the taught (as opposed to the APEL) parts of the BA and MA degree programmes, it was possible to go a considerable way to holding the line against the 'academicization' of the COMEX approach to work-based learning and assessment.

COMEX provided a fully developed rationale for the accreditation of non-traditional forms of knowledge, but the academic system fundamentally undermined this when differential weighting was given to 'conceptual' competencies over 'interpersonal' and 'impacting' competencies. What is of interest, although it can never be more than speculation, is the extent to which this partial emasculation of the COMEX APEL system, thereby considerably reducing its appropriateness to work-based experiential leaning, was intentional on the part of specific powerful individuals in the university or was merely a demonstration of the way in which a complex system such as a university has in-built mechanisms that come into play almost automatically to re-establish the status quo whenever it is disturbed. We did not demolish the ivory tower although we went a little way towards deconstructing it.

Looking back: a retrospective commentary

COMEX clarified for me how action research can provide a broad framework for carrying out exploratory, creative work within a complex, politicized project. We worked with so many different kinds of partners – the representatives from the participating companies, our students who were employees of these companies, colleagues in EDU, and senior staff of both the academic and administrative arms of the university. Action research gave me a belief in our own agency through drawing on the support of powerful individuals who knew how to make things happen.

What strikes me as most amazing about the COMEX project, on re-reading the data, is that we managed to develop the BA and MA programmes in professional development, enrol students and commence teaching, all within a nine-month period. Knowing what I do now about the procedures for developing new degree programmes in universities – even ones like UEA that do not have the tradition of extensive paperwork inherited by some other universities from former CNAA accreditation – I now realize that we could never have achieved as much as we did without the support of both senior academics and administrators. We had the benefit of wise and visionary advice as well as practical help.

The COMEX action research also allowed me to develop the very creative strategy of recasting barriers as interesting research data: I learnt how to stand back from confrontations and view them with the detachment of a researcher, understanding that they originated largely in institutional culture and structures and were not primarily personal. I found that problems could often be overcome through careful analysis and reflection followed by tentative strategic action that attempted to demonstrate empathy for colleagues. This is a technique that is particularly useful for those in management roles.

Learning to lobby for support and manoeuvre through the committees proved to be extremely useful experience for me when I later became a dean at another university. In Project INTENT I had supported others in forming strategic alliances and positioning themselves socially and politically to enable them to have agency within the constraints of organizational structures. In COMEX I had to undertake these processes myself and learn the same kind of generic competences that we hoped to develop in our students. Having by this time developed an understanding of the self as multiple and responsive rather than essential and unitary, based on my reading of Mead (1934), Goffman (1959) and Garfinkel (1984), I learnt that action research provides the opportunity to construct your 'self' as powerful rather than powerless and to seek for ways of manoeuvring towards a goal rather than accepting that it is going to be unachievable (see Chapter 1). I learnt from COMEX that when people construct themselves as powerless they are taking on the role of the victim and this provided me with useful understanding. When I became a dean several years later, I realized that one of the most destructive forces in an organization can be the phenomenon of individuals who create their own manipulative victimhood, seeking subversive power through continuing recourse to complaint and accusation of oppression by 'them', the managers.

The most disappointing aspect of COMEX, looking back, was that only one significant publication sprang from it. Dave published an important article on 'Universities, work-based learning and issues about knowledge' (Ebbutt 1996) but there was the potential to publish more widely than this. My move to a new post with senior management responsibilities, in February 1995, coincided with the start of a new project with funding from the European Union. COMEX's work was only half completed when I left UEA and my attention was drawn in too many directions by other things. A particular disappointment was the failure to secure publication in 1997 of an article on the development of COMEX's new procedure for accrediting experiential learning, jointly authored by Dave and myself. We worked on many revisions to this paper in response to comments from peer reviewers and never understood at the time why the journal concerned finally rejected it. Reading it again with hindsight I can see that the problem was not our lack of an original contribution to accrediting experiential learning, but our insufficient awareness of other achievements in the field taking place in other universities during 1992–97. We sound distinctly 'old university', couching our claim for the originality of our work in a rather naïve and patronizing comparison with the work of 'new' universities ('They tend to conform to established norms for the award of credit rather than priding themselves on their own academic standards.') While this may well have been true – and even beneficial in possibly reducing the problem we faced at UEA of entrenched resistance to accrediting non-academic forms of knowledge – it was not likely to endear us to peer reviewers who would have been drawn from those with greatest experience of devising APEL procedures at the time – and therefore mainly from 'new' universities. There was an extensive body of work on work-based learning of which we were largely ignorant. In some ways this enabled us to address the issues with freshness, but in other ways it limited our understanding of those issues.

7 Action Research in the Evaluation of a National Programme[1]

What kind of contribution can teachers' action research make to the evaluation of a large-scale national innovative programme? Is this one way of giving the teaching profession a voice in the policy-making process? What are the methodological implications for 'insiders' carrying out action research in 'a blame culture'? This chapter is about the evaluation of the ICT Test Bed project, starting in April 2003 and projected to end in December 2006, two years after the time of writing this chapter. The ICT Test Bed Evaluation, funded by the UK government's Department for Education and Skills and managed by the British Educational Communications and Technologies Agency (Becta), is a joint project of Manchester Metropolitan University and Nottingham Trent Universities. Writing about work in progress, rather than a completed project as in the previous chapters, means that I can invite readers to share my thinking about methodological issues that are currently engaging me. The chapter will end with both reflections back on the first two years of the evaluation and forward to possibilities yet to come. At a time when evaluation contracts are rarely for more than two years, and often for a considerably shorter period, the ICT Test Bed evaluation, covers a period of almost four years. This offers a unique opportunity because, for the first time in my experience, the evaluation will have two years to focus on the impact of the investment after the installation of infrastructure and equipment – parts of which have taken almost two years – has been fully completed (Somekh *et al.* 2005a and b).

Reading the invitation to tender (ITT) for the ICT Test Bed Evaluation in November 2002 I was amazed to find that, in addition to measurement of gains in pupils' test scores, action research was a required component of the research design:

---

[1]   The action research work reported in this chapter has been carried out jointly with Andy Convery, Cathy Lewin and Diane Mavers. I would like to thank them for their enormous contribution to the ideas contained here. I would also like to thank Tim Rudd and Di Matthews-Levine of Becta for their valuable advice and support.

The main evaluation will also identify and demonstrate, through *action research*, how the appropriate deployment of ICT may impact upon standards, improve added value, refocus teacher workloads and enable greater internal and external collaboration across the Test Bed institutions. (emphasis added)

Seeing action research specified in a government ITT, as far as I knew for the first time since I had completed work on the PALM project in 1990, I felt a rush of adrenalin in my blood. This was a contract that I very much wanted to win.

I had been inducted into evaluation of government policies for IT in education through working with Barry MacDonald at CARE/UEA in 1987 on a retrospective evaluation of the Department for Trade and Industry's Micros in Schools initiative, 1981–84 (MacDonald *et al.* 1988). Evaluation was always very highly regarded at CARE because of its focus on critical engagement with policy and the operation of power (Wildavsky 1993). Researchers at CARE believed that education, as an essential liberating asset of a civil society, should not be left in the hands of politicians and bureaucrats without scrutiny. Evaluation, in the tradition of MacDonald (1974) and House (1974; 1993), who was a regular visitor from the USA, focused on critical scrutiny of both policy formation and bureaucratic control of policy implementation. Its purpose was to hold government and its agents to account for the spending of public money. Evaluation itself should operate democratically to serve the needs of all stakeholders, rather than merely serving the bureaucratic needs of government administrators or taking upon itself autocratic power. My interest in the special problems of ICT initiatives grew during the course of conducting evaluations under government contract both at CARE and later at SCRE in Scotland. I became increasingly interested in means of maximizing the educative function of evaluation studies, and in the necessity for evaluators to engage in what I have characterized as *supportive evaluation* in order to ensure excellence in innovative ICT programmes (Somekh 2001). Immediately on my arrival at Manchester Metropolitan University, at the end of 1999, I had established the Centre for ICT, Pedagogy and Learning with my colleague, Diane Mavers, and we had already developed a track record for evaluation work. The contract for the ICT Test Bed Evaluation was, therefore, doubly attractive to me, as an evaluation of a major national ICT initiative and one that offered the opportunity to develop a research design incorporating action research.

Designing a 'supportive evaluation' of the ICT Test Bed project

The overall aims of the ICT Test Bed project are focused on whole school improvement (limited in the colleges to three curriculum areas) across five themes: teaching and learning, leadership and management, workforce development, collaboration between the cluster schools and colleges and improved links with pupils' homes and the community. The three clusters, comprising in all 28 schools and three further education colleges, are located in: an inner suburb of a West Midlands conurbation with a large number of ethnic minority and asylum seeker families; a rural district in a former coal-mining area; and a suburb in the east end of London. All are areas of high social deprivation and the aim is to see if very high levels of ICT equipment can make a significant difference to the educational opportunities of children in the area and raise their levels of achievement. Overall project funding in the first year was for £20 million, rising to a total of £34 million over a four-year period. The very large scale of this funding is significant because of the high expectations it raises in the minds of sponsors. Although the schools and colleges were specifically chosen because of the extreme difficulties they faced in achieving high levels of attainment for their pupils, staff fear that the scale of the funding will be expected to produce miracles. Improvements in national test scores and examination results is the expressed aim. These are outcomes that would transform the life chances of the children concerned, but, although they include a measure of 'value added' in relation to socio-economic data, they are crude measures that may not capture fully the different kinds of learning resulting from a technology-rich education.

Supportive evaluation requires a careful balance between adopting an independent stance in order to provide fair and honest judgements and sympathetic engagement with the complexities of the ICT initiative. It involves bringing knowledge from previous evaluations of similar initiatives to assist project participants in overcoming problems and to inform sponsors of the practical difficulties and systemic barriers that are likely to make their initial expectations somewhat unrealistic in practice. This strong emphasis on formative feed-back and knowledge transfer draws evaluators closer to the project participants and has the potential to endanger their independence. However, the alternative of withholding knowledge and watching an initiative fail – or even more likely, watching the project director and participants being blamed for 'failures' beyond their control – is clearly unethical. Evaluators also need to resist the sponsors' instinctive desire to reduce complexity and their tendency to rely too much on quantitative measures of outcomes such as test scores without the benefit of theoretical understandings, developed from qualitative data capable of contextualizing and illuminating the meaning of those outcomes. The subtlety of the evaluation process and the need for evaluators to engage robustly with naïve assumptions that could undermine the reliability and utility of evaluation outcomes were encapsulated more than 20 years ago by Cronbach, himself originally a statistician, who realized that he could not use these methods alone when he was asked to evaluate social programmes:

> The evaluator should almost never sacrifice breadth of information for the sake of giving a definite answer to one narrow question. To arrange to collect the most helpful information requires a high degree of imagination, coupled with the flexibility to change plans in midstudy.
>
> (Cronbach 1982: xii)

The ITT for the evaluation of the ICT Test Bed project required a mixed methods approach, combining quantitative with qualitative methods. This kind of approach is commonly required by sponsors and enables evaluators to provide clear information on the extent of the change achieved in measurable indicators such as test scores, examination results and pupil attendance/exclusion rates, as well as exploring the *process* of change and describing and deepening understandings of the *nature* and *extent* of change. Although a relatively new approach, mixed-methods research in evaluation studies has been well-documented and is now widely accepted (Greene and Caracelli 1997; Greene *et al.* 2005).

In partnership with Jean Underwood, of Nottingham Trent University, we designed a study that combined three quantitative measures including test score comparisons against 'benchmarked' institutions and maturity modelling (Underwood and Dillon 2005) and both 'external' (independent) and 'internal' (action research) strands of qualitative methods. Action research, carried out by teachers, school managers/leaders and support staff, was a crucial element of the research design, but it was to be balanced and triangulated by focused studies of aspects of ICT Test Bed's work carried out by members of the project team. Participants' involvement in action research would be voluntary and, since its extent could not be predicted in advance, the extent of the externally conducted studies could be varied to take account of any gaps in coverage. The merging of action research and independent evaluation in the design of a single study was unusual and, some would argue, foolhardy. The problem lies in the conduct of the work on a day-to-day basis, which requires members of the evaluation team to adopt two rather different types of role: the informality and supportive challenge of a facilitator of teachers engaging in action research; and the detachment and critical questioning of an independent evaluator presenting a fair and balanced account of achievements and problems, albeit adopting a non-judgmental, explanatory stance.

Action research in the ICT Test Bed Evaluation: the first two years

In starting the process of engaging teachers and their colleagues in action research I was unavoidably influenced by my previous experience of co-ordinating the PALM project (see Chapter 4). The differences between the two studies are very great: one an exploratory action research project, the other an evaluation; one with three full-time project officers to work with six–nine schools each, the other with three 'link researchers', appointed on a part-time, 0.6 basis, who must each divide their time between facilitating teachers' action research in a cluster of 9–12 schools and one further education college and collecting their own data for the independent strand of the evaluation. Nevertheless, many of the issues of embarking on leading an action research project involving ICT remained the same.

Action research in the ICT Test Bed Evaluation had three purposes:

1 a source for the larger evaluation team of unique, 'insider' knowledge, developed through engagement in the change process in the context of an established educational system and institutional cultures;

2 a means of supporting the effectiveness of the ICT Test Bed initiative, in pursuit of excellence, by encouraging participants to engage at a much deeper level with its purposes, possibilities and practical problems;

3 a strategy for the professional development of the action researchers themselves, through the cyclical process of inquiry, reflection, evaluation and improvement. This has the potential to raise the self-esteem of teachers and re-establish professional leadership in a major national initiative.

The three original link researchers supporting action research were Diane Mavers, Cathy Lewin and Andy Convery. Tanya Harber Stuart joined the team to work with Cathy in November 2004. Di and Cathy brought to the team extensive experience of researching ICT in education, whereas Andy brought extensive experience of action research, including many years as a member of the editorial panel of *Educational Action Research*. Each of the link researchers worked primarily with one of the clusters, but from the start Andy played a leading role in developing the action research. He and I provided some inputs at an action research study day for the team and he produced the first draft of the support materials more specifically related to action research while Di and Cathy drafted those on qualitative data collection generally. An important occasion for building the team understanding of action research, and the process of facilitation, was a two-day seminar with Susan Noffke, who visited from the University of Illinois,

USA, in September 2003. Other visitors from the international action research community during the first two years were Allan Feldman from the University of Massachusetts, USA, and Dennis Sumara and Brent Davis from the University of Alberta, Canada.

The biggest challenge during the first six months was building relationships with schools, explaining the role of action research in the evaluation, and recruiting volunteer teachers, leaders/managers and support staff to undertake action research studies. Travel time to the Midlands and London from Manchester was a constraint for Di and Cathy but Andy lived only a few miles from the schools he was working with. Since each was employed on the project for only three days a week, an average of about a day and a half was all they could devote to facilitating action research. This time could be used flexibly, allowing visits of two or even three days on occasions, but it was clear that we could not offer a level of support anywhere near as extensive as that enjoyed by teachers in the PALM project. Even Andy, although he could visit the schools and college much more easily, would not have the time for extensive and frequent visits. Our first step was to visit each school, talk through with heads and ICT Test Bed managers/co-ordinators an information leaflet about the evaluation and negotiate with them our draft code of practice. This set out the values and principles by which we would be conducting the evaluation, including that we would: treat all data as confidential but use them as the basis for written reports; always report to the DfEs/Becta in written not oral form (to avoid informal, covert reporting); negotiate case study reports with those concerned in advance of their wider circulation; allow a 'right of reply' in cases where a participant disagreed with any statement in our reports; and publish teachers' action research with their name and the name of their school. In view of the importance to the schools of being publicly accredited for their ICT Test Bed work in a system where education is strongly politicized, we were asked by the ICT Test Bed Evaluation steering group, convened by the DfES/Becta, to change the anonymity clause in the first draft of the code of practice. Originally this read: 'In the reports, schools and individuals will not normally be referred to by name.' The revised version read: 'In the evaluators' reports, schools and colleges will have the right to decide whether or not they wish to be named. Anonymity will be assured where requested. If schools and colleges wish to be named the evaluators will let key people see draft reports at least a week in advance of wider circulation.' Although this clause of the code did not refer to the action research work on which I am focusing here, it was to be important in setting the tone of our relationships with some schools and is further discussed in the section on issues below.

Very soon we realized that to recruit teachers to participate in action research we would have to make exceptional arrangements for the first four months. Di, Cathy and Andy would have to make far more visits to schools than originally planned to get things started, so we negotiated an additional travel and subsistence budget with the sponsors to enable this. I accompanied them on some visits, including attending a meeting of heads in each cluster. They started by asking heads and ICT Test Bed leaders/managers to tell colleagues about the opportunity to get involved in action research and to help them organize meetings with interested individuals during visits to schools. However, it was soon obvious that this was too piecemeal and time consuming, and did not sufficiently signal the importance of action research in the research design. So we decided to hold an action research workshop in each cluster, presented by all three link researchers (and myself on one occasion). These were organized as 'twilight sessions' after school in a central venue and each was attended by between 12 and 20 tentative volunteers. They took place in the second half of October 2003, giving us time to produce support materials to be distributed on the day. The materials contained two sections: Getting Started and Research Methods and Approaches. The Getting Started materials began with basic information in response to the questions 'What is "Action Research"?' and 'Why are ICT Test Bed teachers and leaders being encouraged to do "Action Research"' and went on to give practical advice on 'finding a focus' and 'planning your research', ending with two alternative pro-formas, one for planning action research on teaching and learning, the other for planning action research on organizational change. The Research Methods materials included sections on seven methods of data collection, another called 'making sense of it all' on analysing data and one on 'writing up the research for ICT Test Bed'. These materials were packaged in smart folders branded with ICT Test Bed Evaluation art work and we gave each volunteer a ring binder, similarly branded, to hold their notes and data. The packaging was mainly to distinguish the evaluation from the work of the team at Becta, which was responsible for supporting implementation of the project itself, but it was also intended to symbolize the importance of action research work and give the volunteers a sense of belonging to the larger evaluation team. The evaluation's information sheet, termly newsletters, reports and web pages were all to be similarly branded.

There was real uncertainty in the first six months as to whether the invitation to undertake action research would be seen as valuable by the ICT Test Bed participants. One obvious problem was that they would be expected to focus on some aspect of their work for the ICT Test Bed project, rather than deciding on their own focus for research. Contrariwise, this could be seen as an advantage, since action research would support them in undertaking an innovation to which they were already committed. We offered as many incentives as we could to make the offer more attractive, for example: some supply cover to free them from teaching to undertake research or writing, funding for refreshments at after-school meetings, a flat payment for research expenses in lieu of supply cover if preferred, part-payment of their fees to embark on modules towards a degree (either an MA or a BA – the latter of which was attractive to some support staff). We explored many possibilities for accreditation and, in the end, arranged with Ultralab at Anglia Polytechnic University for ICT Test Bed participants to enrol for modules in their new on-line degree courses. The workshops were very successful as occasions at which individuals made a firm commitment and began planning their study. The link researchers then followed up to provide as much support as they could to those who had produced draft plans on the day, making email and telephone contacts and arranging visits to their schools. We formalized their commitment by publishing a list of 70 names and proposed projects in an appendix to the Annual Report in December 2003. This resulted in an enthusiastic response from the ICT Test Bed Evaluation steering group and offers of extra funding from Becta to support individuals in carrying out their research.

The initial commitment to undertake action research was followed by the demanding task for individuals of carrying out the research. The link researchers made visits, where they could, to facilitate research activities, but their time was limited, and even when appointments were made cancellations sometimes occurred because of illness or pressure of work. Teachers and support staff had to take most of the responsibility for their own research. The first reports were published on the Becta internal Quickplace website early in 2004 and several more were produced by early summer in the rural cluster, where Andy lived close by and, without the need for long-distance travel, was able to provide support more flexibly. Nevertheless, there was a level of uncertainty as to how many of the action researchers would be able to complete and write up their studies. To give a meaningful deadline for ICT Test Bed writing as well as acknowledging the work done, 'celebration events' were organized in the clusters in the Midlands and London during June 2004.

In the rural cluster, where action research work had proceeded at a more rapid pace, a meeting was held to start building a team of research leaders to take on a different role. This new support strategy was piloted from September 2004. A significant group of teachers, college lecturers and support staff in this cluster had by then completed one or in some cases a second or even third report and had acquired significant new skills that we believed could be used to support colleagues. The idea was to maximize the available support and encourage new people to become involved. This pilot strategy appeared to work well and by January 2005 research leaders had been appointed and started work in both the other clusters. In each case a small payment was made, either to the research leaders individually or to their schools, to cover expenses and give formal recognition to the importance of their contribution.

By the time of writing the Annual Report for the second year, in December 2004, the contribution of the action researchers to the work of the ICT Test Bed Evaluation had been significant. During 2004 action researchers had presented their work at several conferences: six at the IT in Teacher Education (ITTE) conference in Chester in July, nine at the CARN conference in Malaga in November, and six at the ICT Test Bed stakeholders' conference, also in November, hosted by Becta in Sheffield. We were also able to include in the Annual Report a cross-case analysis of 23 action research studies, all of which were individually cited in the report.

Research issues for the action research support team

Facilitating action research requires different skills from other forms of research and to learn these skills we needed to organize qualitative team meetings as research events rather than administrative meetings. Administration is important in projects, especially projects that have a large team, because there is so much to be done, often involving quite complex logistics to co-ordinate activities; work for individuals can usually be greatly reduced if it can be efficiently shared. However, in our team we always try to minimize the time spent on administration in team meetings so that we can use them to explore innovative approaches to methods, discuss methodological issues and rekindle our fascination with the process of research. In the ICT Test Bed Evaluation, a key part of these early discussions focused on sharing extracts from reflections in our research journals. The extent to which each member of the team kept a regular journal varied, since journal writing depends a lot on an established habit, but the breakthrough moment was our first 'sharing' experience: the deeply personal nature of our writings and the issues they contained relating to pressing practicalities and demands, the force of the need for interpersonal sensitivity in working with heads and teachers, and the anxieties and loneliness of being the agent for engaging other people to work with us as – what felt like – a favour, were mutually revelatory and deeply reassuring to each other. We had got under the skin of the facilitation process and begun to understand that it has common features for all but has to be carefully customized by each individual facilitator, to maximize the strengths of personalities and relationships and ensure a 'fit' with school and cluster cultures.

Over the first two years, several problematic research issues emerged from these discussions or thrust themselves upon us demanding action. Since the work is on-going these are not issues of historical interest, but the focus of on-going debate. In this section I will explore five of them.

Learning from action research in the context of a society with a blame culture

The present climate of schooling in England includes a great deal of publicly reported inspection and the outcomes of national test scores and examinations are published in the newspapers in league tables that show how schools 'perform' in relation to one another. This has given rise to a culture of blame that is likely to affect the kind of action research that teachers carry out. This issue, which is clearly of importance to all teachers carrying out action research at the present time, has required particularly careful handling within a national, high-profile evaluation.

Action research is sometimes characterized by higher education tutors as research focused on the question, 'How can I improve my practice?' This approach is strongly embedded in a deficit model and reports of this kind of action research tend to focus on the uncovering of problems and actions taken to overcome them. The underpinning assumptions are closely linked to the culture of the student teacher's 'reflective journal' in which, as I was once told by a student in my role of external examiner of a BEd degree, it is hard to judge the amount of 'self-flagellation' to include – it needs to be enough to signal self-evaluation, but not enough to undermine the tutor's confidence in the student's performance: clearly a difficult and risky game to play.

Action research in the ICT Test Bed Evaluation has a different starting point. The focus is on developing new practices to make the most effective, and ultimately transformational, use of new ICT equipment and software. The evaluation team suggests to teachers that they should experiment with using ICT to increase pupils' opportunities for creativity, critical thinking, learning about the learning process and taking responsibility for their own learning. We support the project itself by inviting teachers to take risks and try out new approaches, testing out the new equipment to see if it makes new ways of teaching possible. Some teachers have risen magnificently to this challenge, but almost all have started by simply trying to see how they can use the new ICT, make it 'work' in their classroom, and fit into their current contexts. It is our function as facilitators to help them go beyond the 'practicality ethic' (Doyle and Ponder 1977) and focus on students' learning at a deeper level. We want them to write about the process of inquiry and discovery, probing problematic issues and the difficulties they have encountered, and explaining what they have learnt.

But, there is a real question relating to the extent that teachers can write about problematic issues raised by their action research, in the existing culture of English education. They will be named authors of their reports – since their research is their intellectual property – and the schools where they have carried out the work will also be named. We want them to write about their learning, explaining the problems they have encountered so that other teachers can benefit from their experience; but there is always a pressure on them, varying between schools and clusters in relation to local culture, to write success stories that show their own work and the work of the school in a good light. This is completely reasonable, since the ICT Test Bed schools and colleges are very conscious of their public image. They need to be, in an education system with high-profile, publicly reported inspections that may identify 'major weaknesses' or result in a school being 'placed in special measures'. League tables of test scores and examination results are published in newspapers, parents use them to choose the best schools for their children and if this results in a school experiencing falling numbers, its funding will be reduced and it will need to 'lose' staff. The massive scale of ICT Test Bed funding also means that schools and colleges feel themselves to be the subject of great expectations. They have four years to demonstrate a significant shift in children's achievements as a result of their ICT equipment. In the first year there was a climate of real anxiety in many schools, as they became increasingly aware of the sponsors' expectations for quick results while at the same time experiencing considerable delays in the arrival and installation of new equipment.

Action research reports written by ICT Test Bed teachers and support staff have to, therefore, follow a middle path between explaining how problems were identified and addressed and celebrating the students' and teachers' achievements. Each author has control over the balance between these components, but the context is not neutral as they are aware that identification of a problem could be seen as an implied criticism of the management in their school. As facilitators we have a role in pushing for the writing to highlight the learning that resulted from the action research, but ethically there is a limit to how far we can push authors towards addressing problems. In this context, it is an important feature of our approach to facilitation that we bring with us no assumptions of a deficit model of teachers and teaching.

Adopting the double role of action research facilitator and independent evaluator

I knew when I designed the research to include both action research facilitation and independent evaluation that this might be problematic. What I had not anticipated was that the ICT Test Bed Evaluation steering group would request that we made the naming of schools and colleges the default position in our 'external' qualitative reports. With hindsight I can see that we should not have agreed to make this change. The qualitative reports were originally designed as a series of small-scale case studies, to 'fill gaps' left by the participants' action research. In the kind of politicized education system described in the previous section, publishing case studies of work in named schools and colleges that engaged honestly with the massive problems inevitable in an innovatory ICT project such as ICT Test Bed was bound to be extremely problematic. Reflecting back I can see that during the first 18 months we only managed to make this work properly in one of the clusters, due to the exceptionally open attitude of the LEA in question and its heads. In another cluster the LEA officers were desirous of openness but criticisms raised in an Ofsted inspection a few years earlier made it essential for them to keep a careful watch on how their work was reported. In this and the third LEA, we walked a tightrope between, on the one hand, taking excessive care in the wording of reports that dealt with problems and, on the other hand, engaging in negotiations with heads or LEA officers to make large numbers of subsequent changes to these wordings. The code of practice started with the statement:

> This code of practice will be the basis for establishing a relationship of trust between the evaluators and project participants. It will enable the evaluators to work with participants with respect and sensitivity whilst safeguarding their public responsibility to report fully to the DfES/Becta. It will also help to assure the reliability of data.

The changed code of practice had conflicting implications that potentially undermined these core principles: the relationship of trust was destabilized by sensitivity to exposure in public reports; respect and sensitivity for participants began to erode our duty to fulfil our public responsibility to report fully by making us tone down or gloss over problematic issues in the finally negotiated texts; and the reliability of data was also in some cases undermined by heads' anxieties. The relationships of the link researchers with action researchers were excellent, but in some schools, heads were unwilling for teachers to participate in action research and in some other cases, they needed to be sensitive to teachers who felt the need to write up their research predominantly as success stories.

We found ourselves at the end of the first year needing to restructure some important features of the research design. In the interim report presented to the DfES/Becta in May 2004 we outlined some significant changes to our working methods: from now on we would carry out 'overarching' qualitative studies with a common focus across all three clusters, rather than case studies in one cluster, and schools and colleges would not be named; the role of action research facilitator and external evaluator was split into two in one of the clusters by bringing in an additional experienced researcher, Derek Woodrow, to undertake the 'external' elements of the evaluation work. This had the great advantage that we were able to reallocate more link researcher time to the facilitation of action research across the three clusters. There were financial implications to this decision as the additional appointment had to be made out of current resources, but the gains achieved in terms of establishing trust with participants and reducing the stress on the link researchers made this excellent value for money.

Overcoming assumptions about the purpose and focus of action research

This is another issue that has implications well beyond the evaluation of the ICT Test Bed project. There appear to be very narrow assumptions embedded in English schooling about who are the appropriate people to engage in action research. It appears to be seen as something carried out by teachers in classrooms, rather than by heads and members of the senior management team into their own activities as leaders. These assumptions severely limit the possibilities for action research to support organizational change.

Action research in the ICT Test Bed project is designed to be of two kinds: research carried out by teachers and support staff into teaching and learning in classrooms and related issues; and research carried out by heads and managers with different levels of responsibility into issues relating to organizational development and the management of change. Two separate pro-formas, with prompt questions to assist in research design, were included in the 'Getting Started' section of the support materials and all the link researchers have talked to ICT Test Bed participants about the importance of engaging in action research that covers issues from all five ICT Test Bed themes. Yet, of the first 23 reports published, 12 are by class teachers in primary schools, seven are by class tutors (teachers) in one of the FE colleges, one is by a support assistant in a primary school, one is by a head of department in a secondary school, one by an FE course co-ordinator and one by an FE developer of web-based materials. All 23 studies focus on issues related to teaching and learning with ICT and of these 18 provide insights into the processes of teacher professional development. A further six focus on issues related to improving links between homes, schools and the community. There are no studies focused on leadership and management issues. There are some such studies in the pipeline at the time of writing, but it is significant that this important area of ICT Test Bed work is not covered in the first batch of published reports. Moreover, in these first 23 studies, some schools are well represented and others not at all: the 14 school-based studies are drawn from just eight of the 28 schools and all nine FE-based studies are from the same college.

There seem to be a number of factors that shaped this profile of the early action research studies:

- One appears to be an assumption that action research is something that teachers do in classrooms; there appears to be little knowledge, at least among heads, of action research as a methodology for researching the management of change and organizational development. Our approach to overcoming this problem has been to promote the idea, in the second year, of heads and managers reflecting back on what they have achieved in the first year, the problems encountered and the means by which they were overcome, and writing retrospective accounts of this important process before their 'insider' knowledge of the process is lost. Although this is not the usual approach to action research, if such studies involve the collection of data they have the potential to deepen understanding and influence future action. Retrospective reflections can be collected easily from colleagues to extend and triangulate the managers' own memories of events and much documentary data exists in the form of records, reports and minutes of meetings produced at the time.

- We have also been met by the assumption, on the part of one of the secondary heads, that action research is something that primary teachers engage in, but not secondary teachers. There are only five secondary schools participating in the ICT Test Bed project but they are all much larger than the primary schools, so this imbalance in participants cannot be by chance. The crucial factor in all the research-active schools seems to be the active support of the heads – who may not be interested in doing action research themselves but are clear about the value of members of their staff undertaking it. This is very much in line with what is already known about the crucial role of leadership in ensuring the success of innovatory programmes. A strategy which has been very successful in increasing action research activity in the case of one secondary school (but not in another) was our drawing its importance as a mechanism for supporting ICT Test Bed implementation and teacher professional development to the attention of the head during the course of meetings or interviews on other matters.

- Other factors that have acted as systemic barriers to participants engaging in action research have been Ofsted inspections and disruptions in ICT Test Bed management due to a key member of staff leaving and a delay in making a new appointment.

In the end, however, a considerable body of action research was carried out and reported in the first two years and, as in a steeplechase, the field is likely to become very spread out. Teachers and heads/leaders in several more schools are now engaged in action research and part of our job as facilitators is to encourage more ICT Test Bed participants to take part, so that the published reports over the next year cover a much larger proportion of the issues related to the five ICT Test Bed themes. The back-up strategy of carrying out our own independent qualitative studies has proved to be essential, however, most of all because it means that we have no need to attempt to pressurize staff of the ICT Test Bed schools to take part. Action research in ICT Test Bed is essentially, and importantly, a voluntary activity.

Integrating action research in the evaluation with ICT Test Bed project work

In May 2004, at the same time as we made some important changes in the design of the qualitative studies and split the roles of facilitator and independent evaluator in one of the clusters, we found the need to look again at the relationship between the evaluators and those supporting the project itself (LEA personnel and members of the Becta team).

Shortly after we started work on the evaluation the DfES transferred its management to Becta, the organization that was already responsible for leading the implementation of the ICT Test Bed project. I was aware that there were serious implications for the independence of the evaluation in having it managed by the agency whose work in leading the project we were, in part, contracted to evaluate. I took various very specific steps to try to draw a demarcation line between the evaluation and the project itself, such as: developing a separate evaluation 'brand' for materials we gave to schools/colleges and our publications; communicating always with the manager of the evaluation at Becta rather than the manager of the project; and dealing directly with schools rather than ever going through the Becta support officers who were working with each cluster. At first my approach was interpreted by some Becta staff as a form of empire building, particularly in relation to the 'branding' as the project itself had nothing equivalent. However, once I had fully explained the reasons, our Becta manager and the project staff appreciated the importance of signalling our independence. They strongly supported us, for example, in the need to use our ICT Test Bed Evaluation identity on the Becta research website – a considerable achievement given the insistence of website managers in all companies on presenting a single corporate identity.

However, the curious features of a research design, incorporating both 'internal' and 'external' elements and, in the former, adopting the most participatory approach possible – action research – made this separation result in a dislocation of the action research activity from the development activity in the schools and colleges. The 'support for development' role that Becta was undertaking would more normally in other projects have been part of the role of the action research facilitator – as it was in the PALM Project. When we began to find that some heads were not supporting their staff's action research activities, and seemed to be regarding action research as an optional extra with no integral connection with development work in the ICT Test Bed project, we realized that the separation between the internal element of the evaluation and the implementation of the project itself was untenable. We needed the help of the Becta implementation team, without which the action research would fall into what we called 'a hole in the middle'. We had to go back and ask for their help.

At a meeting with the Becta implementation team and LEA representatives, early in May, 2004, we presented a discussion document that included the following:

Questions:
Do all school management teams realize that their staff's action research contributions to the ICT Test Bed Evaluation are a central part of the ICT Test Bed project's work?

Do those responsible for ICT project implementation see it as part of their role to encourage staff of the schools to undertake action research?

Who is responsible for ensuring that the internal evaluation work being undertaken by schools (as per their action plans) is passed on to the evaluators?

Ways forward:
The evaluators need help from LEA personnel and the Becta team to ensure that the action research work is carried out effectively and the benefits of this approach are maximized.

The evaluators are also embarking on new strategies to get the action research work embedded. This term is crucial.

The meeting accepted the need to emphasize the importance of the action research within the evaluation as a support mechanism for the ICT development work in the project. It was agreed that henceforward the link researchers would keep in much closer contact with both the Becta representatives and LEA personnel in each cluster and that they would assist in encouraging headteachers and their staff to get involved in action research, as well as in practical matters such as setting up meetings and organizing venues. In practice, this worked well in two of the clusters but there was little difference in the third. However, the overall effect of inviting closer collaboration with those supporting the project's implementation was beneficial.

The nature of action research reporting in the ICT Test Bed Evaluation

Writing is a particularly important part of carrying out action research but many teachers regard it with anxiety as a difficult challenge. For some, the fear of writing acts as a barrier that prevents them from getting started. It seems certain that this has been largely caused by the association of writing with academic accreditation and a range of related assumptions about the nature of the writing that should be produced. This is a pity because action research reports written for an audience of teachers and policy makers do not need to be of the same kind as those written for masters degrees.

A crucially important aspect of the ICT Test Bed action research has been the reports written for publication. Our strategy evolved over time but always included the requirement for a short written report as a contribution to the evaluation that would be published on the web. Initially we asked for reports of between 500 and 700 words, keeping them short both to reduce the work load for action researchers and make them readable for visitors to the website. In the end, reports have tended to be nearer 1000 words in length, because making them any shorter would, paradoxically, have involved more work for their authors and made it impossible to include important background information.

Several issues have arisen in relation to our evolving understanding of the purpose and nature of the teachers' writing during the first two years:

- First, it was clear that a large part of its value would lie in its early publication, to give the voices of teachers prominence in the ICT Test Bed Evaluation and to allow teachers to read each other's reports while the project was still in progress. This meant we had to seek permission from the ICT Test Bed Evaluation steering group to exempt the action research reports from the contractual restrictions placed on reporting the main evaluation work. This was agreed in principle in June 2003: action research reports could appear in cluster newsletters or the ICT Test Bed Evaluation newsletter as well as being placed on a public website once this was developed.

- The next important decisions related to ensuring the quality of action research reports published in the public domain. It would be important for the authors, as it was for the ICT Test Bed Evaluation as a whole, for the quality of the writing to be as good as possible. The procedure that eventually evolved was for link researchers to advise authors on the improvement of first drafts, and for revised drafts to be read and commented on by the team of link researchers, myself and our Becta manager. The drafts are then revised and improved to the author's satisfaction – depending upon the amount of time the author is able to give. In practice this process becomes one of taking each report as far as the author is prepared to go: the link researchers have to make sensitive judgements as to what it is fair or possible to ask of very busy people, and whether the revised report, as it stands, is of sufficient interest to warrant its publication, despite what might be added or edited in a perfect world.

Initial discussions with our managers at Becta raised a number of issues/decisions with which both Andy and I were very familiar from teachers' writing in previous projects, articles submitted by teachers to EAR, and the work of teachers with funding for DfES Best Practice Research Scholarships, which had been an important strand of national education policy in the years immediately prior to the start of the ICT Test Bed Evaluation. These issues included: whether or not writing should be in the first person; the level of formality/informality of the tone; acceptability or otherwise of colloquial English with regional variations; the nature of knowledge claims; and 'what counts' as evidence to support knowledge claims. These issues were hotly debated both within the team itself and with our Becta managers. It was clear that there were two important jobs to be done: first, to take decisions on methodological grounds to ensure that the teachers' writing presented what might be called their 'authentic voice' and would provide us with the unique 'insider' knowledge that we could otherwise not access; second, to find a way of informing evaluation steering group members and other ICT Test Bed stakeholders of the kind of teachers' writing they should expect to see. The strategy we agreed with our Becta managers, following very full discussion of all the issues, was for the nature of the action research writing to be clearly described and explained in the autumn 2004 Interim Report, the first 23 action research reports to be included as Part 2 of that report and published one month later unless anyone from the evaluation steering group had come back to us with queries in the meantime. We also had the opportunity to raise awareness of the issues surrounding teachers' writing, and the reasons for the approach we had adopted, in a presentation to the ICT Test Bed Stakeholders Conference organized by Becta in November 2004. This was well attended and the audience included senior representatives from both the DfES and Becta's 'communications' directorate, the two groups that might have been most likely to question our approach. We characterized the teachers writing in this presentation as follows:

- Written for teachers, parents, policy makers and the evaluators
- Short (normally around 1000 words)
- Outcomes of work undertaken alongside carrying out a full-time job
- Normally first-person narratives

- Incorporating an account of the initiative and the research process
- Intended to give a sense of what anthropologists call 'being there'
- Sometimes generating questions as well as knowledge
- Often leading the author into follow-up action research

In a second slide we added:
- Action research reports should offer 'engaging evidence that will excite identification and discussion'
- Should employ the language of the staff meeting

Generating knowledge from action research in the ICT Test Bed Evaluation

A main purpose of the action research in the ICT Test Bed Evaluation is the generation of 'insider' knowledge that would otherwise be inaccessible to the evaluators. The vision is of teachers' action research reports contributing to the evaluation on two levels: first, as research case studies in their own right and, second, as 'second-order data' on which the evaluators can carry out cross-case analysis. This reading of the reports in the light of one another, including systematic mapping of contents, cross-checking of themes and meta-analysis to look for trends and gaps, is a process intended to generate more reliable knowledge about the process of ICT innovation than can be produced by a single action research study.

In October 2004, 23 completed reports had been included as Part 2 of the autumn term Interim Report and by means of the strategies outlined above, these gained evaluation steering group approval for publication on the ICT Test Bed Evaluation's pages on the public Becta research website. Although the setting up of this website took some time, due in part to the need for it to have the evaluation's branding, these reports were all in the public domain by Easter 2005.

In preparation for writing the Annual Report in December 2004, Andy produced the first draft of a cross-case analysis and we worked together on a final version that was included in the report as Chapter 4, entitled, 'ICT Test Bed from the inside – evidence from action research carried out by ICT Test Bed teachers and para-professionals' (Somekh *et al.* 2005b). The process we adopted was similar to that we had used in the PALM Project, itself based on my experience of participating in cross-case analysis of the teachers' research studies in the TIQL project. The difference this time was that we did not involve the teacher–authors in this meta-analysis.

The theoretical underpinning for cross-case analysis of action research comes from the work of Stenhouse. He had a vision of teacher–researchers and professional researchers working together to develop educational theories as the basis for the improvement of teaching and learning (Stenhouse

1975: 142–65). Stenhouse urged the importance of teachers' research studies being written up and published to provide a core of professional knowledge. He compared the accumulation of teachers' reports of their own work with the accumulated knowledge from case studies in medicine and believed they would provide a unique core of knowledge to assist 'professional researchers' in developing explanatory theories:

> Professional research workers will have to master this material and scrutinize it for general trends. It is out of this synthetic task that general propositional theory can be developed.
>
> (Stenhouse 1975: 157)

The outcomes of the cross-case analysis supplemented and extended the knowledge generated by the external strand of the qualitative evaluation. For example, across all the action research studies it emerged that the main value primary teachers saw in using an interactive whiteboard was the clarity with which it enabled them to present concepts and information to the whole class, and their ability to gain the sustained attention of children who normally had very short attention spans, including those who had been diagnosed as being on the autistic–asperger continuum. These teachers' action research studies did not focus much on uses of interactive whiteboards which gave children opportunities to be creative, to take a lead in interacting with the board, and to take responsibility for their own learning. Other teachers' action research studies focused on children's creative activities, problem solving and independent learning, but these were in the context of student-led use of ICTs such as laptops, digital cameras and video-recorders. This finding was immensely useful to us in our continuing exploration of the impact of ICT on pedagogic change, as opposed to improving the effectiveness and increasing the pace of delivery of knowledge and information through traditional pedagogies. This issue was important because the quantitative data from the pupils' responses in questionnaires had identified an apparent trend towards greater variety in teaching methods and we needed to investigate what pupils understood by greater variety. Was the use of the interactive whiteboard *itself* seen by pupils as a radical change, rather than them meaning to refer to changes in pedagogy that might, for example, make their learning more interactive or more personalized? The results of our observation study in the 'external' evaluation, when put alongside this strong trend in kinds of IWB use reported in the teachers' action research studies, confirmed our suspicion that half way through the ICT Test Bed project's lifetime this was probably the case.

Reflections on future possibilities

The process of writing this chapter has been generative of considerable reflection. Rereading the data from the early days of the project and reviewing the stages we have gone through within the central team, our analysis of problems as they arise and the necessary actions we have taken, has revealed the extent to which we, as a team, are engaging in our own action research into both elements of our work: our facilitation of the teachers' action research and our conduct of the evaluation as a whole. The close working relationships established in the central qualitative team, of whom Di, Cathy and I have now worked together for five years, and Andy and I have collaborated at various times over many years prior to the two years on ICT Test Bed, have made it possible to address even the most problematic and emotionally draining issues arising from our work directly and honestly, providing each other with considerable support.

Lots of questions emerge

How can we best take forward the process of cross-case analysis, in particular, can we draw the teachers into this process, perhaps by producing succinct summaries of the outcomes and asking them for comments? Methodologically, we need to involve them in this process if we can, because analysis from the outside only will necessarily screen out some important insights. But will teachers who have already given up so much of their time be interested in this meta-analysis (especially remembering that on the whole the PALM teachers appeared not to be)?

Could we make better use of the action research support materials we developed in the first year. Could these be used by research leaders in their current form or should they be reduced and rewritten in a simpler form. Such a decision would need to be taken carefully as there is a danger of reducing the materials to little more than outline 'tips'.

There is also the question about how best we can report the outcomes of the teachers' action research in future reports. In our next Annual Report we want to present the outcomes of the quantitative and qualitative research holistically rather than in two separate parts. For the first two years this was not possible as the year two quantitative data were not available to make comparisons with year one data. Next year we will need to find the best way of presenting the outcomes of both strands integrally, in an appropriate form. Will it also be important to integrate the outcomes of the action research with these other two strands, rather than presenting them in a separate chapter as we did in the 2004 report? And how will that influence our choice of the most appropriate form and tone of reporting?

The ICT Test Bed Evaluation steering group members have already said that they would like us to conduct a follow-up interview study with those who have carried out action research to identify the impact of their involvement. Some teachers have already spoken of feeling 'transformed' by the process, one said something along the lines of, 'I can't go back to being the same as I was'. This teacher felt the urge to build on her new skills and was unsure how this would be possible. We need to track what happens to this teacher and others like her. Maybe we also need to find out if those who have written up their action research have gained something significantly different from others who carried out data collection but failed to bring their work to a written conclusion.

Over and above building on the action research studies already undertaken and encouraging others to begin participating, there is an enormously important job for the central team in finding ways of bringing teachers' voices to the forefront of our reporting. It will be important to develop different kinds of reports for different audiences and it may also be important to integrate the outcomes of both the 'inside' and 'external' evaluation work in various kinds of publications, so that we do not risk the danger of teachers' publications being accorded a lower status.

Two issues of possible methodological significance also emerge

The low level of facilitation for the ICT Test Bed action research may be important in increasing its independence and giving participating action researchers a higher sense of ownership than they would otherwise have achieved. The low level of staffing to support this aspect of the evaluation's work has posed a problem for us throughout the first two years, but this has pushed us to develop approaches to facilitation that are necessarily different from those in previous project such as TIQL and PALM. The strategy of appointing teachers as 'research leaders' appears so far to be very successful and in the remaining two years we will be able to track its impact on the nature of the action research and the quality of its reporting. It may be that it will lead to studies that reflect teachers' discourse and culture more accurately and, in that sense, can be said to have greater authenticity.

It may also be that the involvement of teacher–evaluators, in an extended evaluation team, will give us better leverage to influence future policy development. In the current climate of an education service in the media spotlight, in which there is an increasing emphasis on the need for government and the DfES to be sensitive to teachers' needs and in which educational researchers based in universities are not always highly regarded, the findings from the action research could be a means of gaining media attention. Our effectiveness in promoting the voices of the ICT Test Bed teachers and heads may not only be important in restoring status and control to the profession, but important also as a strategy for greatly increasing the impact of the evaluation on future national policy.

8 Action Research and Innovative Pedagogies with ICT[1]

Could we organize teaching and learning in radically different ways now that we have the internet, internet-look-alike CD/DVD materials, digital imaging, video and other new technologies? What kind of action research partnerships can support this kind of radical change? Since 1984, when I first took a BBC 'B' computer into my classroom and worked with children on how it helped them improve the quality of their writing, I have known that computer-based technologies disrupt classroom behaviour patterns and have the potential to change teacher–learner relationships and give learners greater autonomy. Over the intervening 20 years I have traced the process of promise and disappointment, been excited by Papert's claims that through logo programming children could develop high-level thinking abilities (Papert 1980), been fascinated by exploring with teachers how computers could enable pupil autonomy (see Chapter 4) and delighted by the innovative work of teachers and students in the Apple Classroom of Tomorrow schools (Sandholtz *et al.* 1997), become inspired by Alan November's vision for transforming schooling (November 2001), but have been forced ultimately to recognize the reality that in the majority of schools very little has actually changed. At the IT in Education conference in the USA in 2000 I heard a keynote presentation launching the US federal government's Teachers Training with Technology (T3) initiative in which the programme's director spoke of 'being on the launchpad' to begin using technology in education. It was as if the previous 15 years of investment in computers in schools, and support and action research by people like myself, had never been. I felt incensed by his assumption that we had achieved nothing. Yet, the ImpaCT2 evaluation of the impact of the UK government's substantial investment in information and communication

---

[1] The research reported in this chapter was carried out jointly by myself and Matthew Pearson. I would like to thank Matthew for his enormous contribution to the ideas contained here. I would also like to thank Lesley Saunders of the GTC for her great encouragement and support.

technologies for schools (ICTs), which I co-directed in 2000–02, found little evidence of gains in pupils' educational attainment resulting from ICT (Harrison *et al*. 2002); indeed, most pupils across the age range 9–16 ticked the 'never' or 'hardly every' boxes when asked how often they used computers in English, maths and science lessons.

Many social scientists have written about this mismatch between vision and practice: Becker's US-wide survey in 1998 found that computers were hardly used in the teaching of academic subjects in schools (Becker 2000); Cuban (2001) provided evidence of widespread failure to implement technology innovations; and this American work has been replicated in the findings of Selwyn (2002) in the UK as well as in the ImpaCT2 study itself. Meanwhile ICTs have made an obvious, extensive impact on all other aspects of social life, with computer networks changing working practices, on-line access removing the need to go physically to offices, banks and shops, and mobile cell phones and internet messaging services radically changing the patterns of social life. Take up of these changes remains very variable depending on individuals, but schools are the only *institutions* that appear to be largely resistant. Moreover, there is considerable evidence that many children are making extensive use at home of the internet, communication technologies and other digital technologies such as cam-corders and digital cameras. They are developing high levels of ICT skills and many aspects of their lives outside school are being transformed (through extended 'connectedness' with friends and easy access to popular culture, leading to increased personal autonomy). By comparison, ICT as presented to them in school is seen by many as boring and irrelevant (Somekh *et al*. 2002b; Facer *et al*. 2003: 26–33).

Contemplating these strange mismatches, I felt both frustrated and fascinated. What was it about schools which made the impact of technology investment so disappointing? Could human agency – supported by so many policy initiatives – overcome this settled resistance? The Pedagogies with E-Learning Resources Project (PELRS) was designed as an action research project to see how radical change in teaching and learning with ICTs could be realized in English schools.

This chapter explores the process of change through discussion of the PELRS work in progress. PELRS is an experiment in focused experimental intervention in the English school system, adopting action research methodology. It is a qualitative empirical study that is exploring the nature of transformative learning through investigating what it might look like in practice for children in schools. It draws on cultural psychology and activity theory to provide an underpinning theoretical framework for understanding change for individuals and organizations. Its research design is innovative and perhaps inherently problematic, but the knowledge it is generating is a powerful basis for scenario building to show what is possible.

The Pedagogies with E-Learning Resources Project: an introductory overview

PELRS is co-funded by the General Teaching Council for England (GTC) and Manchester Metropolitan University, from 2003 to 2006 (www.pelrs.org.uk/). It addresses the question with which this chapter opened: Could we organize teaching and learning in radically different ways now that we have the internet, internet-look-alike CD/DVD materials, digital imaging, video and other new technologies? PELRS is led by my colleague Matthew Pearson and myself, working in partnership during the first two years with teacher-researchers and pupil-researchers in four schools[2] in Manchester and Bolton. The schools were invited to join the project because they were relatively well equipped with ICT, some of their teachers were already using ICT innovatively in teaching and learning, and in some cases they had worked with our research group previously. These teachers joined the project knowing that our focus would be on exploring new approaches to teaching and learning with technology, rather than – in the often used phrase – 'starting where teachers are at'. We developed with them an overarching framework for innovative pedagogies, and a small number of more specific, themed frameworks, together with exploratory case studies of putting them into practice. The PELRS frameworks and case studies were put on a password-protected area of the project website as they emerged, so that reporting and dissemination of the work was in the form of a digital ethnography emerging incrementally. In the third year PELRS worked with a larger network of schools, across the UK, who were invited to engage with the case studies, try out new ways of using the overarching and themed frameworks, and contribute new exploratory case studies to the website to enlarge the range of the digital ethnography. With the assistance of teachers and pupils from the four original partner schools, Matthew and I provided regional start-up workshops and continuing on-line support in the third year.

The intention of PELRS was to work with a wide range of stakeholders, including not only teachers and pupils, but school principals, senior managers and policy-makers. The GTC set up a PELRS Advisory Board which included representatives from two key government agencies: the National College for School Leadership (NCSL) and the Qualifications and Curriculum Authority (QCA), and the project also had links with researchers at the University of Cambridge Local Examinations Syndicate

---

2 PELRS partner schools are: Sandilands Junior School, Wythenshawe, Manchester; Seymour Road Primary School, Clayton, Manchester; Medlock Valley High School, Ancoats, Manchester; and Westhoughton High School Specialist Technology College, Bolton.

(UCLES), one of the main bodies responsible for setting and marking national examinations such as the General Certificate for Secondary Education. These links with key individuals, including Lesley Saunders, Policy Adviser for Research at the GTC, provided us with the possibility of indirectly influencing policy development.

Designing action research into innovative pedagogies with ICT

The starting point for designing PELRS was my knowledge of the processes of educational change from years of exploratory praxis. I am using Susan Noffke's definition here of praxis as 'the continuous interplay between doing something and revising our thought about what ought to be done' (Noffke 1995: 1), which she links with the practice of 'critical scholarship.' My research has all involved this seeking for understanding, probing to find possibilities for exercising effective agency and moving towards what 'ought' to be done. The projects explored in the earlier chapters of this book have been one part of that process. Exploratory, eclectic reading of theories and ideas drawn from a range of disciplines has been the other part. There have been times when reading has been crucial in opening up new ways of looking at the world and in some ways the process could be described as a personal tussle between the world of action and the world of ideas. Ideas taken from reading – and from dialogue with colleagues – have been a form of data that I could weave into my action research practice, both in funded projects and my own larger identity project.

To illustrate this process I will focus on five areas of theory that shed light on the complex issues arising from the introduction of ICT. These were all crucial in the design of PELRS, because they provided me with an underpinning rationale for specific features of the research design. They also helped to extend the conceptual framework for the exploratory action research.

Action research in the design of PELRS

Action research itself, with its impetus towards reaching for the possible and overcoming barriers to change through strategic action is the first of these theoretical perspectives and the focus of the book as a whole. In PELRS, as in the projects presented in other chapters, the research was focused on generating local knowledge, opening up possibilities, experimenting with putting ideas into practice and identifying barriers emerging from daily experience, building on the unique knowledge of teachers and pupils, who are the only real experts in their own experience of schooling.

In the design of PELRS we sought to work with teachers as co-researchers rather than asking them to take the leading research role and providing external facilitation and support. Primarily this was because we started with a strong vision of the possibilities for transforming the learning process with ICT and the knowledge that most previous research into ICT use in which teachers had taken a leading role had focused on ways of using ICT more effectively to support traditional pedagogy rather than using it to support the introduction of new pedagogic practices (Sutherland *et al.* 2004; Ruthven *et al.* 2005). We believed this was because teachers, encultured by the education system into practices they had developed and refined through experience, would inevitably be agents of cultural reproduction. We started with the intention to intervene in existing practices and question prevailing assumptions and experiment with possibilities and we recruited teachers who were interested in working with us to this end. Two of the schools we originally approached had very strong traditions for innovatory uses of ICT, two others were participants in an education action zone, which had a vision for technology as a means for transforming education and had created the role of 'ICT innovator' for selected teachers, the fifth, recruited to replace one that had dropped out, was a school where the head wished ICT to be a key driver in the school's success and saw the project as a means of strengthening its proposal to become a specialist technology college.

The second reason for wanting to work with teachers as co-researchers, rather than facilitating *their* research, was our consciousness of the extraordinary pressures under which teachers now work in England, compared with their work conditions at the time of the PALM project (see Chapter 4). It made sense to suggest that we should work in partnership, developing as far as possible a culture of equity and dialogue between 'insiders' and Matthew and myself, and consciously dividing up responsibilities for each stage of the research so that teachers could participate and exercise some control without having to take on too much additional work. First, we developed a draft framework for innovative pedagogy and then discussed and adapted this with the teachers before working with them to develop further frameworks with specific themes ('pupils as teachers'; 'pupils as producers of media'; 'learning on-line'). The teachers then took a leading role in planning and implementing a learning event with the children, on an aspect of the curriculum of their choice, using one of the pedagogic framework themes. Matthew collected data having first consulted teachers on the specific areas of focus and the kinds of data likely to be most useful (usually involving videoing the learning event as it took place, conducting brief, informal interviews with pupils while they worked, and consulting/interviewing pupil researchers in focused follow-up sessions). From the very extensive data collected, Matthew selected video-clips and key points from interviews with pupils (with the pupils' help) and presented these to their teachers for interpretation and analysis (identifying the group as a whole with their permission, but not individuals). The meanings the teachers drew out from these data were centrally important in both developing research knowledge and planning how to adapt and improve the strategy next time. We did not clearly specify the role that the teachers would take in writing (would their increased sense of ownership and the deepening of their understanding resulting from writing justify the imposition on their time?), but it was clear that our success in inducting other teachers into PELRS in year 3 would depend to a great extent on these teachers taking a leading role at the induction seminar for interested schools, midway through year 2, and the regional workshops with participating schools in year 3, as well as providing follow-up support on-line.

Structuration theory and the design of action research in PELRS

The second body of theory that influenced the design of PELRS relates to the nature of institutions that gain their stability from their established structures of roles and relationships and the formal allocation of power and responsibilities (Mills 1959: 29). I have been particularly interested in Giddens' structuration theory (see Chapter 1: 20), which explains the inter-relationship between structure and agency as a process of mutual construction and conformity by participants that, nevertheless, always has the potential to be open to agency and change (Giddens 1984). More recently, however, Bidwell (2001) has shown how resistance to change in schools is often rigidly embedded through oppositions between groups operating within rigid hierarchies. He argues that at times of strong external threat (an example of which might be the punitive system of inspections in England which places schools at risk of being shown to have 'serious weaknesses', or needing to be 'placed in special measures') the internal networks of teachers function as mechanisms that expertly adapt externally imposed innovations to existing practices.

These theories are powerful in providing explanations of the consistent resistance of schools to any radical change resulting from the introduction of ICTs. The core of resistance lies not in any consciously expressed – or even consciously practiced – negativity towards ICT on the part of heads or teachers, but in the instinctive maintenance and continuity of roles and practices. Technology is welcomed but expected to 'fit in' to existing norms and structures. Two examples illustrate this process very clearly:

- First, the early struggle between those who promoted ICT as a 'subject' in its own right, and those who saw it as a set of tools to be used for learning in all subjects, was not played out on equal grounds. The introduction of computers into all classrooms, their use in all teaching and the changes in pupils' learning practices that this implied were too great. By comparison, the structuring of ICT as a separate subject which can be taught in a specialist room (computer lab or ICT suite) and lead to specialist examinations, so that it can become the role of particular teachers – and not others – to use computers in their teaching, has a good 'fit' with current practices. This was what led to the misunderstanding on the part of policy makers who invested in the National Grid for Learning, expecting that this would have a major impact on pupils' attainment in subject learning, only to find through the ImpaCT2 evaluation that the computers and internet links had been used almost entirely in specialist teaching of the subject IT or teaching of (mainly low-level) ICT skills – with the result that there was no significant impact on examination results and test scores in English, maths and science (Somekh *et al.* 2002b: 2–3).

- Second, the successful widespread introduction of interactive whiteboards (IWBs) to English classrooms from around 2003 could probably have been predicted since this was the first kind of ICT that had a perfect 'fit' with current pedagogy. For the first time teachers used this ICT equipment and its specialist software immediately and developed considerable skills in their use surprisingly quickly, because IWBs focused pupils' attention on the teacher's presentation and supported a transmission model of pedagogy seen by many teachers to be essential in preparing pupils for national tests and examinations. By contrast, computer use that involves moving a class to a specialist room, computer use at the side of a classroom by a group of pupils while the rest of the class works on something else and even the use of laptops at a time when wireless connectivity is still often problematic, simply does not provide this 'fit', particularly since 'whole class teaching' has been strongly promoted by policy makers and is embedded in the prescribed pedagogy of the literacy and numeracy hours.

In the design of PELRS we addressed these kinds of unconscious resistance in various ways. For example, by the involvement of heads and managers as well as teachers and pupils, so that different constituency groups within the school would participate in different ways in the action research; by using every opportunity offered by our sponsors, the GTC, to make the work of the project known to those in a position to influence policy development; by making the use of ICT in the teaching and learning of subjects, rather than specialist ICT, the main focus of the project's work, so that there was no danger of it coming to be seen as part of the role of the ICT specialists in the project schools, out of bounds to subject teachers; and by making brainstorming of ideas for teaching with ICT in radically new ways the starting point in planning project work with teacher groups and individuals. Another important mechanism for change was a direct appeal to teachers' primary motivation to help pupils learn: we focused the action research on not just using ICT in subject learning but using it to 'transform learning' and we developed what we called 'an operational definition of transformative learning' to be the core issue in our discussions with teachers. The process of learning would be transformed and the outcomes would be 'transformative' of the learners by allowing them to:

- learn creatively (e.g. contributing, experimenting, solving problems);
- learn as active citizens (e.g. acting autonomously, taking responsibility);
- engage intellectually with powerful ideas (e.g. using thinking skills, grappling with ideas/concepts);
- reflect on their own learning (e.g. evaluating it through metacognition).

This focus in PELRS on specific kinds of learning was important because it by-passed the kind of low-level memory work that can sometimes be seen as effective in preparing pupils for high-stakes tests and examinations. There was also the great advantage that each of the kinds of learning listed drew directly on a current area of policy focus. Educational policy development at the national level, in the same way as educational practice in schools, was a site of struggle. The larger structures of curriculum, attainment targets, test regimes and inspection were inscribed in law and maintained and enforced by quality assurance procedures and, to a large extent, by the vigilant attention of the media. In the spaces between these large structures, however, there was room for visionary policies to develop and be adopted – often despite their inherent conflicts with the larger structures. Hence, government policy documents for ICT promoted visions for the transformation of learning (DfES 2002) and these were often specifically linked with an emphasis on new kinds of learning that forefronted concepts such as creativity (NAACE 1999), active citizenship (DfES 2003) personalized learning (DfES 2005a) and thinking skills (DfES 2005b). Teachers in the PELRS schools liked the approach to learning we were suggesting not only because of their own fascination with the learning process, but because PELRS gave them an opportunity to try out approaches that they had already been asked to adopt, such as promoting the notion of 'pupil voice'.

Theories of pedagogy and the design of action research in PELRS

Theories about pedagogy were the third strong influence on the design of PELRS. My understandings of pedagogy sprang from my early immersion in the concept of the 'process curriculum' (Stenhouse 1975). For Stenhouse, curriculum consisted of the process of teaching and learning, not a set of written prescriptions. It is not a syllabus drawn up by experts outside the school that counts, but what is enacted in the classroom by teachers and pupils. Curriculum is, therefore, all the knowledge resulting from the interactions between learners and teachers in an educational setting. Curriculum includes both what is planned and intended by the teacher and what is modelled by the teacher's practice and norms of the institution. A child will learn what the teacher and school value in terms of relationships from the way they are treated by adults: this is an important feature of the 'enacted' (as opposed to the specified) curriculum, which will always include elements that are unplanned and largely unnoticed and may have unintended consequences that undermine the teacher's espoused values. Pedagogy is the interactive process through which this curriculum is enacted. It is through the interactions of teacher–learners(s) and learner–learner(s) that pedagogy stimulates the intellectual curiosity that is the core element of learning: it is not merely through doing a task, but through consciously tracking the task's process, meaning and outcomes that learning takes place. ICT intervenes strongly in this process of teacher–pupil interaction, partly because it draws the focus of attention away from the teacher to the screen, and partly because the software and/or the special features of the ICT (e.g. digital camera, internet) offer opportunities and interactions from which the teacher will be partly or wholly excluded. Whether through the agency of the software designer or the learner's (skilled) use, the technology intervenes in the teacher–pupil interactions and creates a new process of three-way interaction (Somekh and Davies 1991).

In PELRS one of our main aims was to redirect computer use from specialist ICT lessons focused on skills acquisition to subject learning within the national curriculum. Since the national curriculum was expressed as a set of syllabus specifications and learning outcomes, profound changes in pedagogy, drawing on Stenhouse's concept of a 'process curriculum', could be implemented alongside it provided that assessment procedures were not very rigid. The only real incompatibility came during the literacy and numeracy hours where teaching methods were prescribed as well as subject content. PELRS adopted a combined strategy of affirming teachers in their responsibility for specifying the learning outcomes (often taken from the national curriculum) but asking them to negotiate with the pupils the methods to be used for this learning. After first explaining the curriculum focus and the learning outcomes expected, the teacher invited the pupils to suggest how they should work towards their goal. ICT resources such as the internet, CD-ROMs, digital cameras, interactive whiteboards and laptop computers were available for the pupils to use as they chose and their learning could either be assessed by evaluating what they had produced or, if the teacher found it necessary, addressed in a separate, later task. By adopting this approach, PELRS classrooms changed dramatically in terms of a considerable reduction in teachers' use of administrative and control language: pupils decided how they worked in groups so there was very little need for the teacher to give orders; and they were much more highly motivated and on-task – apparently with much greater investment of mental effort – so that teachers had no need to spend valuable lesson time on issuing reprimands or punishments. These were effects that supported the differentiation of learning tasks to suit individual needs and the flagship policy to personalize pupils' learning (TLRP 2004).

Technologies as mediating tools and the design of action research in PELRS

The Vygotskian concept that all human activity is mediated by the use of tools is the fourth theoretical insight that influenced the design of PELRS (see Chapter 1: 21). We can imagine a very distant past when, without tools – including the essential cognitive tool of language – our ancestors had very limited capabilities. This is akin to the state of a new-born baby. Language, as it develops, transforms possibilities, allowing us to develop 'mind', first through the inter-mental processes modelled in early childhood through question and answer with adults, merging into the intra-mental processes of independent thought. Other tools and artifacts such as levers, wheels, printing presses and steam engines are historically and socio-culturally constructed in traditions of use and practice, and cognitive tools such as the periodic table in chemistry, double-entry book-keeping in accountancy and iambic pentameters in poetry are likewise constructions of our culture that enable us to achieve excellence in specific disciplines through traditions of their skilled use. But it is clear from these examples that tools developed in one historical period will not transfer with equal usefulness to the generations that follow. They endure into obsolescence with a momentum of their own: hence, double-entry book-keeping continued to be taught to accountancy students long after its use had ceased in most offices. Equally, the introduction of a complete new tool set – of computer-related hardware and software – produces new affordances for mediating human activity, but these only become fully available once their use has become socio-culturally embedded in sets of practices. Transformations in human activity will occur in some situations but not others, since their integration depends on transformations in socio-cultural constructions of expectation and possibility, as well as the acquisition of new skills in their use.

In PELRS, one of our main aims was to draw young people into the research as co-researchers with us and their teachers, in order to gain access to their unique sets of practices, socio-culturally embedded in their use of ICT in the home (Pearson 2004). We wanted to learn from them. Matthew was able to select the most technically expert pupils from those the teacher suggested by sitting beside them and asking them to show him the software on the school computer and what it could do. The way they used the mouse and manipulated icons, pull-down menus and buttons, as well as their easy use of the keyboard, indicated established patterns of use and enculturation into computer literacy. At any one time, at least four pupils in each of the four schools worked with us as researchers, commenting on current usage of ICT in the school, suggesting new strategies for its use drawn from their experience at home and participating in analysis of video data from their classroom. They were often able to uncover our misinterpretations of data and explain puzzles such as why they did not tell the teacher that they found a particular piece of maths software boring ('If we did we might not get to use the computers at all, and that would be worse') (Pearson, 2004: 7). There was, of course, an equity issue here as we were spending more time with some pupils than others, but the expert knowledge of these individuals was crucially important to the research, so we worked with them occasionally and intensively while trying to find other ways of involving the rest of the pupils. In addition to their expertise in computer use, we looked for a balance of gender and ethnicity in the four we selected; it also happened often that the pupil–researchers were not all obviously clever and socially advantaged by comparison with their classmates, since fascination with computers seemed to be a classless phenomenon and spending a lot of time on computers at home was not necessarily charac- teristic of children who were high achievers in the school system.

Activity theory and the design of action research in PELRS

The fifth area of theory that influenced the design of PELRS is activity theory, which incorporates the Vygotskian concept of tools *mediating* human action within larger organizational structures. Its first principle is that human activity is never individual and isolated, but is always integrally part of an activity system. Human activity is not carried out by the *agent* alone but by agents held in tension with mediating tools and focused on a socio-culturally constructed *object*: the affordances of the tool may either enable or constrain particular kinds of activity and the object of the activ- ity is constructed not only by what the agent sets out to achieve, but by what the *mind* sees as possible/expected/desirable in that particular setting under those particular circumstances. The notion of *situated cognition*, with its insight that learning is shaped by the context and is most often a joint and *distributed* process between different minds is a key to understanding activity theory (Brown *et al.* 1989; Salomon 1993). Activity theory does not distinguish between learning and activity but assumes that learning is not something special, separated from activity, but is a necessary and continu- ing outcome of all experience (Lave 1996). Yet, the situated experiences of here and now are always located in a cultural–historical tradition that shapes and constrains the way that minds engage with them. In this sense there is no independence of mind from context and context has a historical dimension, promoting in the present the possibilities offered by structures and tools developed in the past (see Cole 1996: 104).

This basic tripartite relationship between agent, object and mediating tools or artifacts is often represented in a simple triangular model. To represent an activity system, Engeström has added an organizational/ institutional dimension by extending the model to incorporate a number of overlapping and interacting triangles (Engeström 1999):

Figure 8.1: *Model of the activity system, adapted from Engeström (1999)*

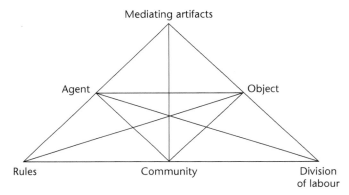

The new points on the extended diagram of the activity system are rules, community and division of labour. They represent the organizational dimension within which human activity is always located. At the centre bottom is *community*, which incorporates the cultural norms and structural hierarchies of the organization, the bedrock of 'belonging'. To the left is *rules*, which govern the behaviour of the agents in the organization, both the explicit and unspoken behaviours to which agents in this organization are expected to conform. To the right is *division of labour*, which governs the roles of individual agents, allocating specific tasks, ascribing expectations of specific behaviours, according different levels of status, categorizing and compartmentalizing the joint organizational endeavour.

Like all models, the activity system diagram is extremely simplified and Engeström was later to develop an extended diagram showing how activity systems interlock with one another and should not be seen as self-standing, separate entities (see Daniels 2001: 92). But for me, as always with models, its simplicity is its great strength. In the design of PELRS action research the activity system model acted as a heuristic device to allow Matthew and myself to play with ideas and formulate possibilities. My starting point was reviewing my experience of schools, looking for evidence of the rules, community practices and divisions of labour that were preventing the power of new ICT tools from being used effectively. They were easy to identify: the system of high-stakes tests and examinations was embedded in the culture of the community with the consequence that teachers often suggested leaving innovative work with the children until 'after SATS' in the last six weeks of the school year; rules regulated a host of matters such as children's movement around the building, their access to computers and the internet and many related matters such as permission to save to the server, print out hard copies, and download new versions of software to enable resources accessed over the internet to run; divisions of labour governed who was a learner and who was a teacher (with the unhelpful assumption that teachers should model 'knowing' rather than 'learning'), who had responsibility for keeping control and who contested that control and who was expected or not expected to have knowledge – constructing through this assumption a sense of threat for teachers who knew less about ICT than the children in their classes (as indeed often happens).

In the design of PELRS, we started from the assumption that the four schools, despite their having been selected for their innovative use of ICT, would conform to the norms of schooling in England, and we looked for ways in which we could disturb these patterns and unlock new opportunities by deliberately changing things like *roles* and *divisions of labour*. One of the most constraining features of the *community* of schooling, we decided, was the system of lesson planning, which was normally done using a proforma with prescribed headings, developed by the Qualifications and Curriculum Authority (QCA). Teachers were not forced to use this planning tool, but if not they had to be ready to explain to the inspectors on their next visit why they were not doing so. This lesson-planning tool was well suited to the emphasis in English education on efficiency, coverage of pre-specified content and testing of outcomes. ICT offers *mediating tools* that have affordances that support exploratory, self-directed learning, but these can be emasculated by enforced containment within the very different affordances embedded in the lesson planning tool. If the aims of 'the lesson', the methods of teaching/learning and the resources to be used, have to be stated in advance that means that the teacher takes all the decisions without consultation with the pupils and greatly increases the danger that teacher and pupils will not share the same *object* in their activity. Without a common focus on an object that has been negotiated, and is at least partially shared (though situated cognition suggests that every individual will always bring different interpretations and expectations to the object), there are very unlikely to be satisfactory outcomes. This risks giving the space for pupils to develop alternative *rules* ('never answer the teacher's questions because it makes you look too keen') and *roles* (clown, gang leader, teenage sex symbol) and occupy their energies in meeting very different *objects* from the teacher (getting through the work as quickly as possible, using the computer multi-tasking facility as an opportunity to play games under cover of an Alt+Tab flick of the wrist, acquiring high status with peers, attracting the admiration and attention of the opposite sex).

To combat these negative features of classroom practices, we developed what we called a *generic pedagogic framework* (GPF), as a model of the kind of innovative pedagogy we wanted PELRS to promote and a heuristic device for planning innovative learning events. Since this was a pedagogic model its basic triangular structure represented the three-way interaction between teacher, pupils and ICT tools described earlier in this chapter, rather than directly invoking the activity system model. It is reproduced here as it appears on the PELRS website (www.pelrs.org.uk). An early version of the GPF was discussed with PELRS teacher–researchers and collaboratively developed and refined. It then became the basis for the development of four 'themed' frameworks which the teacher–researchers used to plan learning events; 'pupils as teachers', 'pupils as media producers', 'learning online' and 'pupil voice'.

Figure 8.2: Reproduction of the 'generic pedagogic framework' from the PELRS website

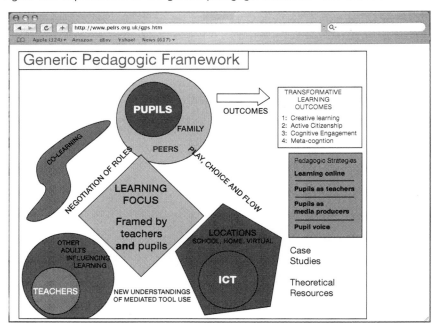

A key feature of this model was that it deliberately avoided some of the discourse of schooling. For clarity, the terms teachers and pupils were retained, but teaching and learning were replaced by *pedagogy*, school was placed in the larger frame of *locations*, the curriculum was replaced by *learning focus* and lessons were recast as *learning events*. The concept was of learning with ICT taking place in a larger frame, incorporating the home and virtual environments as well as the school. *Roles* of teachers and pupils were to be *negotiated* with the implication that these roles could be interchangeable or shared and that *co-learning* rather than individualized learning was assumed. Both pupils and teachers were placed in a social rather than an isolated environment, with the *family* and *peers* interacting with pupils and *other adults influencing learning*. This forefronted the concepts of situated and distributed cognition, emphasizing the social nature of learning. ICT was a set of *mediating tools* over which pupils could exercise *choice* and through which they could learn through *play* and experience *flow*; and through whose exploratory use teachers would develop new understandings of the power these tools offered rather than instinctively taking action to limit their disruptive power and recast them as a limited set of preselected resources. The model intentionally contained an object expressed in terms of the PELRS *transformative learning outcomes*, since PELRS was a project focused on reconstructing schooling rather than de-schooling and the starting point of each learning event was the specification of learning outcomes and a curriculum focus by the teacher. The pupils' role in planning how their learning would take place was given a central position, however, within the *learning focus framed by teachers and pupils*, and the outcomes were not listed in narrow behaviourist terms but in terms of aspirations for deep learning. Wider reading of learning theories by myself and colleagues at MMU and our exploratory praxis in using these ideas in other projects, particularly the evaluation of the GridClub website for 7–11 year old children (Somekh *et al.* 2003), strongly influenced the development of this *generic pedagogic framework*. These included, in particular, Claxton's (2000) work on learning styles, Csikszentmihalyi's (1996) concept of intensive engagement in activity or flow, Lave and Wengers' (1991) vision of learning in a community of practice and James and Prout's (1997) concept of according children the same status as adults by respecting them as full beings rather than merely beings en route to adulthood.

Issues and practices in PELRS action research

In this section I describe some of the methodological issues arising from the PELRS approach to action research. I am drawing on a wide range of project data and some published articles by my colleague, Matthew Pearson.

Issues of power and ownership in PELRS action research

It was central to the design of PELRS that Matthew and the teachers should work as co-researchers and partners, rather than the teachers deferring to him and perceiving PELRS as *his* research rather than *theirs*. We expected difficulties in making this work in practice because of the power differentials likely to be embedded in all the participants' perceptions of the roles of 'teacher' and 'researcher'. However, it remained a key aim.

At the start the teachers participated fully in the development of the 'themed' frameworks and they easily and naturally took a lead in planning the learning events. However, they assumed that Matthew would bring expertise in how to use the technology and concentrated themselves on the logistical problems (booking equipment or rooms for particular time-slots). They were excited from the start at the possibilities offered by the PELRS approach and were able to change their practice by 'letting go' of control and giving pupils real choices over how they learnt and what ICT tools they used for learning; but they adopted these practices initially because we suggested them, without any prior feeling of a need to change, since they were used to conforming with expected practices and doing this very well. They demonstrated, as expected, very strong acculturation in current pedagogical practices, such as 'winding up a lesson' at the end by reviewing what had been learnt and hence seeing each lesson as a separate event rather than part of more extended project work, but were happy to adapt and change these practices following discussion if they could see the possible benefits. In viewing clips of video data, they easily identified what they judged to be gains and moved from speculative trials to embedding the new approaches in their practice. For example, two teachers when watching video-clips from a lesson in one of their classrooms noted that the teacher's voice was not often heard addressing the whole class when the pupils were working in groups, which appeared to indicate an extraordinary drop in the need to give instructions or admonish pupils for going 'off task'. As the video was an extension of their experience of being there, and they could review their memories of the lesson and others in which they had adopted the same approach, they could confirm from extensive evidence that this was indeed a clear gain and *they interpreted* this as resulting from the pupils' enhanced motivation and genuine engagement with the task. *Our interpretation*, which complemented and theorized theirs, was that the *object* of the lesson had been sufficiently negotiated to orient the pupils towards it as their own object and that this then enabled the teachers to adopt a genuinely different *role*, moving towards a *co-learning* stance and away from an authoritarian stance.

It appeared to us that in participating in this action research the PELRS teachers had taken ownership of the new pedagogies they were developing. For example, some engaged without our prompting in a classical action research cyclical process, by using the same themed framework a second time, incorporating changes in the design of the learning event and monitoring the impact on children's learning. Several used the frameworks to develop approaches that went a long way to overcoming endemic problems, such as the use of digital video to record group drama as a means of supporting pupils in speaking a foreign language (pupils as producers of media framework). The power of digital video, in this case, had a dramatic impact on pupils' engagement with the task and the teacher's ability to discuss their work with them while also tracking their learning at both levels of outcome. It seemed that the teachers would almost certainly continue to use the pedagogies they had helped to develop after the project came to an end. Their ownership of PELRS existed in their own classrooms, however, and did not go beyond the school. They probably had not perceived the need to assist us with promoting the project nationally, leaving us with the important job of finding a way to make this meaningful for them so that leadership of PELRS in year 3 could be genuinely shared with us by the teacher–researchers. But the extent of their leadership role in year 3 had to remain theirs to decide.

Issues of discourse and inter-cultural dialogue in the PELRS action research

This inter-linked process of analysis and interpretation of data illustrated the advantages of carrying out co-research led by those inhabiting the different cultures of the school and the university. Matthew's role had often included brokering of language between the two cultures. Partly this had been through his own consciousness of the need to adopt different language when talking to teachers not closely involved in PELRS work. With PELRS teachers, however, he was able to express his ideas without constantly deferring to a perception of difference, knowing that they would immediately ask him to explain anything they did not understand. The generic pedagogic framework (GPF), as an intriguing and pleasing diagram, was a powerful mechanism for opening up debate (Pearson and Somekh 2006, in press). Its colour, inter-related shapes and clear labelling with words in everyday use, immediately captured the attention of teacher and academic audiences alike. It appeared to teachers as a bit of a puzzle, whose meaning needed to be teased out, and it seemed to Matthew, from his experience of discussing it with them, that teachers found it 'opens up a space for reflecting on their practice'. The multi-modality of the image, especially in its dynamic form on the website, where you could move between it and the specialist 'themed' frameworks, was satisfying semiotically and invited adaptation and speculation. Some of the word labels, such as 'mediated tool use' and 'flow' had specialist meanings but in both cases they could be easily explained and opened up intriguing theories that deepened understanding of human activity and learning. The only word label that remained fundamentally problematic was *outcomes*, which, at least at the start, had rather different meanings for the teachers and for Matthew and myself. The GPF had the learning focus at its core and the teacher's primary responsibility for selecting and planning the knowledge on which the learning would focus was a key part of the PELRS action research design.

Since the national curriculum is expressed in terms of learning outcomes these had to have a place in the GPF, but PELRS overlaid the national curriculum with a Stenhousean process curriculum, which extended and broadened it. The outcomes of the learning event were, therefore, at two levels: the deep transformative level of creativity, active citizenship, cognitive engagement and meta-cognition and the more technical and functional level of the national curriculum attainment targets. What you set out to learn is important, of course, but the *process* of the learning experience is what will shape the depth of learning and understanding achieved and the extent to which it is embedded in a transformed learner identity empowered to use this new knowledge. The PELRS GPF diagram and the themed frameworks provided a heuristic device for discussing the dual nature of the outcomes with the teachers and pupils, so that it was itself a good example of a mediating tool with affordances that helped to shape our shared activity.

Issues of power and autonomy in the role of the PELRS pupil–researchers

The role of the pupil–researchers and their contribution to generating knowledge and understanding was shaped by their relationship with Matthew. Schooled by our education system to expect that adults are generally uninterested in the views and opinions of children, and encultured into various assumptions about the relative power of adults and children in a school environment, which dictated, for example, what they were permitted or not permitted to say, the selected pupils did not immediately take on the desired role. Matthew had to persuade them that when he asked them a question it was a 'real' question to which he did not have any predetermined answer and that he really wanted to know their views. Through a process of trial and error he found that the first key thing was to explain who he was ('Matthew' and not a teacher) and tell them that he came from a university whose business was finding out things through research. Their starting point was to assume that there were no unanswered questions, so his first task was to persuade them that there are many things that are not 'cut and dried' and that researchers like himself want to explore problems and try to develop new ideas. The next step was to tell them that 'there are things you know that we cannot possibly know', particularly when it came to their experiences of using computers at home. Starting by talking to pupil–researchers about their home experience with ICT, rather than their school experience, opened up a conversational space where they could see they had an authoritative voice – what ICT did they use at home? What did they do with it? How did they find out about it and learn how to use it? were all questions that led to extensive and interesting data about home use. Once the conversational relationship between them and Matthew was established, it was possible for him to turn their attention to the school and the shared understanding they had begun to construct between them provided points of comparison to help the pupils comment upon their use of ICT at school. When it came to school they did not have any desire to criticize, partly because they took school as a 'given' that could not be changed and partly because they probably did not want to turn this serious – and probably very enjoyable – conversation with an adult into a complaining session. But once these barriers to talking about ICT use at school had been overcome all the pupil–researchers had many important points to make. They confirmed their enjoyment of using ICT to find things out, their frustration at the limited use often imposed by trivial, repetitive software and their additional frustration at knowing the equipment they could be using often remained locked up in cupboards. Other insights and comments emerged, such as the boredom of spending all their time on such a narrow curriculum: 'All we ever do is English, maths and science' (Pearson 2005).

Matthew negotiated with the pupils that he could discuss what the groups of four told him with their teachers, without naming individuals, but that they could ask him not to tell their teacher something if they wanted to. The children made this judgement sometimes, but mostly they were happy for him to pass on their insights and comments, finding it a novel idea that their voices were being heard.

Barriers to change: could PELRS action research provide models of transformative learning in schools?

PELRS was an ambitious project that attempted to co-construct with teachers pedagogic strategies with ICT to transform learning. The theories of institutional formation and human activity discussed earlier in this chapter make it clear that these aims could perhaps be seen to be naïve and over-ambitious. By the same token, following Giddens (1984), we can see ourselves as co-constructors of the institutions and systems in which we are constrained. There are always spaces of possibility.

So what could we claim by the end of the second year when this book was going to press? PELRS had been successful in developing some innovative pedagogic strategies for using ICT in new ways, but inevitably it had also run into barriers to change. Many of these were well known. The short time-frames of teaching periods, particularly in the secondary school, made it impossible for pupils to make full use of the internet. The internet is fundamentally an individualistic, exploratory medium that encourages users to find information for themselves, without placing any constraints on its provenance or any controls on its quality. It opens up access to knowledge so that, regardless of the dangers of picking up misinformation, school children have the opportunity to find out things as yet unknown to their teachers. The significant factor here is that the power differentials embedded in formal knowledge structures are removed; and while this is potentially liberating it also means that there is a crucial set of 'information literacy' skills for children – and adults – to acquire in distinguishing between trustworthy and untrustworthy websites (November 2001: 2–3). Schools have traditionally had a primary function to select and filter information so that education is time efficient and task oriented, preparing young people to take up positions of responsibility in the future that will be of service to the community. By contrast, the internet invites all users, regardless of their age and status, to surf and explore. ICT, therefore, has the potential to disrupt the procedures and practices embedded in the traditional values of schooling (Sharples 2002).

The specific barriers we encountered in PELRS included some that would affect any major educational innovation, such as lack of teacher time and the culture of schools (in England) that discourages teachers 'boasting' about their achievements, thus making it initially difficult for them to take on a leadership role with other teachers. We had little success in setting up meetings between teachers in the four participating schools and, while this was partly due to the very heavy traffic in Manchester at the end of the school day, it might also have been due to teachers' unwillingness to take time out of school during the day for something that could be seen as making them 'special'.

The other barriers related to the technology itself, which was subject to frequent technical problems, especially in primary schools that did not have such robust firewalls and virus protection systems as secondary schools (Pearson 2004: 14). Conversely, robust system security in secondary schools meant that it was often impossible to put new software on the system, making experimental work that used specialist software impossible without considerable negotiations in advance. In primary schools teachers had less difficulty in adding software of their choice to the system, but it was also easier for someone to mess about with the system and remove a file (perhaps unintentionally) so that suddenly Word no longer functioned or to download some software from the internet that interfered with existing software and made it malfunction. This may be one of the reasons why so much ICT use has been focused in the past on whole class teaching of skills in a specialist room, because it is much easier to check in advance that everything you need for a lesson like that is functioning. PELRS' more open-ended lessons, giving pupils choice over the technologies and software they used, were more demanding of everything to function unproblematically and made it more likely that something would 'go wrong'. Most seriously, in some schools, at various times, access to the internet was so restricted by safety filters that PELRS needed to divert its focus to using other kinds of ICT.

Despite these barriers, the PELRS teachers all engaged in exciting innovative teaching, working with enthusiasm to embed ICT use across the curriculum and explore with the children how to use digital cameras, cam-corders and editing software. ICT in PELRS classrooms was over-whelmingly a positive experience in which teachers experimented with new ICTs and new pedagogies and children responded with enjoyment and real engagement. At the time of going to press, towards the end of the second year of PELRS work, I am confident that there will be substantive knowledge outcomes from our research partnership including models of successful innovative teaching and learning with ICT.

9 Reflections on the Process of Writing this Book and its Purposes

> *When we turn to look back, like Orpheus looking back at*
> *Eurydice, experience ceases to become the thing it was before we*
> *looked.*
> *[...]*
> *The point is that life continues to unfold in the accounting of it,*
> *and the account-making is, in that sense, always a new event, a*
> *new experience.*
>
> (Davies and Davies 2005: 3–4)

This quotation is taken from a paper on the nature of experience in the social sciences, given by Bronwyn Davies at a seminar I attended while I was finalizing work on this book. It encapsulates the problems and the fascinations I have experienced in re-presenting the action research I carried out as a teacher and writing about six subsequent research projects spanning a period of 17 years. What exactly is the nature of my remembered experiences? The experiences themselves slip back to second, third, fourth remove, on each revisiting; but the very act of looking back on the past from a quite different present, re-creates the memories and turns them into something new. And this contradiction is mirrored in the two parts of the quotation. The negative connotations of loss in Davies' Orpheus and Eurydice image are balanced by the emphasis on making new meanings and gaining new insights in the second half of the quotation, taken from the end of the same paragraph. The meta-reflective process of immersing myself in the data of each of these projects in turn gave me new ideas for writing their stories. In a very real sense the data took me back into the past, conjuring up strong visual images and replaying long-gone emotions. So it would not be right to say that this writing is based on memories alone; in each case the impetus to write the chapters has been fuelled by new ideas.

From the start there were so many decisions to be made. What kind of text would be most in line with the eight methodological principles for action research I had set out in the Introduction? What should be the balance between personal narrative and the 'red thread' of an intellectually engaging line of argument? (The 'red thread' is a metaphor commonly used in this way by writers in German.) Should the other participants in the research be named? And above all, how could I justify the creation of a series of narratives that purported to re-create the experiences of the past while remaining, inescapably, products of the present?

A naïve belief in telling stories that would represent what truly happened was not open to me. Writers such as Van Maanen (1988) have exposed the crafted nature of the ethnographic text; in particular, Geertz (1988) has uncovered the persuasive power of discourse that is available to authors in writing about people and cultural contexts. I may not have the skills of an Evans-Pritchard or a Ruth Benedict, but there is a pressure to do the best I can with the skills I have, since narrative remains the only way to give a sense to readers of 'being there'. But beyond that, the insights that I drew from my colleague Maggie Maclure's work into the way that texts conceal the 'essential spaces and gaps in the foundations of qualitative research' (Maclure 2003: 3), raised my awareness of the 'weird' nature of writing and made me aspire to be open about the writing process.

The creation of a voice and a text would need to be conscious and crafted – and sufficiently flexible to leave me room to move between description and theory without artificially separating them. Beyond that, the peculiar challenges of writing narratives about action research turned into a kind of hide-and-seek game as I reread my colleague, Ian Stronach's article, 'This space is not yet blank', in which he describes the process of creating a text as 'gingerly picking my way, tensely, across this page, step-by-step, leaving word prints here and there' (Stronach 2002: 293). Action research, as he points out at the beginning of his article, poses particular challenges for contemporary social scientists because of the assumptions it carries of uncovering cause and effect and moving forward to what 'ought' to be. Indeed, in Stronach's sense, the nature of the action research narrative was already inscribed on the blank page before I started: there was a strong sense for me of being compelled towards creating realist narratives.

The process of writing this book was relatively easy once I had taken some decisions to answer my own questions. To write a text in line with my eight methodological principles there would need to be a strong personal voice, predominantly an 'I' rather than a 'we', so that I could engage in reflection and interpretation without presuming to speak for my colleagues. My aim was to create texts that would enable readers to experience events from the inside, engaging vicariously in the experience of needing to take decisions and responding to issues as they arose. My colleagues over the years would as far as possible be named, partly to give them credit for their work and partly to embody the text in a larger network of participants and highlight the importance and diversity of the relationships between people that gave each project its energy. Naming meant sending chapters to former colleagues for 'clearance' and brought responses which varied from quick 'permissions', to expressions of pleasure in being re-immersed in past experiences, and in one or two cases speculative comments on the long-term impact of being involved in the project itself. In one case where I had given an account of an event that had been fraught with tension I had the enormous privilege, after the passage of 14 years, of sending my account to the two people who were, so to speak, on the opposite side, which in both cases led to telephone conversations giving me new information to triangulate and extend my own understandings.

The text remains problematic, however. In two cases, from two different chapters, comments from colleagues alerted me to ways in which my words had created meanings I had not anticipated. The 'slipperiness' of words is intriguing: in each of these cases the comments brought me to recognize ways in which words – written by me but in another sense flowing through me – had introduced connotations of power or critique that were not consciously intended. These were neither mis-readings nor in some senses mis-writings (since I had chosen the words carefully), although in each case, once pointed out, I was sure of the need to rephrase and alter the tone of what I had written. Further, turning my attention beyond the choice of words and syntax to the presentation of my interpretations of events, it is certain that these are necessarily partial. Except in cases where I was able to contact current or former colleagues and get their responses, my meaning making has not been cross-checked and is likely to be different from how others would have made meanings from memories of the same events. Even where I have been able to cross-check, colleagues have often been content to accept my interpretation without wishing to change it, on the grounds that it is a personal point of view, necessarily different from theirs. In the case of one of my current projects, which will not end until after this book is published, the participating schools and LEAs have been anonymized in line with our agreed code of practice and the chapter has been 'cleared' with the three LEA project managers.

Readers will notice that each of the project chapters is written to a similar pattern, starting with key questions and in most cases including sections on 'design' of the project, 'research issues' or 'working tensions' and 'knowledge outcomes.' The intention is to allow readers to make comparisons between chapters and perhaps trace the development of ideas between one project and the next. For me, writing the sections on 'knowledge outcomes' was particularly important and led me to realize that in many cases the knowledge generated in these projects had not been fully written up and published. This was because of the roller-coaster nature of my research career over the years – the narratives track two occasions when my energies were diverted to new projects before old ones were properly 'put to bed', in one case involving a move to a management job where I had limited time for my own research and writing. The realization that I would not have time to publish as I should was depressing each time, and this book is intended to go some way to putting that right.

The first two chapters are intentionally different from the others. As far as possible I have included a personal voice in these chapters, by writing passages of narrative to keep the more theoretical passages closely linked to accounts of experiences which these theories enlivened and illuminated. My constant attempt in these chapters is to engage in critical scholarship without dislocating it from the praxis of action and reflection (Noffke 1995: 1), action in this sense having a wider meaning of the actions of the mind in exploratory engagement with ideas. The metaphor of 'living through the looking glass and looking back on Wonderland', described in the Introduction, was an essential device to enable me to understand how to position myself vis-à-vis the text. Perhaps this is an example of T.S. Eliot's 'objective correlative' because it enabled me to identify and understand my own emotions (Eliot 1920). The metaphor certainly had the force to allow me to start writing. The development of eight methodological principles then became an essential strategy to relocate my looking glass self vis-à-vis action research theory. Ideas which had been crucially important to me in Wonderland could then be more fully explored through this reflexive lens in Chapter 1. Chapter 2 develops and extends the theoretical framework for the whole book by illustrating the flexibility of action research methodology and its sensitivity to different contexts. It is intended to pave the way for the six narrative chapters, each one of which describes a project in which action research was designed to fit local needs and combine support for development with the generation of actionable knowledge.

The eight methodological principles embody my aspirations for action research and the narrative chapters provide accounts of striving to put them into practice – while inevitably falling short. My hope is that others will engage critically with these accounts of action research projects and use them to design new work that will surpass my own for creativity, reflexive sensitivity and transformative impact.

References

Almond, L. (1982) Containable Time, in *Institutional Self-Evaluation, Block 2 Part 2 of Course E364 (Curriculum Evaluation and Assessment in Educational Institutions)*, Appendix. Milton Keynes: Open University.

Altrichter, H. and Holly, M.L. (2005) Research Diaries, in B. Somekh and C. Lewin (eds) *Research Methods in the Social Sciences*. London and Thousand Islands, CA: Sage.

Altrichter, H. and Salzeber S. (2000) Some elements of a micro-political theory of school development, in H. Altrichter and J. Elliott (eds) *Images of Educational Change*. Buckingham and Philadelphia, PA: Open University Press.

Altrichter, H., Posch, P. and Somekh, B. (1993) *Teachers Investigate Their Work*. London: Routledge.

Arendt, H. (1978) *The Life of the Mind*. New York: Harcourt Brace.

Argyris, C. (1993) *Knowledge for Action: a guide to overcoming barriers to organizational change*. San Francisco: Jossey-Bass.

Argyris, C. (1999) *On Organizational Learning*, 2nd edn. Oxford and Malden, MA: Blackwell.

Argyris, C. and Schon, D. (1974) *Theory in Practice: increasing professional effectiveness*. London: Jossey-Bass.

Argyris, C. and Schon D. (1991) Participatory Action Research and Action Science Compared: a commentary, in W.F. Whyte (ed.) *Participatory Action Research*. Newbury Park, CA and London: Sage.

Aristotle (1955) *Ethics*, translated by J.A.K. Thomson. London: Penguin Classics.

Bacon, F. (1625) Of Custome and Education, in F. Bacon, *Essays*. London: Oxford University Press.

Bebbington, W.G. (ed.) (1978) *Famous Poems of the Twentieth Century*. Huddersfield: Schofield and Sims.

Becker, H.J. (2000) Findings from the Teaching, Learning, and Computing Survey: Is Larry Cuban right? Paper presented to the School Technology Leadership Conference of the Council of Chief State School Officers, Washington DC, 16–18 June.

Berge, B-M. and Ve, H. (2000) *Action Research for Gender Equity*. Buckingham: Open University Press.

Bidwell, C.E. (2001) Analyzing Schools as Organizations: long-term permanence and short-term change, *Sociology of Education* 74 (Extra Issue: *Current of Thought: sociology of education at the dawn of the 21st century*): 100–14.

Bion, W. (1946) The Leaderless Group Project, *Bulletin of the Menninger Clinic* 10: 77–81.

Bridges, J. and Meyer, J. (2000) Older People in Accident and Emergency: the use of action research to explore the interface between services in an acute hospital, *Educational Action Research* 8(2): 277–90.

Brown, J.S., Collins, A. and Duguid, P. (1989) Situated Cognition and the Culture of Learning, *Educational Researcher* 32 (Jan–Feb): 32–42.

Bussis, A., Chittenden, E. and Amarel, M. (1976) *Beyond Surface Curriculum: an interview study of teachers' understandings*. Boulder, CO: Westview Press.

Carr, W. and Kemmis, S. (1983) *Becoming Critical: knowing through action research*. Victoria, Deakin University Press. (Republished by Falmer Press (1986) as *Becoming Critical: Education, Knowledge and Action Research*.)

Carroll, Lewis (edited by Donald J. Gray, 1992) *Authoritative Texts of Alice's Adventures in Wonderland, Through the Looking-glass, The Hunting of the Snark: backgrounds, essays in criticism*. New York: Norton.

Chiu, L.F. (2003) Transformational Potential of Focus Group Practice in Participatory Action Research, *Action Research* 1(2): 165–83.

Claxton, G. (2000) What would Schools be like if they were Truly Dedicated to Helping all Young People become Confident, Competent Lifelong Learners?, in B. Lucas and T. Greany (eds) *Schools in the Learning Age*. London: Campaign for Learning.

Coghlan, D. (2003) Practitioner Research for Organizational Knowledge: mechanistic- and organistic-oriented approaches to insider action research, *Management Learning* 34(4): 451–63.

Cole, M. (1996) *Cultural Psychology: a once and future discipline*. Cambridge, MA and London: Belknap Press of Harvard University Press.

Coulter, D. (2002) What Counts as Action in Educational Action Research, *Educational Action Research* 10(2): 189–206.

Cronbach, L.J. (1982) *Designing Evaluations of Educational and Social Programs*. San Francisco: Jossey-Bass.

Csikszentmihalyi, M. (1996) *Creativity: flow and the psychology of discovery and invention*. New York: Harper Perennial.

Cuban, L. (2001) *Oversold and Underused: computers in classrooms*. Boston, MA: Harvard University Press.

Dadds, M. (1995) *Passionate Enquiry and School Development: a story about teacher action research*. London and Bristol, PA: Falmer Press.

Daniels, H. (2001) *Vygotsky and Pedagogy*. London and New York: Routledge/Falmer.

Davies, B. and Davies, C. (2005) Having, and being had by, 'Experience'. Or, 'Experience' in the Social Sciences after the Discursive/Poststructuralist Turn. Paper presented at an Education and Social Research Council Seminar within the Research Capacity Building Network, Institute for Social and Educational Research, Manchester Metropolitan University, 3–4 February.

Davis, N., Desforges, C., Jessel, J., Somekh, B., Taylor, C. and Vaughan, G. (1997) Can Quality in Learning be Enhanced through the use of IT? in B. Somekh and N. Davis (eds) *Using IT effectively in Teaching and Learning: studies in pre-service and in-service teacher education*. London and New York: Routledge.

DES (1989a) *Information Technology in Initial Teacher Training. The Report of the Expert Group chaired by Janet Trotter*. London: HMSO.

DES (1989b) *Initial Teacher Training: approval of courses*, Circular 24/89. London: HMSO.

Dewey, J. (1944) *Democracy and Education*. New York, Free Press.

Dewey, J. (1973) The Child and the Curriculum, in J.J. McDermott (ed.) *The Philosophy of John Dewey*. Chicago and London: University of Chicago Press.

DfES (2002) *Transforming the Way We Learn: the vision for the future of ICT in schools*. London: Department for Education and Skills.

DfES (2003) *Working Together: giving children and young people a say*. London: Department for Education and Skills.

DfES (2005a) www.standards.dfes.gov.uk/personalisedlearning/ (accessed 2 April 2005).

DfES (2005b) www.standards.dfes.gov.uk/thinkingskills/ (accessed 2 April 2005).

Doyle, W. and Ponder, G. (1977) The Practicality Ethic in Teacher Decision Making, *Interchange* 8(3): 1–12.

Dreyfus, S.E. (1981) Formal Models vs Human Situational Understanding. Unpublished manuscript, US Air Force Office for Scientific Research under contract F49620-79-0063 with the University of California, Berkeley.

Ebbutt, D. (1996) Universities, Work-based Learning and Issues about Knowledge, *Research in Post-Compulsory Education* 1(3): 357–72.

Ebbutt, D. and Elliott, J. (eds) (1985) *Issues in Teaching for Understanding*. London: Longman for the Schools Curriculum Development Council.

ED (1992) *Learning Through Work*. Sheffield: Employment Department.

Eliot, T.S. (1920) *The Sacred Wood: essays on poetry and criticism*. London: Methuen & Co. Ltd.

Elliott, J. (1976) Developing Hypotheses About Classrooms from Teachers Practical Constructs. Mimeo, North Dakota Study Group on Evaluation, University of North Dakota, Grand Forks, ND.

Elliott, J. (1980) Implications of Classroom Research for Professional Development, in E. Hoyle and J. Megarry (eds) *Professional Development of Teachers: world year book of education*. London: Kogan Page.

Elliott, J. (1985) Educational action-research, in J. Nisbet (ed.) *World Year Book of Education: research, policy and practice*. London: Kogan Page.

Elliott, J. (1988) Educational Research and Outsider–Insider Relations, *Qualitative Studies in Education* 1(2): 155–66.

Elliott, J. (1989) Educational Theory and the Professional Learning of Teachers: an overview, *Cambridge Journal of Education* 19(1): 81–101.

Elliott, J. (1990) Teachers as Researchers: implications for supervision and for teacher education, *Teaching and Teacher Education* 6(1): 1–26.

Elliott, J. (1991) *Action Research for Educational Change*. Buckingham and Bristol, PA: Open University Press.

Elliott, J. (1993) *Reconstructing Teacher Education*. London and Washington: Falmer Press.

Elliott, J. (1998) *The Curriculum Experiment: meeting the challenge of social change*. Buckingham and Philadelphia, PA: Open University Press.

Elliott, J. (2000) Towards a Synoptic Vision of Educational Change in Advanced Industrial Societies, in H. Altrichter and J. Elliott (eds) *Images of Educational Change*. Buckingham and Philadelphia, PA: Open University Press.

Elliott, J. (2004) The Struggle to Redefine the Relationship between 'Knowledge' and 'Action', *EDUCAR* 34 (Universitat Autonomia de Barcelona, Servei de Publications, Bellaterra, Spain).

Elliott, J. (undated) The Qualities of a Good Patrol Constable. Mimeo, Centre for Applied Research in Education, University of East Anglia, Norwich, UK.

Elliott, J. and Ebbutt, D. (eds) (1986) *Case Studies in Teaching for Understanding*. Cambridge: Cambridge Institute of Education.

Engeström, Y. (1999) Activity Theory and Individual and Social Transformation, in Y. Engeström, M. Reijo and R.-L. Punamäki (eds) *Perspectives on Activity Theory*. Cambridge, New York and Melbourne: Cambridge University Press.

Engeström, Y. (2005) *Developmental Work Research: expanding activity theory in practice*. Berlin: Lehmanns Media.

Facer, K., Furlong, J., Furlong, R. and Sutherland, R. (2003) *ScreenPlay: children and computing in the home*. London and New York: Routledge/Falmer.

Fals-Borda, O. (2001) Participatory (Action) Research in Social Theory: origins and challenges, in P. Reason and H. Bradbury (eds) *Handbook of Action Research: participative inquiry and practice*. London and Thousand Islands, CA: Sage.

Fals-Borda, O. and Mora-Osejo L.E. (2003a) Context and Diffusion of Knowledge: a critique of Eurocentrism, *Action Research* 1(1): 29–38.

Fals-Borda, O. and Mora-Osejo L.E. (2003b) Shaping the Future, *Action Research* 1(1): 29–37.

Feldman, A. (2003) Validity and Quality in Self-Study, *Educational Researcher* 32(3): 26–8.

Foucault, M. (1970) *The Order of Things: an archaeology of the human sciences.* London and New York: Tavistock/Routledge.

Foucault, M. (1972) *Power/Knowledge: selected interviews and other writings 1972–77.* Bury St Edmunds: Harvester Press.

Foucault, M. (1977) *Discipline and Punish: the birth of the prison.* London and New York: Penguin.

Freire, P. (1972) *Pedagogy of the Oppressed.* London: Penguin.

Freud, S. (1986) *The Essentials of Psycho-Analysis.* London and New York: Penguin.

Fullan, M.G. (1982) *The Meaning of Educational Change.* Toronto: OISE Press, Ontario Institute for Studies in Education.

Gadamer, H. (1975) *Truth and Method.* London: Sheed and Ward.

Garfinkel, H. (1984) *Studies in Ethnomethodology.* Cambridge: Polity Press.

Geertz, C. (1988) *Works and Lives: the anthropologist as author.* Cambridge: Polity Press.

Gergen, K.J. (2003) Action Research and Orders of Democracy, *Action Research* 1(1): 39–56.

Giddens, A. (1984) *The Constitution of Society.* Cambridge: Polity Press.

Glaser, B. and Strauss, A. (1967) *The Discovery of Grounded Theory: strategies for qualitative research.* Chicago: Aldine.

Goffman, E. (1959) *The Presentation of Self in Everyday Life.* London: Penguin.

Graves, D.H. (1983) *Writing: teachers and children at work.* London: Heinemann.

Greene, J.C. and Caracelli, V.J. (1997) Defining and Describing the Paradigm Issue in Mixed-method Evaluation, in J.C. Greene and V.J. Caracelli (eds) *Advances in Mixed-method Evaluation: the challenges and benefits of integrating diverse paradigms*, pp. 5–18, New Directions for Program Evaluation, No. 74. San Francisco: Jossey-Bass.

Greene, J.C., Kreider, H. and Mayer, E. (2005) Combining Qualitative and Quantitative Methods in Social Inquiry, in B. Somekh and C. Lewin (eds) *Research Methods in the Social Sciences.* London, Thousand Oaks, CA and New Delhi: Sage.

Greenfield, T.B. (1981) Theory about Organisations – a perspective and its implications for schools, in T. Bush (ed.) *Approaches to School Management.* London: Harper & Row.

Griffiths, M. (2003) *Action for Social Justice in Education: fairly different.* Maidenhead and Philadelphia, PA: Open University Press.

Groundwater-Smith, S. (2005). Painting the Educational Landscape with Tea: re-reading, *Becoming Critical*. *Educational Action Research* 13(3): 329–45.

Habermas, J. (1970) Towards a Theory of Communicative Competence, *Inquiry* 13: 372.

Habermas, J. (1973) A Postscript to Knowledge and Human Interest, *Philosophy of the Social Sciences* 3(168).

Habermas, J. (1974) *Theory and Practice*. London: Heinemann.

Habermas, J. (1979) *Communication and the Evolution of Society*. London: Heinemann.

Habermas, J. (1984) *The Theory of Communicative Action: volume one: reason and the rationalization of society*. London: Heinemann.

Haraway, D. (1991) *Simians, Cyborgs, and Women*. London: Free Association Books.

Harrison, C., Fisher, T., Haw, K., Lewin, C., Lunzer, E., Mavers, D., Scrimshaw, P. and Somekh, B. (2002) *ImpaCT2: the impact of information and communication technologies on pupils' learning and attainment*. www.becta.org.uk/research/research.cfm?section= 1&id=539 (accessed 2 April 2005).

Hinsdale, M.A., Lewis, H.M. and Waller, H.M (1995) *It Comes from the People*. Philadelphia, PA: Temple University Press.

HMI (1989) Information Technology from 5 to 16, *Curriculum Matters* 15. London, HMSO.

Hopkins, D. (1985) *A Teachers' Guide to Classroom Research*. Milton Keynes: Open University Press.

Horton, M. and Freire, P. (1990) *We Make the Road by Walking*. Philadelphia, PA: Temple University Press.

House, E.R. (1974) *The Politics of Educational Innovation*. Berkeley, CA: McCutchan Publishing Co.

House, E.R. (1993) *Professional Evaluation: social impact and political consequences*. Newbury Park, CA and London: Sage.

Hutchins, E. and Klausen, T. (1996) Distributed Cognition in an Airline Cockpit, in Y. Engeström and D. Middleton (eds) *Cognition and Communication at Work*. Cambridge, New York and Melbourne: Cambridge University Press.

Ireland, D. and Russell, T. (1978) Pattern Analysis, *CARN Bulletin*, 2: 21–5.

James, A. and Prout, A. (eds) (1997) *Constructing and Reconstructing Childhood*. London: Falmer Press.

Kemmis, S. (2001) Exploring the Relevance of Critical Theory for Action Research: emancipatory action research in the footsteps of Jürgen Habermas, in P. Reason and H. Bradbury (eds) *Handbook of Action Research: participative inquiry and practice*. London and Thousand Islands, CA: Sage.

Kemmis, S. and McTaggart, R. (1988) *The Action Research Planner*, 3rd edn. Geelong, Australia: Deakin University Press.

Kemp, P. (2000) Empowering the Supporters: enhancing the role of unqualified support workers in a housing scheme for people with mental health problems, *Educational Action Research* 8(2): 261–76.

Knijnik, G. (1997) Popular Knowledge and Academic Knowledge in the Brazilian Peasants' Struggle for Land, *Educational Action Research* 5(3): 501–11.

Lave, J. (1996) The Practice of Learning, in S. Chaiklin and J. Lave (eds) *Understanding Practice: perspectives on activity and context*. Cambridge, New York and Melbourne: Cambridge University Press.

Lave, J. and Wenger, E. (1991) *Situated Learning: legitimate peripheral participation*. Cambridge, New York and Melbourne: Cambridge University Press.

Lewin, K. (1946) Action Research and Minority Problems, *Journal of Social Issues* 2(1): 34–46.

Lewin, K. (1951) *Field Theory in Social Science: selected theoretical papers*. New York: Harper & Row.

Lukes, S. (1974) *Power*. London: Macmillan.

MacDonald, B. (1974) Evaluation and Control of Education, in *Innovation, Evaluation, Research and the Problem of Control*. Mimeo, IFS. Project, CARE, University of East Anglia, Norwich, UK.

MacDonald, B., Beattie, C., Schostak, J. and Somekh, B. (1988) *The Department of Trade and Industry Micros in Schools Support 1981–84: an independent evaluation*. Norwich: CARE, University of East Anglia.

Maclure, M. (2003) *Discourse in Educational and Social Research*. Buckingham and Philadelphia, PA: Open University Press.

Maclure, M. (2005) 'Clarity Bordering on Stupidity': where's the quality in systematic review? *Journal of Education Policy* 20(4): 393–416.

Maclure, M. and Norris, N. (1990) Knowledge Issues and Implications for the Standards Programme at Professional Levels of Competence. Unpublished report available from CARE, University of East Anglia, Norwich, UK.

Malen, B. (1994) The Micro-politics of Education: mapping the multiple dimensions of power relations in school polities, *Journal of Education Policy* 9(5/6): 147–67.

Marshall, M. (1990) *Developing Image: developing child creativity and autonomy with computers*. Norwich: PALM Publications, CARE, University of East Anglia.

Marx, K. (1977) Wage Labour and Capital, in D. McLellan (ed.) *Karl Marx: selected writings*. Oxford and New York: Oxford University Press.

McCormick, R. and James, M. (1988) *Curriculum Evaluation in Schools*, 2nd edn. London and Sydney: Croom Helm.

McClellend, D. (1978) *Guide to Behavioural Event Interviewing*. Boston, MA: McBer and Co.

McNiff, J. (1988) *Action Research: principles and practice*. London: Macmillan Education.

Mead, G.H. (1934) *Mind, Self and Society*. Chicago: University of Chicago Press.

Mills, C.W. (1959) *The Sociological Imagination*. London and New York: Oxford University Press.

Murray, D. (1990) *Shoptalk: learning to write with writers*. Portsmouth: Boynton/Cook.

NAACE (1999) *All Our Futures: creativity, culture and education*. London, Department for Education and Employment, National Advisory Committee on Creative and Cultural Education. www.dfes.gov.uk/naccce/index1.shtml (accessed 2 April 2005).

Noffke, S. (1995) Action Research and Democratic Schooling: problematics and potentials, in S. Noffke and R.B. Stevenson (eds) *Educational Action Research: becoming practically critical*. New York and London: Teachers' College Press.

Noffke, S. (1997) Professional, Personal, and Political Dimensions of Action Research, *Review of Research in Education* 2: 305–43.

Noffke, S. and Somekh B. (2005) Action Research, in B. Somekh and C. Lewin (eds) *Research Methods in the Social Sciences*. London and Thousand Oaks, CA: Sage.

Noffke, S. and Stevenson, R.B. (eds) (1995) *Educational Action Research: becoming practically critical*. New York and London: Teachers' College Press.

November, A. (2001) *Empowering Learners with Technology*. Glenview, IL: Skylight Professional Development.

O'Hanlon, C. (1997) The Professional Journal, Genres and Personal Development in Higher Education, in S. Hollingsworth (ed.) *International Action Research: a casebook for educational reform*. London and Washington, DC: Falmer Press.

PALM (1990) *Supporting Teacher Development Through Action Research: a PALM resource for advisory teachers*. Norwich: Pupil Autonomy in Learning with Microcomputers, CARE, University of East Anglia.

Papert, S. (1980) *Mindstorms: children, computers, and powerful ideas*. London: Harvester Press.

Pasmore, W. (2001) Action Research in the Workplace: the socio-technical perspective, in P. Reason and H. Bradbury (eds) *Handbook of Action Research: participative inquiry and practice*. London and Thousand Islands, CA: Sage.

Pearson, M. (2004) Activity and Agency: engaging young people in ICT research. Paper presented to the Digital Generations Conference, University of London Institute of Education, 26–29 July.

Pearson, M. (2005) Let's Have a Look Around: some relfections on recruiting schools and teachers to an action research project. Paper presented to the ICARE Conference: The Social Practice of an Education Research Community, Manchester Metropolitan University, 12–14 September.

Pearson, M. and Somekh, B. (2006, in press) Learning Transformation with Technology: a question of socio-cultural contexts? Under revision for possible publication in *Qualitative Studies in Education*.

Peters, T.J. and Waterman R.H. (1982) *In Search of Excellence: lessons from America's best-run companies*. New York: Harper & Row.

Polanyi, M. (1958) *Personal Knowledge: towards a post-critical philosophy*. London: Routledge & Kegan Paul.

Posch, P. (2000) Community, School Change and Strategic Networking, in H. Altrichter and J. Elliott (eds) *Images of Educational Change*. Buckingham and Philadelphia, PA: Open University Press.

Reason, P. and Bradbury, H. (eds) (2001) *Handbook of Action Research: participative inquiry and practice*. London and New York: Sage.

Ruthven, K., Hennessy, S.K. and Deaney, R. (2005) Incorporating Internet Resources into Classroom Practice: pedagogical perspectives and strategies of secondary-school subject teachers, *Computers & Education* 44(1): 1–34.

Rutter, K.A. (2003) From Measuring Clouds to Active Listening, *Management Learning* 34(4): 465–80.

Salomon, G. (ed.) (1993) *Distributed Cognitions: psychological and educational considerations*. Cambridge, New York and Melbourne: Cambridge University Press.

Sandholtz, J., Ringstaff, C. and Dwyer, D. (1997) *Teaching with Technology*. New York: Teachers' College Press.

Schön, D.A. (1983) *The Reflective Practitioner*. New York: Basic Books.

Schostak, J. (1999) Action Research and the Point Instant of Change, *Educational Action Research* 7(3): 399–418.

Schutz, A. (1967) *The Phenomenology of the Social World*. Evanston, IL: Northwestern University Press.

Schutz, A. (1970) *On Phenomenology and Social Relations*. London: University of Chicago Press.

Selwyn, N. (2002) *Telling Tales on Technology: qualitative studies of technology and education*. Aldershot: Ashgate.

Senge, P.M. (1993) *The Fifth Discipline: the art and practice of the learning organization*. London: Random House Business Books.

Sharples, M. (2002) Disruptive Devices: mobile technology for conversational learning, *International Journal of Continuing Engineering Education and Life Long Learning* 12(5–6): 504–20.

Smith, J.K. (2004). Learning to Live with Relativism, in H. Piper and I. Stronach (eds) *Educational Research: difference and diversity*. Aldershot and Burlington, VT: Ashgate.

Somekh, B. (1983) Triangulation Methods in Action: a practical example, *Cambridge Journal of Education* 13(2): 31–7.

Somekh, B. (1984) Teaching Poetry for Understanding within the Constraints of the 'O' level Cambridge Plain Text Literature Syllabus, *CARN Bulletin* 6: 27–36.

Somekh, B. (1987) The Eyes of a Fly: an experiment in collaborative research, *CARN Bulletin* 8: 169–78.

Somekh, B. (1989) The Human Interface: hidden issues in computer-mediated communication affecting use in schools in R. Mason and A. Kaye (eds) *Mindweave*. Oxford: Pergamon Press. (Reprinted in O. Boyd-Barrett and E. Scanlon (1991) *Computers and Learning*. London: Addison-Wesley in association with the Open University.)

Somekh, B. (1992) *Project INTENT: final report*. Coventry: National Council for Educational Technology.

Somekh, B. (1994) Inhabiting Each Other's Castles: towards knowledge and mutual growth through collaboration, *Educational Action Research* 2(3): 357–82. (Reprinted in C. Day, J. Elliott, B. Somekh and R. Winter (eds) (2002) *Theory and Practice in Action Research: some international perspectives*. Oxford: Symposium Books.)

Somekh, B. (2000) Changing Conceptions of Action Research, in H. Altrichter and J. Elliott (eds) *Images of Educational Change*. Buckingham and Philadelphia, PA: Open University Press.

Somekh, B. (2001) The Role of Evaluation in Ensuring Excellence in Communications and Information Technology Initiatives, *Education, Communication and Information* 1(1): 75–101.

Somekh, B. (2004) Taking the Sociological Imagination to School: an analysis of the (lack of) impact of ICT on education systems, *Technology, Pedagogy and Education (Special Issue on Researching Educational ICT)* 13(2): 163–80.

Somekh, B. and Davies, R. (1991) Towards a Pedagogy for Information Technology, *The Curriculum Journal* 2(2): 153–70.

Somekh, B. and Davis, N. (eds) (1997) *Using IT Effectively in Teaching and Learning: studies in pre-service and in-service teacher education*. London and New York: Routledge.

Somekh, B. and Pearson, M. (2002) Inter-cultural Learning Arising from pan-European Collaboration: a community of practice with a 'hole in the middle', *British Educational Research Association Journal* 28(4): 485–502.

Somekh, B. and Thaler, M. (1997) Contradictions of Management Theory, Organisational Cultures and the Self, *Educational Action Research* 5(1): 339–55.

Somekh, B., Whitty, G. and Coveney R. (1997) IT and the Politics of Institutional Change, in B. Somekh and N. Davis (eds) *Using IT*

Effectively in Teaching and Learning: studies in pre-service and in-service teacher education. London and New York: Routledge.

Somekh, B., Mavers, D. and Lewin, C. (2002a) *Using ICT to Enhance Home–School Links: an evaluation of current practice in England.* London: Department for Education and Skills.

Somekh, B., Lewin, C., Mavers, D., Fisher, T., Harrison, C., Haw, K., Lunzer, E., McFarlane, A. and Scrimshaw, P. (2002b) *ImpaCT2 Final Report Part 3: learning with ICT: pupils' and teachers' perspectives.* London: Department for Education and Skills. www.becta.org.uk/research/research.cfm?section=1&id=539 (accessed 2 April 2005).

Somekh, B., Lewin, C., Mavers, D., Scrimshaw, P., Haldane, A., Levin, C. and Robinson, J. (2003) *Evaluation of the GridClub Educational Service: final report to the Department for Education and Skills, March 2003.* Manchester: Manchester Metropolitan University.

Somekh, B., Underwood, J., Convery, A., Dillon, G., Lewin, C., Mavers, D., Saxon, D. and Woodrow, D. (2005a) *Evaluation of the ICT Test Bed Project: annual report, 2004.* www.evaluation.icttestbed.org.uk/studies/ict_test_bed_evaluation_2004.pdf (accessed 2 April 2005).

Somekh, B., Underwood, J., Convery, A. (2005b) *Evaluation of the DfES ICT Test Bed Project: annual report 2004,* 4: 44–51. Coventry, Becta: British Educational Communications and Technology Agency.

Stenhouse, L. (1975) *An Introduction to Curriculum Research and Development.* London: Heinemann.

Stenhouse, L. (1981) What Counts as Research? *British Journal of Educational Studies* 29(2): 103–14.

Stronach, I. (2002) This Space is Not Yet Blank: anthropologies for a future action research, *Educational Action Research* 10(2): 291–307.

Stronach, I. and McNamara, O. (2002) Working Together: the long spoons and short straws of collaboration, in O. McNamara (ed.) *Becoming an Evidence-Based Practitioner: a framework for teacher–researchers.* London and New York: Routledge/Falmer.

Sumara, D.J. and Luce-Kapler, R. (1993) Action Research as a Writerly Text: locating co-labouring in collaboration, *Educational Action Research* 1(3): 387–96.

Susman, G. and Trist, E. (1993) Action Research in an American Underground Coal Mine, in E. Trist and H. Murray (eds) *The Social Engagement of Social Science: a Tavistock anthology, volume II: the socio-technical perspective.* Philadelphia, PA: University of Philadelphia Press.

Sutherland, R., Armstrong, V., Barnes, S., Brawn, R., Breeze, N., Gall, M., Matthewman, S., Olivero, F., Taylor, A., Triggs, P., Wishart, J. and John, P. (2004) Transforming Teaching and Learning: embedding ICT into everyday classroom practices, *Journal of Computer Assisted Learning* 20(6): 413–25.

Taylor, F.W. (1992) The Principles of Scientific Management, in J.M. Shafritz, and J.S. Ott (eds) *Classics of Organization Theory*, 3rd edn. Pacific Grove, CA: Brooks/Cole Publishing Company.

Terhart, E. (1982) Interpretative Approaches in Educational Research, *Cambridge Journal of Education* 12(3): 141–59.

Titchen, A. (1997) Creating a Learning Culture: a story of change in hospital nursing, in S. Hollingsworth (ed.) *International Action Research*. London and Washington: Falmer Press.

TLRP (2004) *Personalised Learning: a commentary by the teaching and learning research programme*. Swindon: ESRC. www.salsafy.caret.cam.ac.uk/cgi-bin/tlrp/news/news_log.pl?display=1102930510 (accessed 2 April 2005).

Torrance, H. and Pryor, J. (2001) Developing Formative Assessment in the Classroom: using action research to explore and modify theory, *British Educational Research Journal*, 27(5): 615–31.

Tragesser, R.S. (1977) *Phenomenology and Logic*. Ithaca: Cornell University Press.

Trist, E. and Murray, H. (1993) *The Social Engagement of Social Science. Vol 1: the socio-psychological perspective; Vol 2: the socio-technical perspective; Vol 3: the socio-ecological perspective*. Philadelphia, PA: University of Pennsylvania Press.

Underwood, J. and Dillon, G. (2005) Capturing Complexity through Maturity Modelling, in B. Somekh and C. Lewin (eds) *Research Methods in the Social Sciences*. London, Thousand Oaks, CA and New Delhi: Sage.

Van Maanen, J. (1988) *Tales of the Field: on writing ethnography*. Chicago and London: University of Chicago Press.

Wadsworth, Y. (2001) The Mirror, the Magnifying Glass, the Compass and the Map: facilitating participatory action research, in P. Reason and H. Bradbury (eds) *Handbook of Action Research: participative inquiry and practice*. London and Thousand Oaks, CA: Sage.

Walker, M. (1995) Context, Critique and Change: doing action research in South Africa, *Educational Action Research* 3(1): 9–28.

Walker, M.J. (1996) *Images of Professional Development*. Cape Town, South Africa: Human Sciences Research Council.

Walker, M. (ed.) (2001) *Reconstructing Professionalism in University Teaching*. Buckingham: Open University Press.

Waterman, H., Tillen, D., Dickson, R. and de Koning, K. (2001) *Action Research: a systematic review and guidance for assessment*. London: Health Technology Assessment, NHS R&D HTA Programme. www.hta.nhsweb.nhs.uk/execsumm/summ523.htm (accessed 2 April 2005).

Wenger, E. (1998) *Communities of Practice: learning, meaning and identity*. Cambridge, New York and Melbourne: Cambridge University Press.

Wertsch, J.V. (1998) *Mind as Action*. New York and Oxford: Oxford University Press.

Whitehead, J. (1989) Creating a Living Educational Theory from Questions of the Kind, 'How do I Improve my Practice?', *Cambridge Journal of Education* 19(1): 41–52.

Whitelaw, S., Beattie, A., Balogh, R. and Watson, J. (2003) *A Review of the Nature of Action Research*. Cardiff: Welsh Assembly. www.ucsm.ac.uk/chrpd/previous.htm (accessed 2 April 2005).

Wildavsky, A. (1993) *Speaking Truth to Power: the art and craft of policy analysis*. New Brunswick and London: Transaction Publishers.

Winter R. (1982) Dilemma Analysis: a contribution to the methodology of action research, *Cambridge Journal of Education* 12(3): 161–74.

Winter, R. (1984) Social Research as Emancipatory Discourse, *CARN Bulletin* 6: 89–93.

Winter, R. (1989) *Learning from Experience: principles and practice in action research*. Lewes and Philadelphia, PA: Falmer Press.

Winter, R. (2002) Managers, Spectators and Citizens: where does 'theory' come from in action research? in C. Day, J. Elliott, B. Somekh and R. Winter (eds) *Theory and Practice in Action Research: some international perspectives*. Oxford: Symposium Books.

Winter, R. and Munn-Giddings, C. (eds) (2001) *A Handbook for Action Research in Health and Social Care*. London and New York: Routledge.

Zamorski, B., Jonker, L. and Bridges D. (1995) Report of the Formative Evaluation of COMEX. Unpublished report, CARE University of East Anglia, Norwich.

Index

Conducting Educational Research series
Editor: Harry Torrance

BECOMING A RESEARCHER
A Research Companion for the Social Sciences

Máiréad Dunne, John Pryor and Paul Yates

This innovative book combines what most books separate: research as practical activity and research as intellectual engagement. It clarifies and makes explicit the methodological issues that underlie the journey from initial research idea to the finished report and beyond.

The text moves the researcher logically through the research process and provides insights into methodology through an in-depth discussion of methods. It presents the research process as an engagement with text. This theme moves through the construction of text in the form of data and the deconstruction of text in analysis. Finally the focus moves to the reconstruction of text through the re-presentation of the research in the report. Following through each of these stages in turn, the chapters consider either a practical issue or a group of methods and interrogate the associated methodological concerns. In addition, the book also addresses the rarely explored issues of the researcher as writer and researcher identity as core elements of the research process.

The book provides a range of insights and original perspectives. These successfully combine practical guidance with the invitation to consider the problematic nature of research as social practice. It is an ideal reference for those embarking on research for the first time and provides a new methodological agenda for established researchers.

Contents: *Introduction – Part 1 – Distinguishing Data: Constructing text – The Logic of Enquiry – Talking with people: Interviewing – Knowing with Numbers: Questionnaires – Being There: Observation – Part 2 – Dicing with data: Deconstructing text – Breaking Down Data: Routes to Interpretation – Worrying at Words: Discourse Analysis – Pulverizing Policy: Deconstructing Documents – Part 3 – Data with Destiny: Reconstructing Text – Writing Research: Authoring Text – The Selfish Text: Research and Identity – Methods and Methodology*

208pp 0 335 21394 4 Paperback   0 335 21395 2 Hardback

A HANDBOOK FOR TEACHER RESEARCH
From Design to Implementation

Colin Lankshear and Michele Knobel

"This informative book helped me to understand research in general and to bring focus and clarity to my current research project. The text answers questions and provides guidance and support in a manner that is user-friendly and easy to comprehend.... After reading this book, I feel empowered as a teacher-researcher and would unhesitatingly recommend it to other teacher-researchers, graduate students and educators."– Francesca Crowther, teacher and doctoral student, Nova Scotia, Canada.

This book provides a comprehensive and detailed approach to teacher research as systematic, methodical and informed practice. It identifies five requirements for all kinds of research, and provides clear and accessible guidelines for teachers to use in conducting their own classroom-based studies.

Features:

- A clear definition of teacher research which insists on more than 'stories' and anecdotal 'retrospectives'
- Easy-to-use and widely applicable tools and techniques for collecting and analysing data in qualitative research
- Acknowledges the relevance of quantitative and document-based as well as qualitative forms of inquiry in teacher research
- Accessible and informative discussions of key issues in teacher research, such as interpretation, ethics, and validity.

A Handbook for Teacher Research provides everything the teacher researcher needs in order to conduct good quality practitioner research. It is ideal for upper level undergraduate Education programmes and for postgraduate research, as well as for teacher researchers who conceive and drive their own independent studies.

412pp 0 335 21064 3 Paperback   0 335 21065 1 Hardback

THE MORAL FOUNDATIONS OF EDUCATIONAL RESEARCH
Knowledge, Inquiry and Values

Pat Sikes, Jon Nixon and Wilfred Carr (eds)

"A rallying call for ethical self-awareness ... This is a book for everyone doing educational research." – BJES

The Moral Foundations of Educational Research considers what is distinctive about educational research in comparison with other research in the social sciences. As the contributors all agree that education is always an essentially moral enterprise, discussion about methodology starts, not with the widely endorsed claim that educational research should be 'useful' and 'relevant', but with the attempt to justify and elaborate that claim with reference to its moral foundations. Determining the nature of 'usefulness' and 'relevance' is not simply a matter of focussing on impact and influence but involves a radical re-conceptualisation of the moral and educational significance of what is deemed to be 'useful' and 'relevant'. There is no argument with this emphasis on the generation of 'useful' and 'relevant' knowledge, but it is suggested that educational research requires a fuller and more rounded understanding that takes account of the moral values of those who conduct it. Educational research is grounded, epistemologically, in the moral foundations of educational practice. It is the epistemological and moral purposes underlying the 'usefulness' and 'relevance' of educational research that matter.

Contributors: *Pierre Bourdieu, Peter Clough, Ivor Goodson, Fred Inglis, Gary McCulloch, Jon Nixon, Carrie Paechter, Richard Pring, Pat Sikes, Melanie Walker.*

Contents: *Introduction – Educational research and its histories – Towards a social history of educational research – Living research – thoughts on educational research as moral practice – The virtues and vices of an educational researcher – Against objectivism – the reality of the social fiction – Research as thoughtful practice – On goodness and utility in educational research – Method and morality – practical politics and the science of human affairs – Index.*

192pp 0 335 21046 5 Paperback

Printed in Poland
by Amazon Fulfillment
Poland Sp. z o.o., Wrocław